SPEAKING OF FEMINISM

SPEAKING OF

Feminism

TODAY'S ACTIVISTS ON THE

PAST, PRESENT, AND FUTURE OF THE

U.S. WOMEN'S MOVEMENT

RACHEL F. SEIDMAN

THE UNIVERSITY OF NORTH CAROLINA PRESS

Chapel Hill

© 2019 The University of North Carolina Press
All rights reserved

Set in Utopia and The Sans
by codeMantra, Inc.
Manufactured in the United States of America

The University of North Carolina Press has been a
member of the Green Press Initiative since 2003.

Cover illustration: Women's March on Washington, 21 January 2017.
© Jim West/Alamy Live News, image HJ5X39 (RM).

Library of Congress Cataloging-in-Publication Data
Names: Seidman, Rachel Filene, interviewer.
Title: Speaking of feminism : today's activists on the past, present, and
future of the U.S. women's movement / Rachel F. Seidman.
Description: Chapel Hill : The University of North Carolina Press,
[2019] | Includes bibliographical references and index.
Identifiers: LCCN 2019010825 | ISBN 9781469653075 (cloth : alk. paper) |
ISBN 9781469653082 (pbk : alk. paper) | ISBN 9781469653099 (ebook)
Subjects: LCSH: Feminists—United States—Interviews. | Feminism—
United States—History—21st century. | Women—United States—Social
conditions—21st century. | United States—Social conditions—21st century.
Classification: LCC HQ1421 .S46 2019 | DDC 305.420973—dc23
LC record available at https://lccn.loc.gov/2019010825

CONTENTS

INTRODUCTION

"Who needs feminism?" In the spring of 2012 my students asked that simple question, and then we watched, astounded, as the world answered. What started as a class project at Duke University exploded into a transnational social media campaign. People on campus quads, in homes, and in offices around the world held up signs declaring "I need feminism because . . . ," completing the phrase with their own answers scrawled in marker on white-boards or pieces of paper. Thousands posted photos of themselves with their signs on social media, and tens of thousands more "liked" the Who Needs Feminism Facebook page, followed the Tumblr site, and tweeted their approval. Others disparaged the photos in tones that ranged from silly to violent.[1]

The energy behind Who Needs Feminism was the same heady mix of righteous anger and joyful creativity that has always shaped feminist activism. The context for my students' work in 2012 was the "war on women," when Republican state legislatures unleashed a rash of antiabortion bills in the run-up to that year's elections; Missouri representative Todd Akin made his infamous remark about "legitimate rape" not causing pregnancy; and right-wing radio host Rush Limbaugh vilified activist Sandra Fluke on air, calling her a "whore" for arguing that insurance should cover birth control.[2]

Experiencing the Who Needs Feminism phenomenon alongside my students altered my sense of the vitality of feminism and its particular importance to young women and men at that point in time not only in America but around the globe. As a women's historian and a feminist, I knew a lot about the women's activism that had occurred in the past and about the fundamental issues that were still in play. But Who Needs Feminism thrust me deeper into the realm of social media and opened my eyes to a vast world of online activism whose participants were drawing on history but also creatively dealing with the realities of their present. Moreover, it revealed to me the nature of the simultaneous, intense backlash against women's progress that finds particularly venomous expression in the relative anonymity of social media. That experience awakened my curiosity; this book is the result of my desire to learn more about feminists and the state of the movement today.

As an oral historian, I recognized the power of in-depth interviews for understanding past movements.[3] I set out to apply the same tool to explore the activism going on around me in the present. Between 2014 and 2016, I collected in-depth oral history interviews with feminist activists in six different locales: Atlanta, Georgia; Washington, D.C.; the Research Triangle of Raleigh, Durham, and Chapel Hill, North Carolina; Minneapolis–Saint Paul, Minnesota; New York City; and Northern California—all urban locations where there are strong feminist networks and significant numbers of feminist organizations.[4]

In this book, I present a collection of those conversations, edited down into short stories. They offer us highly personal, even intimate, reflections on the individual lives and careers of today's self-identified feminists, with a kind of granular detail and reflective quality that is unique to oral history. Oral history interviews allow people not only to describe events that were important to them in the past but also to reflect on how and why they made the choices they did. Interviewees discuss how individuals—perhaps parents, siblings, friends, or teachers—shaped their lives and outlooks. They admit mistakes, they mourn, they cry, and they display anger and also forgiveness. Some look back with pride on their success and hard work, others more with wonder at their luck or at the surprising turns their lives took. The interview process allows people time to gather their thoughts, to go back and correct themselves, to reflect with the interviewer on issues with which they are grappling. Thoughtful, full of both emotion and deeply strategic thinking, these interviews offer a way for us to hear deeper, more meaningful stories than those that emerge on Twitter or in newspaper articles rehashing the "Is she or isn't she a feminist?" argument.[5] The emphasis in these interviews is on understanding how people make sense of their own paths to feminist activism, the work that they do, the contexts in which they live, and how those contexts shape their thoughts and actions.

These activists' stories give readers a powerful way to understand feminism: by getting to know individual feminists. For young people growing up in communities or families where the word *feminist* is a caricature and a slur, these interviews will shed light on who real feminists are and what they care about. For older people wondering whether feminism today is any different from the movement with which they grew up, these interviews will illustrate significant continuities alongside interesting shifts. For those who want to know how to build a feminist life and career, these activists chart a variety of helpful paths. For activists who want to learn about the issues that still require energy and attention and hard work from feminism, these interviews provide a wealth of detail and hint at road maps for the future. These interviews will also serve as essential primary documents for historians and other researchers years and decades from now who want to understand what feminists at the dawn of the twenty-first century cared about and how they did their work.

So whom did I interview? They are people, mostly women, who earn their living through or center their major activist commitments and actions on feminist work. Some of my interviewees have national reputations; many others may be well known in their communities but will not be familiar to most readers. They include nonprofit leaders, writers, journalists, philanthropists, a labor unionist, budding politicians, media professionals, and students. They share a fundamental belief that women still face barriers and challenges based on their gender and that laws, policies, attitudes, and behaviors need to change in order for society to reach the goal of gender equity. They are committed to working toward that goal. Most of them comfortably claim the label "feminist"; a few offer the perspectives of people who advocate for women's rights and empowerment but do not necessarily identify easily with the feminist movement per se.

I interviewed people who came of age during and after the 1980s, when, during Ronald Reagan's rise to power and the ascendancy of the Right, we witnessed a backlash against the gains made by feminist activists in the 1960s and 1970s. I wanted to know more about the activists who, despite growing up during and after that backlash, have been carrying on the feminist movement. I wanted to know what it means to them to carry on that movement today. What do they care about? How do they undertake the task? How do they relate to previous generations of feminists and to each other? How have the political, economic, and technological shifts of the past thirty years shaped their experiences, their goals, and their strategies? What inspires them? Are they optimistic or pessimistic about the future?

This book begins to fill an important gap in the scholarship—very little has been written so far, outside of popular media, about the feminist movement in the twenty-first century. Thanks to women's historians, we have learned a great deal about the nineteenth- and early twentieth-century "woman's movement" that officially launched in 1848 in Seneca Falls, New York, seeking property rights for married women and higher education and voting rights for all women, among other demands.[6] Excellent scholarship has also described and analyzed what happened when the 1960s and 1970s unleashed the "second wave," what appeared to be a sudden mushrooming of women's organizations, consciousness-raising groups, street demonstrations, and publications demanding equal access to jobs, equal protection under the laws, and "women's liberation" from societal strictures about femininity and family life.[7] When I started this project, most syllabi for women's history courses ended around 1995, relying on books written about fifteen years earlier about and by feminists of the 1980s and 1990s who called themselves "the third wave" and claimed to represent a new, improved version of feminism.[8] Second-wave feminists had believed they were more attentive to race, class, and sexuality than their foremothers; likewise, in the 1990s, third-wave feminists claimed new understanding. Kimberle Crenshaw coined the term *intersectionality* to explain how race, class, sexuality, and other distinguishing characteristics intersect in individual lives, creating different experiences of oppression even among a group that shares a gender identity, like women. The word became a staple of third-wave feminist discourse, along with a new emphasis on the politics of the body, gender, and sexuality.[9] Looking around me in the second decade of the twenty-first century, I set out to see what, if anything, had changed since the 1990s.

Historians argue over whether the wave metaphor is helpful, but as Nancy Hewitt has shown, it has lodged itself firmly in the way people write about and teach the feminist movement and is hard to ignore. Hewitt brilliantly suggests recasting the image of oceanic waves—seemingly arising from unseen natural forces to obliterate and replace those that came before—as one of radio waves instead, allowing us to trace echoes from one century to the next, understanding that "signals coexist, overlap, and intersect."[10] Certainly Hewitt's description is closer to the way many of the activists I interviewed see the world. Writer Soraya Chemaly said, "I'm in my late forties and I take from every wave that I need to."[11] Many narrators pointed to their teachers or their mothers and suggested that because they learned so much about feminism from them, they felt connected to the ideas of an earlier generation. Several who are familiar with how historians had written about women's history argued that "waves" might be a useful academic construct, but it did not figure prominently in their own on-the-ground experiences outside the classroom. While the idea of waves might help describe the past, they suggested, it contradicts effective movement building in the present by dividing people. In ways that would likely resonate with Hewitt and others like her, they assert that it is more important to recognize the achievements of those who came before and identify the goals they shared with those who are still active. I saw no big embrace of the wave metaphor for today; while a few said that they had, at one time, identified with the third wave, none of them claimed to be part of a "fourth wave," a term occasionally used to describe the new phenomenon of online feminist activism.[12] I do not suggest that we are in some kind of new wave today, and neither do my interviewees.

But these interviews do help us begin to see and understand the terrain of feminism in the twenty-first century.

Years from now, historians are likely to identify the rise of the internet as a profound moment of change in our culture. Part of my mission was to see how it reshaped feminist activism. According to one of my interviewees, Elisa Camahort Page—founder of BlogHer, the first national conference for female bloggers—male observers in the 1990s assumed that women would not flock to the World Wide Web. "Investors really said women won't use the internet . . . but we now know that women are the predominant users of most of the social platforms out there. All these guys in hoodies owe their billion-dollar valuations to women for sure."[13] Nearly all of the feminists I interviewed use the tools of social media and the internet, to a greater or lesser degree, to undertake their work. There is little sense among these activists of a strict division between "online" activism and grassroots or political activism. These leaders discuss the need to combine online work with face-to-face gatherings or in-the-streets actions; their sense is that neither can succeed without the other now.

Although the internet enables global activism by instantaneously sharing information and mobilizing outrage, my interviewees conveyed a palpable sense of anger and worry about the myriad ways it also opens up a new arena where women's rights and feminist progress are pushed back. Whether they are anonymous online misogynist "trolls" or well-known media bullies like Rush Limbaugh, those who seek to punish women for taking a stand in the public sphere have found new avenues on social media. The people I interviewed describe the huge personal toll for individuals who may routinely deal with violent threats of rape and murder; they also discuss the cost to the movement as a whole when activists drop out or young women choose not to engage out of fear. Indeed, as the internet becomes a more and more important arena for activist work—a new kind of public sphere—it becomes not only a tool for feminist activism but also itself an essential focus of it. Several of these activists describe nascent global initiatives aimed at making social media safer for women through regulation, enforcement of policies, and coalition building among activists around the world.

Social media provides a bullhorn for people with many different points of view. The resulting challenges that arise in the feminist movement are not all external. My interviewees agree that most of the damage has been done by those on the political right. However, when I interviewed them, many also expressed disappointment and anger at the level of criticism feminists have leveled at each other, especially on social media. They disagreed about the root cause of the tension and whether it was significantly different than what had happened in the past or in other social movements, but they all agreed that the cost—to individuals and to the progress of the movement as a whole—was high. Several of them expressed a profound sense of grievance over the fact that they chose to dedicate their lives to the movement—working long hours, forgoing large salaries, making important contributions to the lives of all women—and yet found themselves attacked online by other feminists for words or actions that failed to live up to a politically correct ideal. They suggested that social media can mask the level of sacrifice required to make a living through feminist activism: you can have a polished website and thousands of followers on Twitter but still be living in cramped quarters, worrying about money, health insurance, and your physical safety. While some admitted that harsh critiques served an important purpose in making them more aware of their own privilege or ignorance, most voiced a strong opinion that feminists would be better served by focusing their outrage on "real enemies," like those on the right who have the power to shape laws and policies through politics or media.

When I was interviewing, tensions were high within the movement, and that was clear in my interviews. Of course, tensions within the feminist movement—or any social movement—are nothing new. Women's rights activists have struggled with internal conflicts since the beginning, and feminism is not the only social movement that faces internecine debates over strategy or approach, nor is it the only one in which tempers flare. In our conversation, journalist Rebecca Traister noted that "feminism is perhaps more susceptible to [conflict] because it's such a massive part of the population, and almost everybody in that population has different other allegiances; it's because of the intersectionality of feminism, which is something we need to emphasize but also one of the things that makes it fragile as a cohesive movement."[14]

Seen in another light, dramatic "Twitter wars" that flare up online illustrate an aspect of the movement's success. Today it matters who gets media attention, because there might be professional consequences—who gets a column, who gets a book contract, who gets speaking engagements. There is a larger professional feminist pie now, and people fight over the slices. Those with higher online profiles garner more attention, which can lead to more money, a possibility that only exists because of new opportunities and audiences for women's ideas and words. But that does not soften the impact of the battles. Some of my interviewees asserted that the "toxic" tone was particularly bad on Twitter, where people try to gain attention by tearing others down.[15] They noted that the "blogosphere" was full of people who are trying to build a personal "brand" and whose individual agendas outweigh their commitment to movement building and allies.

While these interviews demonstrate the challenges faced by the feminist movement and the difficulties that can get in the way of productive dialogue, they also illustrate the progress being made by activists who are grappling with complex and painful issues. While the media at the time of the interviews tended to focus on infighting among feminists, the tone of these long interviews is significantly different than what one might have read in popular articles or seen online during the same period. Anger, frustration, and disappointment certainly appear. But there is also clear commitment to inclusivity and analysis that does not assume all people who identify as women experience that identity the same way. These interviews reveal a willingness on the part of many organizations and individuals to reckon with past mistakes and learn from them and to forgive others who might make missteps. For instance, narrators describe learning not to try to "speak for" communities of people and learning to make sure that those who sit at decision-making tables represent a variety of viewpoints. Although some of my interviewees are defensive or angry at times, overall they come across as generous, creative, passionate people who were seeking improvements in the lives of all, not fame or individual gain.

One thing the activists I talked to shared was a boldness of vision for how the world could be better. To get there, they focused on different but overlapping goals: They were trying to change cultural messages that teach girls that their main value is their sexuality, and they were trying to provide girls with a sense of empowerment and tools for self-actualization. They were fighting against street harassment and online bullying, which prevent women from occupying public spaces comfortably. They were working to stop sexual assault on college campuses and helping victims organize and heal. They were pushing for LGBTQ rights, seeking resources for poor women and women of color, and protecting all women from violence. They were helping immigrant and refugee women adjust to new lives in America and empowering them to advocate on their own behalves. They provided spaces for women to express their opinions and sought to get more women to contribute their voices to major media forums and to run for public office, and they persuaded the media to discuss gender in politics and public life. They sought to protect abortion and reproductive rights and to expand notions of reproductive justice. They were trying to support women students, faculty, and staff on college campuses and to change university curricula and policies to better serve women's interests. They funded grassroots feminist projects and aimed to reshape philanthropy in ways that support such efforts. They used the labor movement to help women with pocketbook issues and used the political system to pass laws to make that easier. Taken together, their strategies, approaches, and visions reveal much about how the feminist movement operates.

In addition to shedding light on the movement as a whole, these interviews also provide access to inspiring individuals who help us see how activism unfolds across the arc of a life. The paths my interviewees followed to working in the women's movement reveal a far more complex story than the widespread assumption that feminists are all white, middle-class, and college educated. While many of these activists came from middle-class backgrounds and discovered feminism in college, that was certainly not true for all. I interviewed women whose families came to America as refugees fleeing war-torn countries; whose single working mothers struggled to provide for their children; and one who barely escaped the consequences of drugs and crime that ravished her Minneapolis neighborhood in the 1990s. For some women, activism with and on behalf of women in their own communities came long before any theoretical adherence to broader feminist concerns or a desire to join a movement.

These life narratives provide us with a way to see how feminist lives intertwine with the political and social contexts in which they unfold. While I found many commonalities among my interviewees, I also discovered intriguing differences between older and younger women. None of the women I interviewed was past her early fifties, and none had reached the end of her career. They were not looking back on a finished story; they were all very much in the midst of their activist lives. But there are differences, for instance, between the women who were in their late forties or early fifties and the youngest women in this book, some of whom were not much older than the older women's daughters. I have grouped these narratives into cohorts based on age; I hope that presenting them in this way allows the reader to get a sense of how feminist work fits into lives differently over the life-span and how it is shaped by the political and social milieu in which one's life unfolds.

Part I focuses on women who, in their forties or early fifties when I interviewed them, came of age in the 1980s, during what Susan Faludi termed the "backlash" against feminists' gains of the 1960s and 1970s.[16] These women entered the world of work at a time when there were almost no models for a "professional feminist." As a result, none of them assumed that she would make a living working on behalf of women's issues. Indeed, in many cases they helped create the contexts in which that became possible. Looking back at how their careers have evolved and the changes they have witnessed in society, they are able to provide a longer view, one that often sees cycles repeating themselves.

For those activists in their thirties when I interviewed them, presented here in part II, generation and age proved to be a recurring theme in their narratives. This was especially true for the directors of nonprofit organizations, often tasked with building bridges between older feminists, who now have money and time to volunteer, and younger activists, who are essential to the vitality of the organizations and the movement as a whole. Some of the challenge revolves around social media, which has been a real problem for established organizations; they have operated for decades with long lists of snail mail addresses, printed newsletters, and donors used to handwritten thank-you notes. Leaders of these organizations have had to figure out how to transition to social media without alienating their oldest and most loyal supporters. But the social media challenge highlights a more fundamental question about who is in charge and gets to decide what the organization should focus on and how it should operate. We are used to thinking of the "sandwich generation" in terms of family—middle-aged adults balancing the needs of older parents and young children—but many of these women are experiencing similar dynamics at work.[17]

Questions about the relationships between older and younger activists also emerge in newer organizations that focus on girls: How do adults support girls' activism and empower them to advocate on behalf of themselves? How do girls navigate the challenge of growing out of the movement that formed such an important part of their activist identities? Some of the young women in part III, most of whom were in their twenties when we talked, started out as girl activists and are trying to figure out how to carry those commitments forward. Shaped deeply by student loans and the shock of watching parents and friends go through the recession of 2008, these younger feminists carry a profound sense of economic anxiety that often affects the choices they make about how to engage in professional careers. Coming of age after 9/11, they have grown up with a different sense of the world—warier, more cynical—than those who were already adults when that horror befell the United States and its social and geopolitical consequences began to unfold.

This book showcases powerful, complicated, beautiful stories of individual lives that, taken together, help shed light on a movement. Through these narratives, we grasp the feminist movement's intricacies and the hard work it takes to sustain it. We see the causes involved, the strategies being employed, the stumbling blocks, and the successes. These interviews allow us to see the women's movement at a particular point in time—a moment which, looking back, appears to have been on the cusp of something new. Reflecting on their work in the two years before the 2016 election, these activists reveal their frustrations and their guarded optimism; discuss the networks they created, the skills they learned, and the coalitions they built; and make known their boundless determination to keep moving forward. The building blocks they laid would prove profoundly important in the future that was just around the corner. These narratives reveal how major new developments like the 2017 Women's March on Washington and the #MeToo movement could flourish so quickly, seemingly coming out of nowhere but in fact drawing on the lessons learned from and connections built by women like those in these pages.

Like the people who create them, movements grow, change, shift, and are remembered and carried forward by new generations. This book seeks to document an important moment in the feminist movement by sharing twenty-five remarkable people's own recollections of their experiences, goals, hopes, sorrows, frustrations, and joys. There are many more stories worth telling, and I hope the ones presented here will inspire others to record and share their narratives. I also hope the pages that follow can shed light on how the feminist movement operates today, provide compelling examples of how activist lives unfold, and offer inspiration to those who are looking for ways to get involved.

PART ONE

Activists in Their Forties

The seven women in this section were born in the 1960s and 1970s, at the height of the burgeoning feminist movement. Their early lives were shaped by the fact that their parents were living through the changes of that era. The stories they tell are inflected not only with discussions about the impact of feminism on their own upbringings but with interpretations of how the movement shaped their mothers' lives as well. Some of these women are now mothers themselves of daughters who range in age from babies to full-grown adults, and they reflect on whether or not the world now is a better place for young women than when they were growing up.

Coming of age in the 1980s and 1990s, these interviewees reached maturity during the rise of Reagan Republicanism and what Susan Faludi termed the "backlash" against feminism. Journalist and writer Rebecca Traister remembers there being very little feminist activity on her college campus; her own feminist outrage was sparked by Katie Roiphe's infamous book *The Morning After*, which argued that young women's expressions of concern about "date rape" were false. Writer and media activist Soraya Chemaly was the only one of my interviewees in this age cohort to graduate from a women's studies program; she was in the first class of the women's studies program at Georgetown University. While the notion of "third-wave feminism" started to gain traction in the early 1990s, none of these women found that to be a particularly useful label for themselves. Several echoed Traister's assertion that the term is "a media way of making categorical distinctions that are fundamentally meaningless."[1]

Unlike some of the younger activists in this book, none of these women set out at the beginning of their careers to be professional feminists; it never crossed their minds as a possibility. There was no "feminist beat" when Traister was a young journalist in New York City; she would create that niche herself in her thirties. Chemaly, an outspoken child with a critical eye who went on to start a feminist journal at Georgetown in the 1980s, shifted from journalism to business in order to make a better living. It wasn't until her forties that she felt compelled to rejoin the feminist fray—and found a new space to do so. Elisa Camahort Page of California drew on a long career in the business and tech world to launch BlogHer in 2005—an organization aimed at creating opportunities for women engaged in the world of blogging and, later, social media. Katie Orenstein was not involved in any political activity in college. Her experiences in journalism sharpened her view of the challenges facing women and minorities, and she set out to make change. Orenstein does not think of herself as "helping women." Instead she draws on the tools and language of the business world and argues that she is "investing in underrepresented brainpower, women's brainpower, for the payoff," which in this case is a strengthened democracy.[2]

About half of the women in this chapter have been involved in one way or another with the intersecting worlds of journalism, academia, social media, and business, and half—all of them women of color—have worked in direct-service and nonprofit organizations. Joanne Smith, who founded and runs Girls for Gender Equity in Brooklyn, sees a divide between black feminists who work online and those who work "on the ground" directly helping girls and women. Both Tara Hall of Atlanta, who ran a program for refugee women, and Patina Park, who works with Native American women in Minneapolis, have long worked on behalf of women's rights and empowerment but hesitate to embrace an identity as a feminist. Hall, age forty-five, says, "I really never thought about it. I just do what I do."[3] As a young woman, Park took a job at an abortion clinic "because it was convenient," and that led her to become a passionate defender of women's right to choose. But in her Native American community, she does not find feminism a useful framework for the work she does—it is not a word or a way of thinking that resonates much with the women she serves.[4]

With long careers and experience in a variety of contexts, these women help us understand how feminism has changed over the past twenty years, where the movement is headed, and some of the reasons why even those who undertake its work do not always embrace it wholeheartedly.

Soraya Chemaly

**WRITER AND ACTIVIST, DIRECTOR,
WOMEN'S MEDIA CENTER SPEECH PROJECT,
WASHINGTON, D.C.**

*I definitely repeatedly bump into older feminist women—usually white—
whom I know and respect, who really think there's no young feminism, and it's
because they're not steeped in the internet, and they're not part of this culture. But
there's so much happening that you can't even wrap your brain around it.*

I met with Soraya Chemaly in the sunny kitchen of her Georgetown townhouse in Washington, D.C. We sat at her small table, under a striking painting—a large, bright orange-red rose on a turquoise background—in a heavy gilt frame. At one point in Chemaly's life, after her twins were born, her doctor had suggested she take up a hobby in order to help deal with stress. Without any formal art training, Chemaly picked up a brush and painted every night. One day a publisher saw one of her paintings and asked to license it; soon 350 retailers around the country were buying her products. Chemaly says, "Honestly, this isn't great art. It's decorative, happy paintings, and people really needed happy things. It was after 9/11, and I think that any kind of bright, happy, joyous thing kind of made people feel good." After the economic crash of 2008, though, half of the retailers went out of business and she turned her attention to other endeavors.

Chemaly grew up in the Bahamas. Her family—originally from Jordan, England, and Lebanon—had settled in the Caribbean. They were an entrepreneurial family—her father ran a successful import-export business—and she led a life of privilege in the complicated racial, ethnic, sexual, and political terrain of the Bahamas. She was an observant, curious child who reveled in her grandfather's extensive library—until her grandmother caught her reading a book about Greek art and declared the paintings on the vases pornographic. Chemaly's sense of outrage over gender inequality grew in part from her recognition of her grandparents' unhappy marriage, including the fact that her beloved grandfather apparently had other marriages in other countries. He once said, "You know, you're a pretty girl. Not as pretty as your mother, but you're a pretty girl, and so you'll find a nice young man who will take care of you." Chemaly burst out laughing and said, "No, I'm going to school, thanks, and I'm going to take care of myself." He asked, "Why? That's so much harder." And she said, "Well, so that if I have to, if I married and he's like you, I can divorce him."

After starting a feminist magazine at conservative, Catholic Georgetown University in the 1980s, Chemaly moved into the world of publishing after graduation. Frustrated by the lack of pay in writing and editing, she eventually crossed over into the business end of the field. She worked in the new media division at the Gannett publishing company, where she tried to get executives to understand the impending impact of their swiftly changing world, "but all these newspapers thought that the internet was kind of a joke, something kids played with." So she moved to the Claritas marketing company, where eventually she became a senior corporate vice president.

Forty-nine when I met her (the same age I was), Chemaly had been a feminist her entire life, but it was motherhood that caused her to focus all her energy on the cause. "I used everything I learned [in business] to fuel the work I've been doing in feminism for the last five years. Marketing strategy, market development, marketing communications, understanding in depth the business world, understanding data."

Chemaly has made a name for herself as a feminist writer, critic, and activist. In 2013, the Association for Education in Journalism and Mass Communication awarded her the Donna Allen Award for Feminist Advocacy and the Secular Woman Feminist Activism Award. In 2014, *Elle* magazine named her one of its twenty-five inspiring women to follow on Twitter.

My grandmother was born in what was then the Ottoman Empire in a Christian-Arab town in what is now Jordan, and her family left when she was three. Her mother was fourteen when her father rode into town and picked her up and kidnapped her. So when I was growing up, I really do remember this story that was a fairy tale—it was a family fairy tale—that she was a beautiful young woman and he was a handsome young man who rode into town and picked her up, and off they went into the sunset. I was maybe five the first time I heard that.

I was eleven the next time I remember actually responding to it, and by the time I was eleven, I was much more acutely aware of physical vulnerability. I lived in a place that had a lot of street harassment and was a tumultuous political environment. So when they told the story that time, I said, "Well, you know, actually, I think she was kidnapped and serially raped, and he should really go to jail." I didn't get much of a response. People just kind of ignored it, and then I said it again, and then I got what I think of in my own mind as my first feminist pat on the head. But my grandmother grew up with a mother who was thought to be mad. She was, the way I think of it, left speechless by trauma. Today, I think we would say she suffered from post-traumatic stress disorder and had all of the symptoms of that.

One day, my daughter, my oldest daughter, who was thirteen—she probably looked like she was eighteen. She's very tall, very pretty. She was wearing her soccer uniform and she said, "Hey, can I just go out and get some ice cream?" She wanted to go by herself. I think, ultimately, when I look back, her asking me that was, like, a triggering event. Because when she asked me, I wasn't really ready for thinking about her being out by herself in a city. She had been before; she'd been out in parks and with friends. But this was, for some reason, different. I looked at her and I was like, "Oh, wait a minute. I have to teach her all kinds of stuff I haven't taught her about navigating public space." And I remember locking myself in the bathroom and feeling just this blind rage because I didn't want to teach my daughters about rape. I didn't want to be the person that transferred that information without objection as it had been transferred to me silently. No one ever talked to me about street harassment or rape. The first time I was harassed, it was not just on the street but in my school yard. I was nine. I was waiting; my aunt had forgotten to pick us up and this boy, he was older than I was, he said, "I could rape you here and nobody could help you."

So my poor husband, he came home, and I said, "I'm doing something really financially irrational. I'm stopping all business-related work, and I'm going to write about feminism. Because writing I can do, and I can do it while still managing life." And he said, "Go for it." So then I actually segmented the writing marketplace the way I would have segmented any market. I thought, "OK, well, there are all these brilliant people writing, but they're kind of writing in a bubble to themselves, and then we have this massive mainstream audience, and maybe I could be useful as a bridge." I set out to do that. I gave myself a column. I wrote twice a week for two or three years in the *Huffington Post* just relentlessly. And then, probably once I had gotten into the practice and habit again, that's when I also started writing for other places.

But almost immediately, like really almost immediately, the harassment online started. At first I was just sort of stunned because I thought I hadn't said anything, really. But I got a hanging threat. I'm sort of ethnically ambiguous to look at: I could be Mediterranean, I could be South American, I could maybe be a little Native American—if you really wanted to stretch— and I am kind of polyethnic in my history. But this hanging threat to me came along with a lot of other things, like content that said, "Go back to Africa or Arabia or wherever you're from," which was fascinating to me. I'm like, "Wow, OK, so there's the racism and the ethnocentrism and the sexism, and they're all in the same pot, right?" You get one, you get the others.

I started then writing about harassment and what it means historically for women to speak in the public space, because clearly the harassment that women are experiencing is meant to just stop women from speaking. I remember sitting with a lot of other feminist writers somewhere and we were exchanging jokes—not jokes, but we were exchanging the fact that we get rape threats or death threats. And I thought, "This shouldn't be funny." Like, it's our way of dealing with it because many women don't deal with it, right? They stop writing, or they don't write about certain topics, or they stop writing in certain places, and those among us that were still talking refused to do that, right? We just keep going. But I thought, "It's really not funny."

Once I started writing about it, readers started sending me things. But not just to say "Look at what happened" but "Please can you help me?" That was overwhelming. I had one woman send me all of her police reports and files because she thought her rapist would kill her. He had been illustrating her rape on Facebook, and Facebook wasn't removing it because, to a Facebook moderator, it just looked like drawings of a woman in a bed, and there was no way for her to get through to them to explain the context for what was going on.

I got video of a rape in progress in Malaysia that had been up on Facebook for a month. It had been reported, but no one had taken it down. I was speaking to Facebook representatives, and they were saying all the right words because they had guidelines. But for some reason, it wasn't applying to what women were experiencing.

Jaclyn Friedman, who is head of Women, Action, and the Media, and I were friends. Laura Bates is another friend; she's in England, she founded [the online feminist campaign] Everyday Sexism. One day, Laura called me and she was very upset because there was a video of a woman being beheaded in a Mexican drug war, and it was going viral. It was horrible; it was really dreadful. I wrote a letter to Sheryl Sandberg that morning saying, "I understand Facebook has stated quite openly that they are interested in free expression and women's rights. These are four things"—I don't know what possessed me, I was just angry—"these are four things Facebook should be doing if you're serious about it. Can you please look at this content and tell me why this is happening?"

Honestly, I was a random woman. I just sent it via email through an intermediary who knew her because she was on the board of a women's rights organization, and [Sandberg] responded right away. She put me in touch with her head of global policy, who was very nice, very responsive, but sent me a lot of boilerplate answers. And I kept saying, "You're not addressing what I said. Thanks so much for your nice note, but maybe we could meet."

By that time, it was very clear that my writing work was advocacy work, because they were one and the same. We didn't have those meetings; they kept dropping off. So Jaclyn Friedman said, "Hey, I know how frustrated you are. Why don't we do a public action?" I said, "Yes, but let's get Laura, because she, too, is experiencing these things." Laura had done something quite brilliant. She had just that day, I think, tweeted to an advertiser on Facebook, "Do you really want your ad next to this content?" We used that as the model for our campaign. We were very deliberate in our campaign. I personally feel very strongly that a hashtag has to be linked to action on the ground. It can't just stand alone in virtual space. We had a website that automated tweets and emails from consumers that linked advertisers directly to this content. This was extremely traumatizing, extremely graphic violence against women that was being proliferated on the platform and not removed and very often was actually slapped with the parenthetical, controversial humor tag because that was meant to somehow—. It literally turned the violence into a joke. So day one of our campaign was a Tuesday. We launched it, and Facebook called right away, and we started to negotiate because we had publicly written a letter—the letter was a lot of the letter that I'd sent to Sheryl Sandberg. We had, in that week, 60,000 tweets, 5,000 emails, and sixteen advertisers drop out.

That was in 2013, and I think that there were a couple of things that were notable about that. One was that it was the first time that Facebook responded to any consumer public action. They responded and they said, "Yes, we've dropped the ball on misogyny." A lot of people thought that we didn't understand free speech and that we were censoring, and that totally missed the point. We weren't censoring; we didn't ask them to create new rules. Companies like Facebook and Twitter and YouTube are moderating content day in and day out. They had rules written down. We just said, "Apply the rules fairly."

I remember on the Thursday of that week, we had over 100 media interviews. The thing just exploded. The campaign, I think, worked because it happened at the right time, at the right moment, and because we were very organized. We worked well together as a team. We each had respective skills. We just had a really positive campaign. Every aspect of it worked. But the thing about that campaign is that once it was over, I was like a dog with a bone. I just wouldn't let go.

It's two years later, and we continue to work weekly on these issues, and that's been very productive. There's been huge change. Huge change in the culture. Not because of this—I just mean in those two years. But I think that that campaign [the Facebook Rape campaign] helped put online misogyny on the map in a way that gave people the ability to talk about it differently. After that they designated a person who had worked at a rape crisis center at Facebook, who was extremely responsive. She knew what we were doing and what we were trying to do. We continue to work with them, and now our emphasis is getting women in the global south front and center. Eighty percent of Facebook's audience is not in the U.S.

The purpose of the campaign was not just to say, "Look at this violent content." It was to say, "Think about the way this violent content suppresses women's free speech and civic participation and ability to equally access everything that the internet has to offer." That's really the emphasis of the work now.

In the early part of 2014, I started this loose organization with no formal structure, because there was no money, but called the Safety and Free Speech Coalition. Initially, it was eight organizations, and I picked each organization because it had an area of functional expertise. Basically, I got everyone together and said, "OK, let's pool our efforts. We're all talking to all of these companies: Twitter, YouTube, Facebook, all the major platforms. We're all talking about violence against women, IT, gender issues, free expression, and it's inefficient. How can we work together to support each other?" At that point, we identified a number-one priority, which was getting companies to change their policies around nonconsensual photography and pornography. No company at that point had clear guidelines or rules. You could take any picture from anywhere and post it in any way you wanted. So that became our priority, and that was, as we started talking, probably in the spring—maybe the early summer. I contacted Facebook and Twitter and said, "Can we have a meeting? This is our coalition."

So by the fall, we had meetings with Facebook and Twitter separately to talk about these issues, broaden this network. My goal was to get people in the room who were doing this amazing work that hadn't ever talked to Facebook or Twitter or any of these companies. There are organizations all over the world, civic society organizations, that are doing this work, but it's like they're in parallel worlds. Because you have these companies that have this incredible footprint around the world and they're making all these decisions, but there wasn't a lot of communication between them. So I thought, "OK, since I have my foot in the door, who can I bring in the door with me?" which was the main purpose of this coalition.

By February of this year, we had a major change, which was that Reddit, Facebook, Twitter, and YouTube all announced policies regarding nonconsensual photography. That's a big deal. Facebook really opened their doors, had lots of people talk to us, and everyone in the room has subsequently then worked with Facebook in different capacities. We've done things like translate safety guides into multiple languages. Those are small but important steps, because one of the major issues on these global platforms is language. Moderators who can't speak some dialect in Pakistan can't tell if a woman's getting threatened. They just don't know, right?

In July, I agreed to work on directing a project for the Women's Media Center called the Speech Project, and our two areas of interest are curbing abuse and expanding expression. And what we will be doing is trying to raise public awareness about freedom of expression issues related to gender, intersectionality, how the abuse—what it looks like, what it means, why it's tied to power and control in intimate partner violence. A lot of people think that online abuse is about people getting their feelings hurt or about bullying the way children experience it, which is awful, but that's not what we're talking about. We're talking about such a broad spectrum of harassment, criminal activity, extortion, trafficking, that we hope to put it in context and give it a place in the broader media conversation about these things.

My professional work experience has been a tremendous asset because in order to engage institutions, you really have to understand how they work. And I was in the corporate world for a long time, and that has been a huge advantage to me.

I wanted very, very clearly to create a model for what I think of as a flip-the-switch campaign that could be global. So during the [Facebook] campaign, for example, I stayed up all night so I could manually roll the tweeting over from being focused in the U.S. to being focused in Europe, to being focused in Southeast Asia, to be focused back in the U.S. There was no automated way to do that then. There was not a Thunderclap that would roll it out that way.[5] So I literally was just tweeting to people in Australia, "Hey, everyone here is asleep. Can you pick this up for the next five hours?" And they would, and that worked. We had over 100 organizations sign on in twenty-four hours.

We started something called the International Feminist Project. We invited feminists around the world to put themselves on a map and join a database, and now there are over 4,000 on that. And we haven't been able to do anything with it. We're all, of course, doing this as second or third jobs; this is the problem, right? But the idea behind that is [that] here we have 4,000 women in organizations who have said, "Yes, we want to be part of this global activism." We had eighty people right away say, "We can translate any material you want." Everybody identified skills that they had. I just think we really have a moment, a moment in time where there's awareness, eagerness, and the transformative power of this technology.

When I did the #FBrape campaign, I had actually outlined ten other campaigns that could generate global support, because a lot of the problems we have in feminism, all the clashes and the friction, come from an inability to work across difference. We're never all going to agree, so what is the single-focus issue that we can agree on ten times over, for example, right? How do we find that? In the case of the #FBrape campaign, even though our off-the-record goal was much broader, we did one thing: we said graphic depictions of rape and domestic violence are unacceptable as humor on your platform. That was easy for everyone to see and understand the wrongness of. And I believe there are other issues that are that laser focused that would enable us to do the sorts of things that we can do, and that's where I'd like to get it to. Comprehensive sex ed—that's a big one. We know that there's a global backlash. It's been measured against providing comprehensive sex ed, and we know how important it is. So if you can create a template where people around the world who are advocates for comprehensive sex ed can support a global movement but act locally, that would be very effective.

I definitely repeatedly bump into older feminist women—usually white— whom I know and respect, who really think there's no young feminism, and it's because they're not steeped in the internet, and they're not part of this culture. But there's so much happening that you can't even wrap your brain around it, and that disconnect is really odd. I think, actually, that it would help if we had some mechanism for reverse mentoring, so that it wasn't just a matter of saying, "Hey, older women, teach these younger women," because that's not the situation we're in. We actually need armies of younger women to be talking to older women and telling them what's going on.

Honestly, today, I'm ambivalent because I'm old enough to see these cycles of boom and bust where there is this kind of momentum. But what I always go back to is the fact that we never pervasively shift the education culture, and so every wave has to relearn everything from scratch, basically. And they're learning through culture, they're seeing their mothers working, they're seeing their fathers taking care of children, they're seeing differences, but they're not actively being engaged to think about these things. They're not, for example, learning to build change into institutions. They're not given the words to confront sexism or racism.

I think that we have still a major problem with what I would describe as living with a hermeneutical void. By that I mean, you know, to go back to my great-grandmother, right? Here was a woman who was kidnapped at fourteen, serially raped for years—I don't care what anybody tells me, that is what happened to her—[and] ended up trembling and speechless and traumatized. But during the course of her lifetime, feminists created the legal framework and the language that enables us to talk about kidnapped brides, rape, postpartum depression. Those things, those words, they didn't exist until the late 1960s, early 1970s.

So [new generations of feminists] learn that way because those things permeate the culture, but it's so slow. The fact of the matter is still [that] today, the higher up any organization or sector you go, the fewer and fewer women there are. It's stubborn. [*Laughter.*] It's very stubborn. So I'm not really feeling optimistic. I'm feeling frustrated, is how I would put it. Not frustrated enough to stop. I always say you have to have a sense of humor, but a friend of mine says that's just a way to deflect my anger.

Tara Hall

EXECUTIVE DIRECTOR, REFUGEE WOMEN'S
NETWORK, ATLANTA, GEORGIA

So when I talk about feminism, I am the captain of my ship, of my boat. It's my life. I've only got one shot. And I choose to make a difference in other people's lives as the captain of my ship because I want to take other people on board and drive them to a place where they can land and begin living the life that they want to achieve and be the captain of their ship, because I didn't get here by myself. It took a lot of people to pray for me and to cry with me and to be there for me and to help me see my potential.

A two-month-old kitten joined Tara Hall during her interview, adding a soft distraction from some of the painful realities of Hall's life. Both Hall and her mother are survivors of domestic violence, and Hall credits experiencing her own home as a "war zone" with making her an effective advocate for her clients from around the world who have faced violence and displacement in many forms. At the time of this interview, Hall was the executive director of the Refugee Women's Network, which provides leadership training, financial education, microlending, advocacy, and support groups for refugee women, picking up where resettlement agencies leave off.

Hall was born in 1969 in Long Beach, California, and spent her childhood in San Diego. At age eleven she moved to Atlanta, Georgia, when her mother fled domestic violence. Hall eventually married and had two children but then fled her own abusive husband. She went back to school at Point University and graduated with a bachelor of science degree in human relations with a specialization in counseling. An internship at a twenty-four-hour crisis hotline set her on a road of helping others in difficult situations. She worked at the YWCA of Greater Atlanta and at the Atlanta Mission. In 2011, she became the executive director of the Forsyth County Family Haven and director of emergency services for Tallatoona Community Action Partnership before joining the Refugee Women's Network.

Hall has worked on "women's issues" such as domestic violence for decades, and she takes great pride in the service she provides. She describes a recent event she organized, an "international women's celebration," where her clients came together for food and dancing, and she thought about how special it was to be "women helping women." But Hall hesitates to claim the label of feminism for herself. She notes, "I was born in the era when they were burning the bras and all of that." She asserts that "as women we could do anything. I mean we're not limited. In terms of feminism, I just don't, I don't allow anyone to put me in a box and keep me there. That's all I can say."[6]

I was born and grew up in California. What brought my mother and me here to Georgia over thirty years ago was my mom was fleeing from domestic violence. I grew up in a very violent home, and in order to stay alive we had to leave. And so we took a Greyhound bus here to Georgia with twenty dollars, a bag of oranges, and a roll of toilet paper. We didn't know where we were going to stay. Mom didn't have job. We just knew we had to step out on our faith and make it here. When I came to Atlanta, I was eleven years old. We had some friends who were here who took us in. Mom was able to find a job, and the rest is history in terms of how we got back on our feet.

I got into this line of work because I was fleeing domestic violence myself, and I knew that I had to take care of my children. At the time, I was working for Supercuts. I was a barber, and I developed carpal tunnel [syndrome] so it was difficult to use my hands. So I said I had to use my mind. I wanted to go back to school. I looked into Atlanta Christian College and enrolled, and then they gave me nontraditional housing for me and my children.

I really had to push myself because it was a learning experience for me in terms of being able to rediscover myself. Because for so long in that relationship, I was so programmed to do what I needed to do to keep the peace in my home so he wouldn't get mad, so I wouldn't feel like I was the problem and there would be another fight. So going back to school, I had to learn how to think and do for myself things that I wanted to do versus trying to please him. Little things like, "OK, after class I'm going to go to the mall, and I'm going to stay as long as I want to without feeling like I have to hurry and get back and cook dinner or else he'll get mad." Little things. Even looking at myself in the mirror and being honest with myself and learning how to love myself and appreciate myself again and tell myself that I was smart, that I was beautiful, that I was a good mother, that none of that stuff that happened to me in that marriage was my fault.

I had to reprogram my thinking and start appreciating who I was for the person that I truly am. Every time I aced a test or aced a class or passed a class, I was patting myself on the back. That day when I graduated, it was more than just a certificate of accomplishment; for me it was life chang-ing. It allowed me to go and tell other women who were being victims—regardless as victims of war or victims of domestic violence or sexual assault, human trafficking—that whatever they truly desire to do or want to be that they could do it.

My first experience on the crisis line [during an internship at the local domestic violence crisis line], it was heartbreaking, especially having come out of it myself. I remembered those moments, so I was able to actually understand from the victim's point of view their fear, their frustration, their anxiety. I understood all that. I even understood why they wanted to stay and didn't want to leave—because they loved the man, they just didn't like his behaviors. But I think that made me a huge advocate, a better advocate, because I wasn't just someone on the other end of the phone that was judging them as a textbook case, if you will. I knew firsthand what it was like, so I was able to help them or coach them how to stay safe, what to do and what not to do to stay alive, and give them the resources they needed or whatever.

I think the most traumatizing case that I had was hearing a woman locked in the bathroom with no way out calling for help, and her husband broke in the bathroom, and all I heard her do was scream and the phone went dead. And I don't know what happened on the other end. So I called the police and sent them there, but I don't know what the outcome is. Those are those scary moments like that.

[In] nonprofit work—especially in the work that we do even here, working with women who are minorities—whether it's working with domestic violence victims or the women that we work with here who are survivors of war, the political climate is always a challenge in terms of advocating for the women we work with or educating the judicial systems or the law enforcement officers or even their community at large, because there's always a level of bias that you have to push through, even with victims of domestic violence: "Oh, she must like it, otherwise she would leave. Why does she stay?" Even with victims of war, the women we work with, [there's] the bias of people not understanding what a refugee or asylee is. I hear this all the time: "Why are those people here? Why don't they just stay where they were?" Or "Americans need jobs, why are we helping other people like them?" When I rephrase it and say, "OK, Refugee Women's Network, we're here to help women survivors of war," then when you hear it that way, then you're like, "Oh, it sounds different."

But to say *refugee*—there's a lot of bias even in DeKalb County. Here, there's a large population of refugees who reside here in the state of Georgia, especially in Clarkston, which is where we are, basically. And the community doesn't want to accept any more refugees because they feel like there's too many. And so what we have to realize, and educate our community and our political leaders [about], is that these families have been uprooted from everything that they've known and are expected to come here to a foreign country, learn a language, find a job, pay their rent within ninety days of getting here, and it's impossible. So here there's a community, a feeling of home, because you have such a wide variety of persons from all around the world in this area, where they set up businesses and set up homes, and they feel comfortable with a support network around them that's familiar to them. But yeah, pushing through the laws and educating and—it's always going to be a challenge.

My role with this organization is I'm the executive director. What I bring to this organization is my experience with working with persons recovering from trauma, basically, that also includes [domestic violence victims and] our sexual assault victims and human trafficking victims. What I bring to this organization is that I'm a survivor too. And it may not be that I've been in another country where I'm a survivor of war because of politics, but I'm a survivor of war in my own home when I'm having to battle a man that said he would love me and our children, and it was a war zone in my own home. So I can understand, from my point of view, some of the post-traumatic stress issues that our families suffered from: the fear of not knowing what your life is going to be like, having to leave your home and go to something new, and wanting to make a better life for yourself and your children and having to start from scratch to do that. So that's what my responsibility, or role, is here for the organization.

This year [this organization] will be twenty years old in September. The primary focus of the organization was to help refugee and immigrant women become leaders in their community. So one of our hallmark programs was creating the leadership program where women from all over the United States were recruited to attend a week-long workshop helping them build the skills to become leaders in their communities. Once they graduated from that workshop, they were charged with going back to their communities and help[ing] other women with that curriculum that they learned. As a result, other nonprofits were birthed and businesses were birthed out of that training all over the United States and even in other countries, because we service women from sixty countries.

But there were other women who had a voice, who wanted something more. And so we talk about the economic crash of our nation and women who came here from other countries, even if they were doctors or attorneys or accountants; unfortunately their skills weren't transferrable here, and they had to resort to working in chicken factories or babysitting or housekeeping. Even women who worked as farmers in their countries or sewed or whatever it was, they wanted to do something for their families, because coming here, if you didn't speak the language and your skills weren't transferable, it was very difficult to find a job. So as a result, our organization started a microenterprise program, where women who wouldn't otherwise qualify for traditional loans could come to us and we would give them loans to help give them capital monies to help them start their businesses. So they were able to get anywhere from $500 to $15,000 to start their own business with the help of us helping to prepare a business plan, provide all kinds of training regarding business in the United States and how they could open up a business, and just everything, technical assistance, once the business is open. That's how we addressed that issue. And as a result there were hundreds of businesses that were established through the organization, from bakeries, hair salons, braiding salons, catering businesses, import-export businesses. All sorts of businesses have been birthed to address that issue because we gave women an opportunity to be able to be self-sufficient by being business owners and entrepreneurs.

We received a huge grant from the [federal] Office of Refugee Resettlement to operate that program. And so as women were given the loans, they would have to pay it back, and that money is recycled. So every woman has an opportunity to apply for a loan with that money. Once a resettlement agency brings people here to the United States, they keep them—they help them stabilize—for about ninety days, and then those families are on their own. So we are not a resettlement agency, but we are an organization that kind of picks up where the resettlement agency leaves off.

One of my staff, she is a survivor of war herself. She is a former refugee from Iraq. And she provides direct services and emergency services for those families who are new arrivals here and even those who have been here awhile. We have developed a core group of women who have been here for some time that have learned our systems. So when we have new people come, we have a network of women that can mentor them or shadow them so they can understand what to do or how to go to the doctor. If you need an interpreter, we have someone who can go to the doctor with you, [help you figure out] how to enroll your children in the school, how to get your prescription filled, and all those kind of things.

The organization was founded by a group of refugee women, and they wanted it to be for refugee women, and even our board—a requirement is at least half have to be refugee or former refugee women. The founder of the organization saw a need in the community, and they wanted to meet that need, and that's how it was birthed.

I feel like [President] Obama worked very hard to create opportunities for minorities in general. And he has a passion for making sure those who are immigrants to this country have opportunities, and I'm really concerned about the next administration and what that looks like. What changes will they try to make? Is the next administration going to come in and cut those funds? Because we've already faced some challenges with that. What does that mean for us if we have to close our doors or cut services when we're already underpaid as staff, and I'm having to beg for resources to keep the doors open? And people aren't giving as much as they used to to nonprofits because everyone is struggling. So I am concerned, very concerned. But that's all in a day's work. I'll just have to figure it out, make it happen. I'm really trying to move us away from being so heavily grant dependent and raise more private donations and corporate sponsorships, because I faced too many times in the last year that I've been with the organization where we were facing funding cuts and not knowing if we're going to be able to sustain that. That is why I'm up at night always thinking about, How am I going to get the word out about the work that we do? How can I engage the community and businesses and corporations and individuals to understand how important our work is? And then how can I get them to be open-minded about the populations that we work with and not be biased or prejudiced? And how can I make it where they feel like they're actually a partner with us and we just don't want their money? We really want them to be a partner with us, to have a hand in what we do out on a daily basis. So that's what keeps me up at night.

I'm restructuring our programs. I think once we rebrand ourselves in terms of all that we're doing and what we're offering, the changes that we made, I think that we can get some community buy-in. For example, I talked about a microenterprise program. I want to restructure that so it's more of a women's economic development program and microfinance is just a component under that, because not every woman is ready to start a business. So we could train women about business, and then for those who are ready to start a business, we can help them to develop their plan and then offer them an opportunity to apply for a loan. But for that woman who says, "I want to go back to school" or "I want a job or career," how are we going to help that woman be self-sufficient or self-reliant? And that will fall under workforce development or economic development to help them do that. So that's just a sample of what I'm trying to do to restructure the work that we're doing here, so that we can meet every person right where they are. And everyone has a place here where we can help them achieve their goals.

I've been blessed to have people with high-level experience and expertise that would normally charge thousands and thousands of dollars for consultation volunteer their time for free to help me in this process. Now that is valuable. That's when I talk about donors and people being engaged with the organization, that's the kind of engagement I like to see. People are passionate about our mission that want to help, and we could all sit back one day and say, "Hey, you remember, and now look at the organization. It's thriving; it's sustaining." That's what I'm hoping.

I want our organization to be a global organization. Right now we're settled here in Georgia, and we're doing great work. But I don't see why we can't be like a CARE.org or YWCA International and have locations throughout the world.[7]

My whole idea is to be able to empower women to recognize their worth and be able to overcome their challenges. I always say your circumstances don't dictate who you are. The circumstances are only temporary. They don't last always. But you have something within you. Every last one of you has something in us to overcome those challenges. But sometimes they can be so difficult and so blinding because you're in it so deep that you just need someone who's been there and done that to kind of guide you through that whole process, and that's what I see myself as: a change agent, as that advocate, as that cheerleader for that person or persons.

I feel like I'm a change agent. I do. I try to think outside the box. This is even more challenging because not only do I have victims, but they're refugees and they're victims of domestic violence, and when you're presenting a case for them or advocating on their behalf, it's just . . . [*sighs*]. The people who are making the laws are primarily men. And to try to get them to understand—they'll never know what it's like to be a woman. They'll never know what it's like to be a minority woman, and they'll never know what it's like to be a minority refugee woman who happens to be a domestic violence victim or whatever issue they're facing. And so the challenge is to get them to understand that place where that person we're advocating for is. They can't relate. They just can't.

I'm trying to create more digital storytelling. Instead of me talking about the work that we do, I want to have a digital story of a woman who we're serving tell her story—talk about how she was raped and beaten in a refugee camp, talk about how she saw her husband murdered right before her eyes or her children murdered right before her eyes, having to flee through the woods barefoot, beaten and bleeding to death in order to survive. I can't tell that story and make it believable to someone who can't understand my point of view. But maybe if they see it from someone who's been there, maybe at some point, they'll have that aha moment where they're like, "OK, this is really happening and we need to do something about it."

For me, my passion is, again, women's issues and girls—whether it's domestic violence, working with refugee women—because I felt the need to do something more of a global work. I can't travel around the world because they don't pay me enough to do that. But I think that working with women from all over the world will have a global impact because they may be here today. They may have an influence on their daughters. Their daughters can go back home or whatever, and that seed I planted, it could make a difference in the world.

I want to make sure that we help stabilize the women and the children in our program to a point where they can learn to live again, laugh again, be happy again, not be consumed with the day-to-day activities of just having to survive in a new culture, a new country. I want them to get to a place where they have a new beginning and can enjoy it.

Back in May, we had a huge celebration for the women that we serve. It wasn't nothing formal; it wasn't advertised. I just told my staff—I said, "Hey, on Friday let's have our own international women's celebration. I want all the women that we serve to come here. We're going to provide food. We're going to dance. We're going to just have fun." Wow, so many women showed up. Different women, from different cultures. They were teaching each other how to dance from their countries. We had all types of international foods here that they prepared, they brought a dish. They were able to exchange conversations and hug each other and laugh and videotape it. They were dancing. It was so much fun, and I didn't realize how much that meant to them. I just wanted to do that for them, but it turned out that it was way more than just a party. They came to me in their different languages, and other staff and other people interpreted for me, and they told me how much that meant to them that I celebrated them. And so this is a place of refuge. They feel safe here because we're women helping women.

I'm one of those people that—I mean, I was born in the era when they were burning the bras and all of that. I just—I don't let anything get in my way. I don't allow anyone to put me in a box and keep me there. I've been there and done that when I was married and that didn't work. I just really feel that we as women, we are—we could do anything. I mean, we're not limited. I think that as a woman I can carry a baby for nine months; I can give birth; I can manage my household; I can manage my children; I can manage my career. I mean, I just, in terms of feminism, I just don't—I don't allow anyone to put me in a box and keep me there. That's all I can say.

I fought so hard in my own upbringing, watching my mom and grandmother and aunts struggle in their own homes and not being free to be who they are, that I just cannot permit that in the work that I do or in my personal life. That if I see that something needs to be done, regardless of what it is, I go after it. Regardless of what the challenges are, I go after it. I don't care if I'm speaking before the president of the United States or president of a corporation and they're both male—I hold my own. I'm going to come up with solutions and expect a plan of action. So when I talk about feminism, I am the captain of my ship, of my boat. It's my life. I've only got one shot. And I choose to make a difference in other people's lives as the captain of my ship because I want to take other people on board and drive them to a place where they can land and begin living the life that they want to achieve and be the captain of their ship, because I didn't get here by myself. It took a lot of people to pray for me and to cry with me and to be there for me and to help me see my potential.

Katie Orenstein

FOUNDER AND EXECUTIVE DIRECTOR,
THE OPED PROJECT, NEW YORK, NEW YORK

*I always say, "It might be socialization, it might be sexism, it might be biology,
it might be the weather—how do we know?" You can't win a game if you're not
playing, and in this case the game is called history.*

I interviewed Katie Orenstein, founder and executive director of the OpEd Project, at the program's office in an enormous coworking building in New York City's SoHo neighborhood. She met me at the building's coffee stand, where she picked up drinks for us and we made our way past millennials chatting with each other over their lattes. Over the next three hours, Orenstein shared a wealth of stories and reflections about her life at a caffeinated speed. Founded in 2008, the OpEd Project seeks "to increase the range of voices and quality of ideas we hear in the world" by getting more women's and minority voices into important commentary forums such as the op-ed pages of major newspapers. Orenstein is also the author of a book about the tale of Little Red Riding Hood and how that story has been told and retold over centuries.

Orenstein grew up in Oakland, California; her father was an attorney on the National Labor Relations Board and her mother a progressive educator and mental health expert. Her extended family was multiracial and included several civil rights activists. She did not see herself as feminist or "civil rights-y" as a young person; she studied art and folklore at Harvard University, where she also swam competitively. Fluent in Creole, she traveled to Haiti after her senior year to study folklore. She lived with a Haitian family who was middle-class by Haitian standards but, she says, would be considered poor in the United States. She had many Haitian friends and spent a lot of time in impoverished neighborhoods, growing to know the area far more intimately than most American journalists. She was there in 1990, when Jean-Bertrand Aristide became the country's first democratically elected president and was then swiftly deposed less than a year later in a coup d'etat by the Haitian army. The violence of that period jolted her conscience, and the skewed way that American newspapers reported on the events—informed mostly by wealthier, privileged people—made her start thinking deeply about who gets to shape the narratives we call history and how she might make a difference in that realm.

Orenstein asserted that she is not in the business of "helping women"; she sees herself as making a calculated investment in women's brainpower, which she believes is a vastly undertapped asset that can help strengthen American democracy.

My family is very mixed. My mom is from a long line of blue-blood WASPs, and my dad is [from] immigrant Jews. My dad's father ran a factory that he started with his father, who had come over from Russia. On my mom's side, I am the thirteenth-generation grandchild of William Bradford, the author of the Mayflower Compact, the first American government. Technically, I could be a Daughter of the American Revolution if I wanted to join that.

My mom and my dad met in training for the Peace Corps. My dad heard John F. Kennedy give his speech at Michigan, where my dad was a law student: "Ask not what your country can do for you but what you can do for your country." So he signed up. My mom was just out of college, and they met in Syracuse, New York. I think they had thirty days of training, and in that thirty days they decided to get married. My parents spent the first two years in Malawi, where they were the first Peace Corps members to go to that country.

I know my mom felt that she missed feminism by a hair. Betty Friedan's book came out when she was in Malawi, already married. She feels as if it was a boat that had just sailed, just moments after she got her footing. You know, I don't feel that my mom missed feminism, actually. My mom opened a school in Oakland [California], a Montessori school. Then later, [she] got a degree in marriage family counseling and then later went back and got her PhD and is a psychologist. She just published a book recently. So I don't really feel my mom missed feminism; she did all these really exciting things. She also founded a nonprofit. All of those things you couldn't have done if you didn't have a good sense of possibility, of creative possibility, in your life. Would my grandmother have been able to do that? It would have been very difficult. I think my mom was pretty profoundly shaped by a new environment.

Playing in the sandbox with my oldest best friend—she wanted to be a mommy, and I'm like, "Are you crazy?" I remember this conversation really well; I really remember it. It was like, "If I'm ever that, it'll come after many other things." I feel like I'd have to have gotten a sense of that from watching my parents and my mom. I was a big tomboy. I didn't really associate with even being a girl.

I went to Harvard. I wasn't political there at all. I wasn't feminist, I wasn't civil rights-y, I wasn't anything like that. I studied art and folklore and I swam competitively. I got a grant in my senior year of college to go study folklore in Haiti. While I was there, quite quickly, there was an election, the first democratic election, of [Jean-Bertrand] Aristide, and then a coup. It was as if somebody had injected adrenaline into not just your body but your conscience. I had my conscience jolted.

The first piece I published that year, in '91—lots of violent things were happening. During this period, 100,000 Haitians marched across the Brooklyn Bridge, and they called the *New York Times* "the voice of the State Department." It was widely reported that no one bothered to check if they had a point. I thought, "Well, this is actually something we could check. Why don't I do that?" There was no internet. I bought the *Times* for several weeks, and I counted the sources and counted the column inches, and they were completely right! It was something like 40 percent of their sources were U.S. diplomats, and another 40 were international NGO heads and things like that. Twenty percent of the sources were Haitian, and they were wealthy, French speaking, typically. [The source disparity] affected what facts [the *Times*] chose. It wasn't the difference in the facts; it was which ones you even chose to privilege and put in history and the historical record.

That year, or couple of years, was a jolt not only to my conscience, my sense of social awareness and justice, but also a jolt to my sense of the world as it is. The world as it's presented is not necessarily—well, it's not even a proxy of the world as it is. It's just one version of the world out of an infinite set of versions. Whereas up until then I hadn't had much reason to question broadly.

I worked for a tiny Latin American affairs journal, *NACLA Report on the Americas*, which is where I published that piece. That piece circulated, and some other pieces I did circulated. I took a delegation of journalists and people down to Haiti during the military regime era to report and study. I went and spoke at different places. I went to the White House with Jonathan Demme, and I spoke at the National Press Club, stuff that today I realize was part of the machinery of getting information out, but at the time it was like, "Wow, I better learn what I'm talking about."

The OpEd Project is based on the same belief that my very first article was about, which is the sources: who tells the story will shape history. It's not simply whether the fact is true or false; it's, Which facts do you choose to represent? We don't have a history; we have an infinite ocean of histories, of facts and events and people and interpretations, and somehow, through that ocean, a very small number of us pick up an infinitesimally thin thread that we call history on behalf of all of us. But we live in an infinite ocean. True and false is only a small part of the equation; it's, How do you choose which things out of that ocean to privilege? If you're not telling the story, who's telling it for you? Which facts are they picking? They won't pick the ones you're going to pick. Which events, which interpretations?

I had a front-row seat to life-or-death issues happening right in front of me, and I could see that I also had a soapbox that many of those people didn't. For me, it was very clear: there is something enormous at stake, and I have the ability to say and do things about it that they don't. There's moral clarity here. If I'd like to say "Oh, not me," that's not—that's not an option.

There was a series of debates starting in 2006 and 2007. Larry Summers had given a speech, famous, infamous. It was a speech about why there are so few women in higher math and science. "Could it be," he wondered, "something to do with biological aptitude?" which pissed a lot of people off. It sparked a lot of parallel debates; one of the parallel debates it sparked is why there are so few women in the opinion pages. Susan Estrich, who is a nationally syndicated columnist, accused the *LA Times* of sexism and started a very public fight with the then editor. Ninety percent of their columns were by men. Then everyone starting weighing in at different outlets, and I watched that with a lot of interest.

I thought, These are big ideas: sexism, biology, socialization. They're all big ideas. There's also a more simple part of the problem that's more mechanical that no one's talking about that could potentially offer a much easier solution, which is submission ratios. Nine out of ten submissions to the *Washington Post* were coming from men. Isn't the obvious solution to get more smart women submitting?

I always say, "It might be socialization, it might be sexism, it might be biology, it might be the weather—how do we know?" You can't win a game if you're not playing, and in this case the game is called history. The *Washington Post* called itself a "rough draft of history" and submissions were predicting publication more surely than fourth grade predicts fifth grade. That's an excellent leverage place to start. If you could increase submissions even a little bit in these forums, you could perhaps have a dramatic shift in representation.

The reason I thought that was worth paying attention to is because I'd been participating in these forums because of what had happened in Haiti. A small number of pieces had catapulted me to [being] somebody who is speaking at universities and on television or at the White House. I knew these forums were the front door into the marketplace of ideas and that they are a very good proxy for which individuals and ideas will shape history. They drive resources, they drive talent, they are highly predictive of which people will rise in influence, will get money, will go on TV, as they were for me, eventually predicting leadership across all industries, not in the media necessarily, but across academia, politics, business.

I didn't imagine I was going to start an organization; I thought this was a project someone else should do, like an immediate, short little intervention. I really didn't imagine the trigger that we would hit. In twenty years there's been a massive shift to digital [media]. A big development from this has been the explosion of outlets and possibilities to have a voice. What's been bad for traditional journalism has also presented a big opportunity for us as an organization, because today far more people understand that they can have a voice than ever before. In the past, in order to have a voice you needed to follow a certain path, look like a certain kind of person, and then be anointed. Today, almost anyone can have a public voice, and that offers possibilities to shatter the old hierarchies.

In the seven years since [the OpEd Project has] been in existence, first of all, the representation of women in these critical forums has improved dramatically. We were 15 percent of the voice; by 2012, we did a byline report and [women] were 21 percent, so that's a 6 percentage point shift that represents a 40 percent improvement for women. We're in the midst of a new and much larger data collection project and working with MIT Media Lab. I can say prototype data indicate another really significant shift upwards. So if we were to say that we'd moved about 10 percentage points, roughly, more or less, that's an enormous shift in a short amount of time. Maybe you're working on a problem that will take decades, but some of us are working on problems that are not only solvable but are imminently solvable. There are five-minute problems, five-year problems, 500-year problems. We're working at somewhere in the middle.

What is it we actually do in our programs? It's not teaching people to write op-eds at all. That was true seven and a half years ago; that was the intervention. Very quickly we began to move into these curious experiments around credibility. We are examining, What are the psychological, environmental, cultural factors that lead us to behave as though we have not just a right but a responsibility to shape history? What makes us feel like we matter? That's the fundamental question in our curriculum. It's really not about writing; it's certainly not about writing op-eds. It is about mattering. What if you really mattered?

The implication is, How would we deal with the things we call "consid-erations"? Considerations are all of the things that might get in the way: "I don't have enough time; I might experience backlash; I might get death threats; I might get laughed at; I don't want to look like I'm bragging." There's a 1,000-item list; some of them are poignant and scary. How will you behave if you realize how much you matter and also what could get in the way? For us, it's about trying to prioritize what matters. We don't want to have a history that doesn't have our voices in it. The easiest way to know if it's a consideration or what matters is, Would you want it on your tomb-stone? "Didn't do what I believed in because I was afraid. Didn't do what I believed in because I didn't have enough time." You know what you don't want on the tombstone.

Sometimes people will say, "Well, what you do is communications." Re-ally? Is that what you think? We are looking at the concentrated pools and systems and delivery mechanisms of power and ideas. We're going to try and turn some knobs to do an intervention to dramatically enhance our democracy. We are not brushing up the writing skills. My goal is to ensure that those of us who are underrepresented will have an opportunity to have as many good ideas that impact the world as the idea-dominant class. That's our endeavor: a core principle of citizenship and democracy. So that's what I think we're doing.

I felt like this was a good idea. If it could change my life, it could change other people's lives, it could change many people's lives. I didn't think it should be about women's leadership. My portfolio is public intelligence, not women's leadership. Public intelligence and democracy. I'm looking for the undercapitalized assets, of which women—women's brainpower—is the prize, a fantastic asset. But I'm not interested in helping women. I mean, there's nothing wrong with helping women or any human being, but I'm interested in investing in underrepresented brainpower, women's brain-power, for the payoff. This is an intelligent investment; it is not a charity prize or charity for someone who needs help. It's the opposite. That's a big difference. I don't see women needing help; I see women possibly able to do a huge help for our system and society and democracy. That's a critical thing that's in some ways different from a lot of other groups.

You know, in Haiti, there was a long time where there was oppression in physical, explicit ways: whips and chains and the most extreme ways. But later, there's different kinds of oppression, still sometimes enforced violently. But more, it's infused the culture so people behave their roles that support the oppression. I feel like a lot of that happens in our culture with gender. We behave the role that supports our oppression. We've internalized oppression as virtues—like modesty, modesty to the point of vanity and irresponsibility; like selflessness: "I don't want it to be about me"; humility. These are the virtues of the underrepresented cultures across every culture that we deal with, including women. So we internalize the oppression. The focus on our bodies and the way we look is another way we internalize, that we willingly embrace. If we're worried about how we look physically, if we're heterosexual women, for example, trying to look attractive to men, to the presumed male standard, how much energy does that take, and who is in charge of our value? We have subjected ourselves to their value.

I didn't study feminism; I didn't study women's studies. I was a tomboy. I studied folklore. I did sports. I did art. Obviously I was a beneficiary of all these things, but I didn't really see myself in them or have much knowledge of them. I didn't have much formal training, none of that. If you asked me, yes or no, I would absolutely say, "Yes, I'm a feminist," like I'd say, "Yes, I'm also a humanist." Because, I think, how could you say no? I believe in a world where we all deserve the full range of our humanity. I didn't grow up in—I wasn't part of that. I wasn't in that club. This organization, like I said, I feel like it's part of this context, but I wasn't following the step one, step two, of how to be feminist. Or ever felt like I was part of organized feminism.

I'm sentimental, but not that touchy-feely about it. Let's get down to business, eyes on the prize, the outcome. When I say we need to change the demographics of voice and we need to change the narrative ourself, it's very much in order to have a bigger voice and bigger influence. You need to have more women in more positions of leadership with more money and more voice, and then the conversation begins to change. You are in a position of power to make those choices. There is power in numbers. It's not enough just to have laws. I just feel like the more women—or insert the demographic of your choice—have political and economic value, power, the more freedom we'll have to do anything, and the less our individual choices will be seen as choices for the whole demographic.

I don't know if that's something that is generational, but people my age were raised in a different bubble. Our universities were co-ed the year I was born, so many of us—not everyone but quite a lot of us—had the training and investment to do things and expect things to be done. We have a kind of agency that didn't exist for other eras of women, so why not start? Why not start to build up? Why not start a venture? Run a company and start to build up money and power? Why not? We have the ability to do that.

Joanne Smith

**FOUNDER AND EXECUTIVE DIRECTOR, GIRLS FOR
GENDER EQUITY, BROOKLYN, NEW YORK**

*In my head, I am fighting for my own life. In my head there's always a little girl
inside of me. . . . It's the reality that girls are dying every day. Girls are missing.
We don't measure the disappeared. Girls are being sexually abused and trafficked,
literally. We don't even know—maybe in this building next door there's a girl
being held hostage. We don't know. The reality is that we don't have the
luxury to wait, and we don't have the luxury to do nothing.*

In 2015, one building in Brooklyn, New York, housed both Hollaback! and Girls
for Gender Equity, two of the organizations whose directors I interviewed. It
was also home to the YWCA, which offers affordable rooms to women, many
of whom have been homeless or faced domestic abuse. The women around
me in the waiting area, chatting together personably, came from many different backgrounds and some were sharing painful stories. I met Joanne Smith,
founder and executive director of Girls for Gender Equity, a nonprofit that serves
mostly black and Latina girls, in her cozy office upstairs, as her energetic staff
worked in the next room. She told me about her path to founding her organization that, through physical education, community organizing, and leadership
training, "encourages communities to remove barriers and create opportunities
for girls and women to live self-determined lives." She hopes she can empower
the youth she works with to combat systemic oppression and advocate for their
human rights. She is, thus, helping them prevent and avoid some of the factors
that shaped the YWCA's residents' lives I glimpsed in the waiting room.

Smith finds inspiration in her maternal grandmother, Ninive Leger, who
raised five children in Haiti alongside her husband, Pierre, an engineer. When
the François "Papa Doc" Duvalier regime came into power, because of their relative class privilege, Joanne's grandparents feared for their economic security
and physical safety, especially when one of Pierre's best friends was murdered.
Eventually they moved to New York, but Pierre's degrees were not recognized in
the United States, and he had trouble finding work. Ninive, who had gone to the
United States first, worked a number of menial jobs and secured her beautician's
license. Struggling to support the family, she wrote to President John F. Kennedy
and asked him for help. Kennedy responded with a letter of recommendation

allowing Pierre to apply for a job at the United Nations, where he was offered a well-paying job in Tunisia. Having already been separated for seven years from her children, who had stayed behind in Haiti under the care of Ninive's adopted cousin, Smith's grandmother decided not to move with Pierre. She managed to bring her cousin and all of her children to live with her in the house she bought in Queens, New York. Smith notes the high costs of the sacrifices she made but also looks to her grandmother and her cousin as models of black feminism, calling them "the real feminists of the family who did what it took to take care of the family but were also innovative and leaders and entrepreneurs."

Smith is passionate about the idea that the feminist movement means on-the-ground work with those who are most affected by the intersecting oppressions of race, gender, and class. She feels at times that activists who focus their work in the academy, journalism, or online activism don't fully respect the work that goes into a direct-service organization like hers. But her hope is that eventually academics, writers, online organizers, and community organizers like her can work more closely together to shape long-lasting change.

M y mom was thirteen when she came [to New York], during adolescence. Being thirteen, it was really traumatic because she didn't speak the language. Both my grandmother and my grandfather are Haitian, but it was a very Dominican community at that time. Many times on the way to school, she would be attacked or assaulted, and most of it was because she didn't understand the language so she didn't answer people. They would pull her hair and fight her. So a lot of the shaping around dealing with conflict is you fight back. I have memories from second grade of coming home and telling my mom that a boy kicked me when I wanted to play soccer. He kicked me in my shin and I cried and told a teacher. The teacher told me to sit down, and I sat down. My mother asked, "What did you do next?" I said, "Then we had to go." "Tomorrow," she said, "you go and you play soccer, and if he kicks you, you kick him back. Just don't let him kick you." So I did; I went, and before he could kick me, I kicked him.

That memory has been at the core of a lot of things that I have done, where—obviously, I don't kick people anymore but definitely understand that, basically, as Assata [Shakur] says, it's our duty to fight and you can't allow people to determine what it is you are going to do if you're determined to do it.[8] [My mother] showed me that, through getting her bachelor's degree at fifty. My mom married my father, Ralph Smith, early. I'm their youngest of three; my mom had my oldest sister at nineteen. We were born in Queens, New York. Raising us, many times she would, little by little, go to school and get credits. I would see her falling asleep at the dining room table as she's preparing for the next class. By fifty years old, she finally got her bachelor's degree and walked across the stage, and it was one of the proudest moments of my life.

She also taught me to really hold on to my value set when it comes to family. In our family, there are no throwaways. As much as we argue or fight, or whatever obstacles there are, there's always a way back in. There's always a way; nobody's exiled from a family, regardless of what they have done. I think that's very much shaped how we do the work here; there are no throwaways. You come into the work, supporting and elevating and leading the way with girls and women of color. Regardless of where you are, we'll meet you there, and you have something to offer. Many times you'll hear it when we talk about our Urban Leaders Academy after-school program for middle school students. We say, "You can be a leader for a moment in a decision; you can be a leader for a day or a lifetime. Leadership comes in many forms and it matters." Even thinking of now, within this movement, or moment, of Black Lives Matter and really the racial justice fight of the twenty-first century, everybody doesn't have to be on the front lines and marching; everybody has a role and everybody's needed.

So I feel like those values were shaped by my upbringing, my mother's core values, as well as what we've seen from our grandparents, and the path it took to get here, the shoulders that I stood on to get here.

I was very athletic in high school; I played soccer, I played basketball, and I ran cross-country. This was in Montgomery County, Maryland. I always had a team and I always had a leadership position. For me, as someone who at the time had so much energy and enjoyed sports so much, it was the ideal place to be. High school is where I was able to explore who I was. It's where I realized I was a lesbian, though I wasn't yet naming myself as a lesbian. It's where I decided I had agency of my body and what I would and wouldn't do. But a lot of that freedom came from playing sports. Sports really shaped how I saw myself in the community and in community with people as a team. How I saw reaching goals, how I saw handling setbacks, and it's what got me to college on a scholarship.

I went to Bowie State University in Maryland, an HBCU.[9] I wanted to try to center myself around black culture and feel more connected to my people, because I grew up in Montgomery County in the suburbs and felt like that was missing. I was a scholar-athlete, so much of the time was spent in the gym and on the road and then in homework help. We did things together as a team, as opposed to having that space to explore and seek mentorship. I was the only player to graduate in four years on the team, which was very sad.

Bowie was fun though. The experience there shaped some of my feminist values around sexuality and sexual orientation. In D.C., being a lesbian or being LGBT was very much based on a heteronormative model—you're either feminine or you're masculine. It was a space where I was like, "Wow, this isn't going to really work, and further reinforces that I need to be in New York," because I've always felt like I'm a New Yorker.

I came to New York after that. I wasn't clear on the path I wanted to take. I worked at the Brooklyn AIDS Task Force, and before that I worked at Rheedlan [Center for] Children and Families, which is now Harlem Children's Zone in Harlem. I explored for myself what it means to do social work service, because I graduated with a psychology degree. My path was to be a psychiatrist, but I realized I did not want to be a psychiatrist. My value was now social work, and I realized that, at the core, it was caretaking and creating an environment and situation where there are options. I knew I loved children; I would create spaces for young people to build, to lend their voice, to share their experiences. Because many times the focus was on the parents and the young people were considered collaterals.

The opportunity came to apply for a fellowship through the Open Society Foundations, and I applied for Girls for Gender Equity in Sports. I looked at taking my experience as an athlete and creating space for girls of color to play but also to be seen differently in the community. Because it became clear right away that, had I grown up in New York, the opportunities and the path that I just went on would have been so different. Sports were so important to me in high school that if I didn't have them, that energy and angst and anger around my [absent] father, anger around whatever was going on in school, would have been taken out somewhere else. On the streets possibly; it could have been in gangs, it could have been in relationships and having early pregnancy, who knows. I'm not different from the other girls; it's a matter of what conditions are created for me to thrive.

I felt like it was very clear that what I needed to do was create better conditions for other girls. The freedom I thought I had wasn't real freedom until I knew others were free; our destiny is tied. I had to do something different and couldn't be part of the everyday business as usual or be complacent within systemic oppression. So the fellowship really changed the trajectory of my life, and many other lives, and is what has us here today.

In 2005 we changed the name to Girls for Gender Equity. Girls for Gender Equity in Sports was about revolutionizing the way that girls of color see themselves, starting from a micro level, understanding their physical capacity and agency, and also being healthy and enjoying sports and having opportunities. Then on a macro level—organizing and bringing community together.

Black girls in particular, and girls of color, don't have access to sports, and cultural competence around sports looks so different. We talk about not wanting our hair to sweat out and what that means in gym class. We're just talking about hair, but it's a very deep, culturally embedded value—here's a space where we can have a conversation about it and have a conversation about, What does it say when your daughter's coming home and her hair is up in the air because she was sweating? Well, it says, "I don't know how to take care of her." It says, "I'm poor." It says, "She doesn't care about what she looks like," and then it reflects on the family in that kind of a way; sweating out the perm means she has to pay more money to go and get her hair done again. This is just one conversation; we all understood it wasn't just about creating opportunities in sports.

The fellowship started on September 11, 2001. Yeah, that was the first day of the fellowship. It was the first day of gathering at the Bed-Stuy YMCA. I asked my partner, "What do I do? Do I still go?" I went. I went, set up, and girls came. I was working with seven-to-twelve-year-old girls from the community. It was the reality—it was the stark reality that what was happening over the bridge did not disrupt their lives. Their parents weren't working over the bridge. The schools kept the TVs off; many TVs didn't even work. They didn't know what happened, they didn't see it, they were in Bed-Stuy, Brooklyn, living their day-to-day, and they were here in the gym. I've seen that consistently as movements have been happening, as international tragedies happen; it's such a disconnect from what's happening in the real world. At that time—so we're talking about 2001, 2002—the access to smartphones and digital access was different.

The news sources, where they get their news and how it is they see their world affected, is still a divide, here, now. I had a meeting with black feminist writers and scholars as well as folks who are social media gurus of Black Twitter, and so many of our girls that they are speaking for, speaking about, creating pathways for, and doing revolutionary work around wouldn't know them if they fell on them. They wouldn't even understand the vocabulary that's being used. It's not the day-to-day, on-the-ground conversation that's being had. The meeting itself was about Black feminism work happening; part of what I was feeling within that meeting was a devaluing [of] social service work and how we hold community.

That digital divide is so real, but it's not only about coding and how to get a job within technology. It's also about being able to communicate and translate ideas and connect to ideas in innovative ways, owning your voice, and cultivating a skill set around scholarship and mastery that you can own and be proud of. For instance, in our Urban Leaders Academy, young people have been learning to develop websites and blogs and storytelling and doing so in-house in the after-school environment. Connecting internationally with other youth organizers in Mexico or Brazil who are fighting against oppression and sharing stories in that way via Skype. Exploring, examining, talking about, having classes about Twitter, classes around social media. Not just "This is what you don't do" but "Here are the possibilities." Let's go deeper in what it is they're saying with this point here in 140 characters. How it is that your comment can help shape dialogue. What feedback do you have or comments do you have? Being able to reply back and feel confident in that reply. Being able to do the research—and not just Wikipedia. The research around developing your own point, and critique, and developing your critical thinking skills—and doing it at an early age with the expectation that, even though you're not in college yet and your frontal lobe isn't fully developed, you can do it. You have something to say and it matters. Your viewpoint from this age in middle school really matters and can add to the conversation—the conversation online and not a separate conversation ("Oh, this is a space for middle school students") but on this conversation around [the murder by Dylann Roof of nine black parishioners in] Charleston, I have something to say about the Charleston Nine and the shooter. I can connect with Eric Garner [who was killed by a New York City police officer] and understand what has happened there and how it has impacted us here.

I thought once that by twenty-eight I was supposed to be rich. For me, at twenty-six, after great tragedy in the program and assaults and threats on my life, I realized, OK, I have to make a decision if I'm willing to die for this. I have to make a decision if this is lifelong work for me. There was an incident in the program where this twelve-year-old girl was a great basketball player and loved it. She reminded me of myself; she was committed. But her job that day was to pick up her little sister at school. She didn't; she came straight to the program. We got the frantic call that she didn't pick up her sister from school. Her parents went to the school and they couldn't find her sister; her sister was missing. The parents came to the program; they had been drinking, and they were looking for her. They threatened me and said, "If we don't find our daughter, we're going to come back and we're going to kill you." They're frantic, so they go off, and I stay with the students, and they ended up finding her at the police station. They came back and they're like, "You're lucky. Still, we're going to kick your ass. You're lucky we found her. Just come outside."

In that moment, I probably didn't make the best decision in talking back to them. I was like, "Why do you have your twelve-year-old picking up your eight-year-old?" So that probably wasn't the best thing; it elevated the mood and the fight, and then the threats came. The front desk threatened to call the police, and they ended up leaving. I ended up leaving and looking over my shoulder and wondering if they were going to jump me. I remember waking up the next morning and wondering, "Am I going to go back?" I realized if I don't go back, then I'll never be able to go back, even if I go back. I'd be telling the girls, one, they're not worth it, and two, when it gets hard, you stop. By that time, we had eighty girls coming. We had teams, we had schools, we had things set up. Not going [would have] disrupted all of that. I also understood I did nothing wrong. If they do shoot me, if they do stab me, if they do jump me, I'm willing to go through whatever it takes to do this work. Just committing to that.

Around that same time, an eight-year-old girl was raped on her way to school in the morning, and it was, again, just the reality that, even within our own communities, we have to recognize that the least valued are black girls. Even a puppy would have been valued more than her, walking from the site of the rape to school, nobody stopping her, at eight years old, in the morning; nobody even seeing her abduction; nobody even seeing her. Like, we're invisible. I had to go deep and deeper and take those risks. Not being a martyr, but taking those risks that really meant something, or it meant nothing—it was just another program or activity. I already had vowed to not do that.

In my head, I am fighting for my own life. In my head, there's always a little girl inside of me. I'm willing to do whatever it takes. I would never burn myself alive in the name of gender equity; it's not going to go that extreme, but it's the reality that girls are dying every day. Girls are missing; we don't measure the disappeared. Girls are being sexually abused and trafficked, literally. We don't even know—maybe in this building next door there's a girl being held hostage. We don't know. The reality is that we don't have the luxury to wait, and we don't have the luxury to do nothing. We have to keep creating conditions for girls and creating awareness and programming as well as addressing policy.

It's more the reality that if I don't do it for myself, if I don't do it for my sisters, nobody will. We feel it now, and I say we feel it—black women in this world right now feel it who are connected to the Black Lives Matter movement, who are connected to what is happening internationally, Bring Back Our Girls, what is happening in Haiti.[10] Even six of the Charleston Nine were black women, and it was in the name of white women that this terrorist killed them. Ain't I a woman? We're still asking. I feel like if I can't even do that for babies—eight years old, young girls—then I'm saying I can't do it for myself and I can't do it for other women. I guess I just feel an obligation to do it and a commitment to do it and a desire to do it and an ability to do it, and I'm willing to do it to the best of my ability.

At the same time, it has come at a cost. I have made decisions that have had me work way more than I ever imagined working. I have a work-life balance that's not quite balanced in the way I imagined it. Doing this work has really come at a cost of fun and life and health and creating that balance, and I have to do better around that. Also, the community has to do better around that, I mean the nonprofit-industrial complex, peers, our own community. There's still a lot of work to be done on many levels.

Rebecca Traister

JOURNALIST AND AUTHOR, BROOKLYN, NEW YORK

The young people, they don't know this has all happened before.
They don't know it happened five years ago, they don't know it happened
forty years ago, they don't know it happened 140 years ago. They just don't
know. That's fine; it's not their job to know. But in an ideal universe it
would be their job to learn.

Rebecca Traister started making a name for herself as a feminist journalist when she worked at *Salon*, where she came up with the idea for the media outlet's feminist blog *Broadsheet*. Her first book, *Big Girls Don't Cry: The Election That Changed Everything for American Women*, about the role of gender in the politics of 2008, was a *New York Times* Notable Book of 2010 and won the Ernesta Drinker Ballard Book Prize. Since our interview, Traister saw the publication and enthusiastic reception of two more books *All the Single Ladies: Unmarried Women and the Rise of an Independent Nation* and *Good and Mad: The Revolutionary Power of Women's Anger*, and won the 2016 Hillman Prize for Opinion and Analysis Journalism from the Sidney Hillman Foundation. Writer Anne Lamott has called her "the most brilliant voice on feminism in the country."[11]

I interviewed Traister in her Park Slope apartment in Brooklyn, New York, where she settled comfortably onto a couch in the small living room. I had met her a few times before, and we talked amicably about our children and personal and professional connections before launching into the official interview.

Traister's father grew up Jewish in the Bronx, New York, the son of Russian immigrants; her mother grew up Baptist on a potato farm in northern Maine. They met at Colby College and went on to obtain PhDs in English; her mother taught at Lehigh University for many years, and her father was a rare book librarian. Traister says she "grew up with 40,000 books in my house."

Coming of age in the late 1980s and 1990s, Traister thought feminism was "finished," and although she was interested in Democratic politics and the issue of abortion even as a young girl, she did not foresee feminism becoming a major part of her life. As for many women, her experiences in the work world—first in film and then in journalism—opened her eyes to the need for, and potential of, feminist analysis and action.

Traister learned to be a journalist at the *New York Observer* with "old-school editors ... [when] people still phoned their columns in, and they set the type and still carried it in a suitcase to the printer." She developed her strong sense of journalistic practice and professional commitments and ethics in this "very old-fashioned" milieu, for which she is profoundly grateful but which she also says was "the ultimate boys' club," where she experienced sexual harassment and objectification.

She sees herself as a journalist, not an activist. "I'm pleased enough if a piece that I write becomes useful to people in the movement, but I would be doing my job badly if I were writing for the purpose of being a part of movement building or activism." She sees the differences in approaches and priorities between journalists and activists causing some of the contentiousness within online feminism.

When I interviewed Traister, she was forty and called herself "an old lady" in the world of online feminism. Her narrative traces major changes in the world of journalism and their connections to the changing nature of feminism in the digital world. But she also posits that many of the issues that arise today can be seen in earlier eras of feminist activism as well as in other social movements and that the changes in media should not be mistaken for a new level of contention in the field.

I grew up in a suburb outside of Philadelphia. I grew up in a blue-collar, largely Republican, Irish Catholic neighborhood, where we were very different from everybody else. We had liberal politics; my parents were white-collar academics, professionals; we spent a lot of time going to New York and we went to the theater. My brother and I were very different from the neighborhood we grew up in. I was very conscious we were the only Jews—and we weren't at all religious, but I was super conscious of it. Then I went to a private Quaker high school starting in seventh grade. There I felt the opposite—I was the only person who wasn't Jewish and who was definitely not rich and everybody else had money. It was an inverse experience at being different, but I was much happier there.

I was very interested in abortion. Not for any personal experience of it but because I went to the 1989 march on Washington with a friend of mine, Abby. My uncles were singing in midnight mass in New York City, and we went. It was a Catholic church, and I wore a pro-choice pin into the Catholic church and I wrote a paper about it. There was a sort of dramatic element to my attachment to that issue; I liked going to the march, I liked being angry about this thing. I didn't have a sex life, I didn't have any sense of what a reproductive life was really like—I was very young. I'm not sure what precipitated my attachment to it; I don't think it was a personal connection. I was already in high school; in my English classes, I was certainly reading things with an eye toward gender. I was interested in women in literature, and abortion seemed to be the contemporary issue that I could attach that interest to and exercise some sort of feminist engagement.

No one cared about feminism. That was true even in my liberal high school; our teachers would talk to us about feminism, we were used to looking at books with a gendered lens, but there was no student embrace of feminism. I have a very distinct memory from high school from an English class. We were reading *Jane Eyre* and I remember one of my friends raising her hand and literally saying about Bertha, "I'm not a feminist, but isn't it weird that he kept his first wife locked in an attic?" I do remember sitting there and being like, "I feel like that's a scenario where you could be a feminist."

So I was aware of it, but it never felt like feminism would reemerge. It felt like it was an antiquated thing and that it was over, and every social message I got was "You might have these critiques, you might talk about it academically, but this is not something that anybody is really identifying with."

I was the opposite of an activist in college [at Northwestern University]. I mostly wanted to survive college. At that point, it was a very active fraternity culture. That moment was, in my memory, the peak of backlash. It was the year after Katie Roiphe's book *The Morning After* had come out. I hated that book; I've often said that Katie Roiphe is the reason I became a feminist, because of my anger at that book. It was kept at fraternity houses as a talisman. I was very aware and very angry, but I did not have any engagement with activism on campus. I had friends who actually founded feminist groups that I didn't participate in. I went once to watch the Take Back the Night march, which existed in an anemic form at that point.

I joke often in speeches when I talk to students—but it was really true— that in college it felt like you could go to the vegan LGBT potluck and you could ask that crowd, "Anybody a feminist?" and not a hand would go up. That was from 1993 to 1997. I never had any sense there would be an application for this lens in any professional or public life or even in my own identity. I cannot tell you if I'd call myself a feminist in those years. I just don't know.

[Bill] Clinton was elected the last year I was in high school. I had no engagement as a young person, really, with Hillary. I knew who she was. I was vaguely interested; she reminded me a lot of my mom and she reminded me of my aunt. But I didn't have any sense of connection to her. She felt very distant and academic and of another time then. I didn't have any sense of personal engagement with her at all.

The other things that were happening in that period when I was a young person—Anita Hill was when I was in high school. It's very interesting because I happened to be on the farm with my very conservative grandparents in Maine the weekend of the Anita Hill trials.[12] We were making cider with a group of people, and I was watching the trials, the hearings, with my grandparents on their little television, and they were like, "This woman is crazy, this is a travesty, she's trying to bring this great man down." I wasn't so engaged that I thought, "No, that's not the case."

As far as feminism goes, when I first graduated from college I worked for Harvey Keitel, who was an actor, and I was his personal assistant for about a year and a half. I decided I wanted to work in film but I didn't know what that meant. I came to New York, I looked for jobs in film, and nobody wanted to hire me. Harvey Keitel needed an assistant, and I went to go interview with him. He asked me, "Do you speak Italian, do you drive, do you cook?" I said, "Yes!" and he said, "Great," and the next day he gave me his keys and his bank cards and everything, and then I was Harvey Keitel's personal assistant. It was in many ways an ideal first job, but it was also a window into an extremely unhappy, ugly world, and the ways in which women are treated badly became very visible.

I went to work for *Talk* magazine as an assistant to an executive editor. When I was there, I met young editors and writers who thought that I could write, so they helped me get a job at the *New York Observer*—which was a weekly, quirky newspaper—as a fact-checker, and then I slowly worked my way up there.

The *New York Observer* was like a 1940s newsroom in an old, falling-down town house on the Upper East Side, and there were a lot of old-school editors, and some people still phoned their columns in, and they set the type and still carried it in a suitcase to the printer. It was an incredible once-in-a-lifetime experience of working in a very old-fashioned kind of newspaper run by an incredibly charismatic editor, Peter Kaplan, who is now dead. But it was also the ultimate boys' club. There were lots of young women there, many of whom I became friends with, but it was not a wonderful place for women. It seems silly—I love a lot of these people—but there was an enormous amount of sexual harassment, just an enormous amount of sexual harassment and sexual objectification. It was all in the name of, like, "Don't be humorless about it."

September 11th was traumatic for me. I was twenty-six years old, and I watched it from my bedroom window. I looked out my bedroom window and I saw a plane fly into the World Trade Center. Literally, I was in bed, late to work. I started taking pictures, and it was like, "That's something you don't see every day." As I was taking pictures, and the radio was saying again, "A plane has flown into the World Trade Center," a [second] plane flew into the World Trade Center. I have a photograph of it. I was taking pictures as it was happening.

I remember each thought as I had them. "That plane must have been coming"—I was a twenty-six-year-old woman—"that plane must have been coming to help people who were trapped on the roof. [*Pause.*] And it must have accidentally crashed. How?" The plane was going to help the people on the roof? That was genuinely the only thing I could think happened. I tried to call people and I realized there were no phones, and I thought, "Oh, I bet this is going to be a big story today. I'm late for work. I have to get to work." So I got dressed, I walked to the train station, and the whole time everyone is standing on the street corners watching. It was visible entirely from this neighborhood. I got on the train—the train was there, and I got on it with other people, and we're going over the high part and everybody is staring at what's happening, and then the buildings fall.

The train stopped. We watched the whole thing from the train windows, although we had no idea. No idea. All we could see was the cloud. I thought the top had fallen off one of the buildings. I did not know for a very, very long time. I couldn't call anybody; I remember trying to call. They kept us on the train, and then the cloud started to blow over directly to us, and they let us off the train. I threw up because there was so much stuff coming. There were papers, clothes, everything, blown over here. I just walked home through it, and then I went to a bodega and I stood in the bodega for an hour and a half trying to decide what I was going to eat for lunch. I got Kraft macaroni and cheese, and I walked back to my apartment and I made Kraft macaroni and cheese and I ate the entire four servings myself, and finally calls began to come through and I began to understand what happened.

Then it was just a scary and surreal time for a while. It was horrible. I feel like the trauma of it for me is borrowed, because I didn't lose anybody and there are so many people who did. I'm sure it changed me in a variety of ways but not in ways I recognized or do recognize now—I wouldn't trace that. It was just a terrible time to be in New York City.

I'd been a junior person at the *Observer* for three and a half years, and I wanted to move on. I had a friend from *Talk* days who was an editor at *Salon*, and at that point, in 2002, I was really just learning what a blog was. *Salon* is an amazing place, because when I got there its editor in chief was a man, but the number two was a woman, the managing editor was a woman, there was a woman film critic, a woman book critic, a woman politics editor; it was actually the only place I've ever worked that wasn't specifically a women's magazine that was completely, effortlessly, justly gendered.

When I got there it was 2003, and there were a whole bunch of movies at that time about men performing oral sex on women. I wrote about that and about how this was some justice in the world or something. It got huge traffic. After that, my editor said there was this Erica Jong thing, the anniversary of *Fear of Flying*. It was so mean and ageist, what I wrote; it was called "The Feminine Antiques." [*Laughs.*] I can't believe I wrote it.

My editor, Lori, and the number two at *Salon*, Joan Walsh—everybody was a feminist. Everybody was a feminist. I wanted to do some other piece about feminism, and they were like, "OK, go for it." At the time, the only person who was writing regularly about feminism in the media was Katha Pollitt—Katha Pollitt and Ellen Goodman, mostly, who were in regular rotation about feminism. Susan Faludi wrote here and there; Anna Quindlen still wrote here and there, but I don't think she was regular at the time. The field was wide open. Any story you wanted to write about feminism, no one else was writing about it. There was no competition.

Around the time I started, a woman who is pretty much my age and who I knew professionally at *New York Magazine* also began to write pieces about feminism. That was Ariel Levy at *New York Magazine*; she's now at the *New Yorker*. In 2004, I came across a blog that was just starting, and that was *Feministing*, and I met Jessica Valenti. It was all coterminous. Around that same time, I would later understand, though I wasn't in the netroots world—but around the 2004 election, there was this community building around, especially, Howard Dean and Democratic politics and within that a splintering off of women in the political blogging scene. Ana Marie Cox, Amanda Marcotte—there were a bunch of fights about gender in the Democratic Party activism that produced and helped to produce another tentacle of what would become the feminist blogosphere.

I know a lot of people would hear me tell this version of the story and they would say, "You are telling an incorrect story. We have been online since 1999. We've been online, we were doing feminism online since the mid-90s" in chat rooms and things I didn't understand. They are probably right. This is my take on how this blossomed, both in my consciousness and in my profession.

I'd been at *Salon* for a while and I'd been writing about feminism, but there were so many stories I couldn't write about. I said to Lori that we should start a blog about feminism. There was a real hunger, a tremendous hunger, to start talking about this stuff again. It had been deadened for so long.

There were a lot of women who were working on this [the *Broadsheet* blog] together, and it was extremely successful. There was a big debate that is a valid one: Were we ghettoizing these things, or were we making more space for them? I think both things were true simultaneously. I don't think there's one right answer. For me, the reason I was pro-*Broadsheet* and in general pro-women's media, even in its own space, is that I am on the side, mostly, of getting more space, more people, more stories out there. I also think it's absolutely true that it ghettoizes a lot of these stories and keeps them out of the "regular," i.e., the male, section of the news. It's true; it's very valid. I don't think there's a good answer for it.

If you had asked me as a twenty-five-year-old, "Would you like to be a feminist journalist?" I would have said, "That thing does not exist." I couldn't have aspired to be it. That thing might have existed in the 1970s. It might've. I understand that Gloria Steinem was a feminist journalist. Nora Ephron was a feminist journalist. It didn't exist [in the 1990s]. Now it exists, and it's something that people want. When I was at *Salon* and when young people would start to come to me and say, "I want to be a feminist journalist," I'd be like, "What are you talking about?" I still couldn't conceive of it as a thing you could be.

A couple things happened, good and bad. The conversation gets expanded, more people enter it, and that's a terrifically democratizing thing about the web. You don't have to have the job at the *New York Observer*, you don't have to have a job at the *New Yorker, Salon*; you can have a blog that you run out of your basement in Waukegan. It brings lots of people into the conversation. Happily, the conversation gets more diverse. Journalism is oppressively white. It's now become slightly more diverse, I'd like to think in part because of some of the pressures that have been applied to it from a feminist media. Those are really good things. The whiteness, the elitism, the coastalism gets interrogated when you expand and democratize, and that's also a great thing.

Some bad things, or complicated things: With this expansion, when you lose the gatekeepers, you also get a diluted profession. You no longer have the people who were subjected to the kind of "learn how to be a reporter" that I was subjected to at the *New York Observer*. You get lots of people who don't report. This is journalism, and blogging means the rise of a lot of people who have terrific writing voices, or at least arresting writing voices, but don't actually know about the ethics, the rules, or how to be a reporter. I'm not saying that's a bad thing. Again, it democratizes the profession and allows a lot more people in. But it is true that it has also caused problems within journalism.

It also makes things complicated in feminism, in part because a lot of the people who want into a feminist media and who should come into a feminist media are activists, not journalists. And academics. Great, except then there are these big fights about what the job is, what the priorities are, what the responsibilities are, what the morals are, what the ethics are. This has created a lot of unfortunate tension and anger in what is broadly referred to as online feminism, because you have a group of people who are activists, and they have a very different set of goals than journalists, even though they might ideologically agree and be in the crowd for the same reason.

Journalists have a different set of responsibilities. They feel different ways about language. I've seen this. A few years ago there were fights about *cisgender* and language around transgender rights. Activists were saying, "You have to use these words. If you don't use these words, you are betraying feminism and trans rights." And journalists were saying, "For my job, the use of these words is not useful right now. It's the activists' job to get the words into the culture, and then I can use them. I can explain what they mean, but to simply throw them in stories alienates readers rather than brings them in if I want to write about trans rights." The activists are saying, "That's crazy. You're silencing me because you're not using the words that I choose," and the journalists were saying, "We can't do our jobs if there's an insistence that we use activist language. Our job is not to use activist language." Now, lo and behold, several years later, I think the activists have done exactly what activists do, which is work the words into the language. I would now not blink using the word *cisgender* in a piece.

The other thing you have when something becomes popular is you wind up repeating a lot of feminist history and the history of social movements where people turn on each other; there's a lot of jockeying about power and control. When something is not popular, nobody cares about who has the most power or the biggest reputation or makes more money. There is an enormous amount of anxiety that is very legitimately tied up to things like privilege, race, class, access, whose voices are amplified and whose voices aren't, but it makes a very difficult, cacophonous atmosphere.

Twitter has also changed a lot because tempers are so high on Twitter. I think a lot of people are angry for a lot of reasons, very legitimate reasons. I think anger is something a lot of people, and perhaps especially a lot of women, feel. There aren't always a lot of great outlets to express anger, but Twitter is the perfect outlet for a lot of people to express anger. It's both direct and anonymous-ish, and you have a different avatar out there in the public sphere. You can get attention from the public world without actually having you yourself be out there. All this stuff people talk about—the culture of silencing, the meanness, the fury that erupts on Twitter—all of that stuff happened in the second wave. It happened in the early part of the twentieth century, it happened around pacifist movements, splits about suffrage. It happened in the end of the nineteenth century, certainly around the Fourteenth and Fifteenth Amendments. It just now has different embodiments.

I remember there was a moment a couple years ago when there was a massive fight happening. I was watching one of these battles unfold on Twitter. It was the same week that the *New Yorker* published Susan Faludi's piece about Shulamith Firestone and the way she was drummed out of feminism; it was just repeated history.[13] It just happens, and it happens in a lot of social movements and not just feminism.

I think feminism is perhaps more susceptible to [conflict] because it's such a massive part of the population, and almost everybody in that population has different other allegiances; it's because of the intersectionality of feminism, which is something we need to emphasize but also one of the things that makes it fragile as a cohesive movement.

Within these conversations, they don't really care what I'm saying. I'm not a young feminist. I'm not an avatar of anything for the young people who are the most active on Twitter. In part, it's because I have a platform that's probably considered elite—that is elite. I'm kind of an old lady. It's OK, I'm happy to be an old lady. I could never have built a career in journalism at this point; I couldn't have afforded to. As far as journalism goes, I was on the last chopper before the wave of underpaid blogging began to wipe out, within journalism, most opportunity for young people. I don't think that the real young feminists, the ones in their twenties now, particularly care what I have to say. They don't see me as connected to them in any way, any more than I saw myself connected to Ellen Goodman, which I didn't.

I hope that young people will respond to the book I'm writing about single women; I think they might. It's not that they don't care; it's just that me as a figure is fundamentally uninteresting to them. I'm not a character in the feminism play.

Young people, they come and they're pushing for feminism to become purer than ever before—they don't have any context for what it was like just fifteen or twenty years ago. They don't know how there was no feminism. They think of the world as a place that has always had a feminist blogosphere, that has always had a feminist media. Fine, that's great, good, that's the way it should be. It's how it should be that people don't know what coat hangers are anymore. That's the idea. Except it creates little bit of a lack of perspective, a little bit of a lack of context, a little bit of lack of depth in a lot of the work. A crumbling media and no economic structures to support this kind of feminism does not help, because it does not encourage anybody to gain that depth.

The young people, they don't know this has all happened before. They don't know it happened five years ago, they don't know it happened forty years ago, they don't know it happened 140 years ago. They just don't know. That's fine; it's not their job to know. But in an ideal universe it would be their job to learn.

Elisa Camahort Page

COFOUNDER, BLOGHER, SAN JOSE, CALIFORNIA

We changed people's lives by creating a livelihood for them that did not exist.

I met Elisa Camahort Page, one of the three cofounders of BlogHer, in the beautiful garden outside her home in San Jose; at the end of the interview, she gave me tomatoes to take home for dinner. BlogHer is an organization that started in 2005 as a conference for women bloggers and grew into a for-profit company that sought "to create opportunities for women to pursue education, exposure, community, and economic empowerment."

Camahort Page grew up mostly in California, the daughter of an Eastern European Jewish mother and a Hispanic father from the Philippines. Her mother remarked late in life that reading Betty Friedan's *The Feminine Mystique* had changed her life—as a young mother, she sought out a job, which led to both a divorce and a long and satisfying career.

A precocious child who was politically engaged from a young age, Camahort Page was determined to seek out a career in theater on Broadway. After graduating from San Jose State University, she earned her Actors' Equity card in summer stock theater and tried her luck in the Big Apple. After a while, discouraged and homesick, she returned to California, where she got a job in commodities trading and then sought out employment in the tech industry. After seven years in the field, the collapse of the tech boom and repeated knocks against "the glass ceiling" led Camahort Page to negotiate a severance package and leave the industry.

At that point, I had started blogging for fun. I had a personal blog that was restaurant reviews, and movie reviews, and book reviews, and music reviews, and stories, and it was just totally whatever I was interested in. I wrote this restaurant review of a little Greek restaurant that was near my former office. If you go over to that part of Silicon Valley, there's all these falafel, Greek deli–type places. Most of them are super greasy spoon, and this place was really nice; it was just a cut above. So I wrote this review of it, and then I sent it to three coworkers at the former company, and I said, "You guys should go here now instead of this other place we used to go to. It's much better." Ten days later I go to this restaurant, and there's ten or fifteen people from the company there, none of whom were the ones I sent the review to. I'm like, "Hey, what are you guys doing here?" And they're like, "Yeah, we saw your review, it got passed around, and so this is our new lunch place." I was like, "Wow, that's super powerful."

That's what I like to call my peanut-butter-chocolate moment about blogging and marketing. There was the social weight of being a real person with a real person's opinion. But if I tell you the Athena Grill in Santa Clara is awesome, six weeks later you're going to think, "What was that restaurant?" Whereas if I wrote it, you're going to go Google, "Oh, what did Elisa say in her blog?" That's it. It's got some findability, discoverability, stability in being published online. So you have this combination of authenticity and a real human giving you their word-of-mouth opinion and the stability and discoverability of it living in a place online; this could really be used as a marketing tool.

My first thought was I should find a way to mix my old passion of theater and this. So I approached someone I knew who was an artistic director at a theater that I'd worked at and said, "You don't have to pay me. I just want to experiment with this." And I got a little case study out of that, which showed they'd gathered more emails for their mailing list; more sales were happening through the online box office versus brick and mortar, which increased efficiency; higher percentage capacities were sold earlier in the run; and they could track exactly how many, the cost per ticket sold, and compare it to other advertising methods. So I took that case study and took it to other theaters, and I had a little consulting firm for a bit called Worker Bees.

That's what I was doing when I met my two BlogHer cofounders. They were both consulting in the space as well. I had realized that theaters and nonprofits had pretty low budgets and didn't pay on time. So by then I had a few enterprise customers, start-up customers. There wasn't a really robust social media "industry"; *social media* wasn't even a term.

I was doing that for a variety of clients when I met Lisa Stone and Jory Des Jardins. At that point, around the 2004 election, I was volunteering for the Santa Clara County Democratic Party and writing their blog. I was a hardcore partisan blogger. Lisa blogged the conventions for the *LA Times*. She was a journalist who had left newspapers for the newsroom at CNN, left that for digital, and then had a year at Harvard doing a Nieman Fellowship and now was consulting with online companies about blog networks and things like that. Jory and I met sitting next to each other at a blogging conference. We bonded because in this session everybody had their laptops open taking notes, but she and I both had paper notebooks; we were kind of joking about being the Luddites of the blogging conference.

Lisa and I, in our very first meeting, got the idea to do the first BlogHer conference as a response to people saying that women would never adopt blogging and women weren't blogging. This was all in the context of post–2004 election. There was a lot of stuff going on about "Where are the women in Congress, the women in politics?" It was post–Carly Fiorina getting pushed out of HP, so we had our regular conversations about "Where are the women in Fortune 500 boardrooms?" We had this public catfight going on between Susan Estrich and Michael Kinsley about "Where are the women on op-ed pages and on the Sunday morning talk shows? Where are the women getting inches and getting airtime?" Liz Lawley at Microsoft wrote a post about why she would go to South by Southwest instead of ETech because South by Southwest actually made an effort to have women and to be welcoming to women. And Kevin Drum, who still is a political writer to this day, wrote a post on a political blog that was "Where are all the women bloggers?" It was a rhetorical question because his post was all about how women would never really take to blogging, especially political blogging, because they couldn't take the rough-and-tumble atmosphere, they wouldn't want to back up their ideas and get into healthy debates, and—it was basically—they were too delicate, I suppose, for it.[14]

So here I was blogging about politics and having a hard time getting prominent male political bloggers to link to me. And Lisa was blogging about politics more from the objective journalistic side in the *LA Times*, and lots of other people were too. So Lisa said, "Maybe we do an event and we cover all the same topics, but all the experts are women." We didn't have a conference about *being* a woman; we were just women having a conference about blogging and the technology that supports it. I have to say that it was easy. The first one we planned—from the day of announcing it to the day it happened was 120 days. Three hundred people came; that was the capacity. We had a waiting list. We sold out. There were people from all over the country and from multiple continents. It was radical at that point.

It was women bloggers from across every discipline. We had to work really hard to find three women who would host a mommy blogger session, and then that room was packed. There were political bloggers. There were tech bloggers. I think the overall attendee base was probably more geeky. I mean, it's 2005, and it was easier than it had been previously to blog, but it wasn't a piece of cake. You had to do some coding. You had to know some HTML. You had to do some stuff. So I think it was maybe a geekier crowd than it evolved to be as it grew.

It was feminist from the beginning. The first keynote was about "Can we level the playing field or do we want to create our own?" It was an explicitly feminist organization and event.

We used to always get "What would you say if I created a BlogHim?" And I would say, "Wow, if you feel super passionate about it and think it's needed in the world, then I totally encourage you to follow that dream." That's my stock response, because they never did feel passionate about it. They never did think it was needed in the world. It was a completely ridiculous question, a straw man.

It was after the first conference that we sat down at Lisa's house and we were like, "OK, wow, there's this passion and energy in the community here. What should we do with it?" And we created this mission statement, which was that we existed "to create opportunities for women to pursue education, exposure, community, and economic empowerment." And we were quite specific about wanting to say we were going to create opportunities for you. We're not going to spoon-feed you education and exposure and all that stuff; we're going to create opportunities. It's up to you what to pursue.

By January of 2006, we launched BlogHer.com, which at the time was designed to be both the Yellow Pages and a *TV Guide* for the women's blogosphere. We knew we didn't want to be, as I always called it, another pink-and-purple silo on the web. So we covered tech and we covered career and we covered politics and we covered news, in addition to food and family and entertainment and all that stuff.

In July of 2006 we launched the ad network, the BlogHer ad network. And from there it kind of grew. We figured out ways to aggregate our community and help them monetize their social platforms too. We developed an analytics platform. We launched new conferences. We did a bunch of different stuff. We bootstrapped for about two years before we got our first round of venture funding. We happened to get our first round of venture funding a year before the recession hit. We ended up with four rounds of venture funding and then having an exit with this larger women's media company, SheKnows Media, in 2014. So the conferences still exist. BlogHer.com still exists. The network still exists.

I've said since we merged that this has been the most productive and smooth merger that I've been a part of. I mean, it is different not to be running the show, so to speak, after ten years of it being our company. It's definitely different. Part of that is freeing—I'm not sad I don't have to go to board meetings, and I'm not sad I don't have to deal with investors. But it's definitely an adjustment.

We were never a nonprofit, and people assumed we were. I don't feel like it was hard for us to raise money; I do feel like we got the woman discount on our valuation. It's because we were women doing woman-y things. If I'd been a man wearing this hoodie doing woman-y things, my valuation would've been higher, and if I'd been a woman wearing this hoodie doing non-gender-specific things, my valuation would've been higher. When we started, people assumed we were going to be a nonprofit because we wanted to create opportunities for women. We said, "No, thanks." Why? We wanted control, and you control your destiny more with a for-profit. So we were always for profit, always about helping people make money.

When you hear people tell you stories about how putting their blog on our network helped them to stop having to choose between medicine and food, I'll match that against anything other feminist organizations are doing. We changed people's lives by creating a livelihood for them that did not exist.

I mean, it is still really hard because the advertising market is changing so radically. It's super hard for a smaller blogger to make good money. But plenty of folks were making money that made a huge difference. I always think about my one friend who's a public school teacher, and she was able to retire five years early because she was making money from her blog. So there's a million stories like that. We, in fact, did a survey several years in a row, and we called it the BlogHer Economy, and we quantified: we paid $36 million to bloggers in five years, I think about 3,000 bloggers. And that was a business that didn't exist for those women that were sort of small to medium, not big superstars of the internet but just really creating great content and having something to say and having an audience who really cared what they had to say.

I feel like if feminism is about equal opportunity and choice, then that's pretty broad—it should be a huge tent, feminism should be. It's not asking for anything narrow; it's asking for, at the very highest level, can we all just have the equal opportunity to pursue what we want to pursue, choose what we want to choose, and be treated the same and respectfully for it if we do? My definition of feminism is pretty broad, I guess.

Back when we very first started BlogHer, one of the questions was "Why does it matter?" Back in 2005, the mainstream media was just starting to pay attention to the blogosphere as being a resource, and they were finding sources there, and they were quoting people, and they were citing people, and almost without fail they were citing white men. We were going to rebuild the patriarchal gatekeeper system of the mainstream media in this new, democratized—it was just going to be a damned shame if we recreated that on the internet. And that was why it matters. And it matters, because if you are less vocal online or less out there online, you are less discoverable online. You are less discoverable by people seeking sources. You are less discoverable by people who have opportunities to offer. You are less discoverable by people who need help or people who need support. I mean, the fact of women getting quiet, why it matters is because it stunts their opportunities. It stunts people's perception of what society is like, and it stunts the opportunity for what is still the most beautiful part of the internet, which is how people come together and help one another and find support and kindred spirits they never knew they had and find learning and find connection and find relationships.

A lot of people find people in the internet who help them live another day. And when we quiet people down, who knows who's not finding that voice who would help them live another day?

I feel optimistic in general. I feel like politically we are going through Dick Cheney's last throes, as they say, of the power structure that has been realizing they can't possibly hold on to this power, that its loss is within their sight line, and they are reacting in the most violent and oppressive way they can think to do to put off the inevitable. I always say that representation matters. Do you want to know why it matters that Hillary Clinton is a woman and why, yeah, I want a woman president? It's because I've gone my whole life without representation in the highest halls of power. I had to start a company in order to work with women's leadership—still never experienced a woman president. And if you look at media, commerce, government, education, women still don't occupy the halls of power to the ratio that they occupy the users or the audience or the consumers or the people doing the work. So that's the work that needs to be done, to make sure we don't somehow create our version of apartheid, where a minority continues to really hold sway over a majority populace that doesn't look like them. And double that for women of color.

We focus a little too much on the pipeline, and somehow we blame the women, that they're not filling the pipeline, as opposed to [the fact that] they *used* to fill the pipeline. The numbers actually have gone down on women studying [computer science]. But that didn't help them achieve representation, or it didn't help them once they got into a company. I mean, it gets tiring. It gets tiring to be maybe the only woman in the room; maybe you're one of a couple. Maybe you get interrupted more. They've shown statistically that women get comments on their reviews talking about their attitude or how they express themselves, which are completely sexist in nature and don't happen to men. That stuff actually and statistically happens, and it's exhausting. And maybe after you do it five or ten years, you're like, "Why am I beating my head against this wall?"

The atmosphere of that kind of constant proving yourself and having to be twice as good to get half as far, that is exhausting. If you can go avoid that and create your livelihood another way, whether it's starting your own business—which women do to a greater percentage—or if you can go do it in another line of work, why wouldn't you? Who wants to be so exhausted from that instead of by your actual job?

From the beginning, BlogHer, we were omnipartisan. We worked really hard to have representatives from every political perspective. When we talked about politics, we were for every kind of blogger. We actively and explicitly sought out diversity, and yes, we were a for-profit company that wanted to make money ourselves and wanted to help women make money. I just think sometimes people have a very limited box that they want to put feminists into. And I think, if nothing else, we kind of show that feminism can look like profit, and feminism can look like fashion bloggers, and feminism can look like conservative Mormon mom bloggers who are pro-life and feminist. And I know there are people who would disagree with me. I know there are people who think if you're pro-life you cannot be a feminist. You don't get to decide what everybody's feminism looks like. None of us do. Because that's kind of counter the whole point, in my opinion.

Patina Park

EXECUTIVE DIRECTOR, MINNESOTA INDIAN WOMEN'S RESOURCE CENTER, MINNEAPOLIS

I think sometimes there's pushback, even in the [Native American] community,
that saying that we're equal [to men] is a lie from the beginning. But it's more about
respect. Are women respected and are they held at a position of equal authority,
equal decision-making, equal competence as men? That said, I would say yes!
I don't want to be an equal with men. I don't. But I do want to be respected.
I want my decisions to be heard, listened to.

Patina Park grew up in North Dakota. She had been born to a Sioux father and white mother and was adopted by Native American parents but didn't identify strongly with Native American culture until later in her life. As we sat in her cluttered office, filled with art that women in her organization's programs had made, Park spoke openly to me of being on the autism spectrum and reflected at times in our conversation about how that might affect her interpretation of events and people's motives as well as her own reactions. As a young woman working in an abortion clinic, and later as an attorney working on behalf of Native children caught up in the child protection system, she saw her role as "an advocate for the individual" rather than as someone taking on systems. More recently, though, as she has taken on leadership roles and become involved in a network of activists through the NoVo Foundation's Move to End Violence, she has begun to embrace the language of systemic oppression and to think about what her role might be in challenging that.[15] Although she works to "empower" women, she does not embrace feminism as a movement that feels relevant to her own community.

I grew up on a farm for the first twelve years, so very independent. I would get up at the crack of dawn with my dad when he'd go out to feed the cow, and I'd go horseback riding. There are pictures of me on horses where my legs are straight out because I wasn't even big enough for my legs to go around. I can remember going horseback riding for hours first thing in the morning. I wasn't in school yet, so I must have been four or five. I'd only come home to eat. My dad working on the farm and my mom busy raising the kids, I spent a lot of time by myself, but on a farm that's awesome.

I moved into Bismarck, and my junior high, seventh grade, had hundreds of kids. So it was quite a shock. My biggest memory of moving to the big city is everyone kept talking about this thing called MTV, and I had no idea what it was, because on the farm we had CBS and NBC, that's it.

I just remember being in a daze. Now I can appreciate, too, how the autism kind of played into where I missed stuff. Probably didn't know better but also had this strong sense of being in a foreign land, that they had rules and stuff that I did not understand at all.

I can remember a very vivid moment. One of my best friends, who was named Amy, lived close to me. We'd hang out at each other's houses. I was at hers, and her dad went off on this tangent, venting about drunken Indians that had been down at this bar in downtown. But I remember just sitting there and thinking, "My dad doesn't drink at all." Not being able to put what he was saying in any kind of context of my experience. I didn't know any drunken Indians at that time. Any. I had no idea what he was talking about. But once Amy told him later that I was Native, he didn't really want me coming around anymore after that. But we remained good enough friends that she followed me her second year of college and moved down [to] Arizona State.

While I was going to college, I was working part-time in a women's clinic and ended up managing the front desk in the front office. I managed the front and then the nurse managed the clinic. We did abortions, too, mostly serving indigenous women. I did counseling. I did phlebotomy. You did just a little bit of everything. I was doing that while I was going to school. Once I got [to the clinic], it just felt so like I was with my people, kind of, I just fit, that I stayed with them the whole time I was in school. They were kind of misfits too. Kind of a different framework of thinking about how people should behave. No judgment, just open-minded. I worked there because it was convenient, and then once I got there, I absolutely supported everyone's right to make their decision. There's no other way I can think of to be. People who are antichoice? I have trouble getting my head around people who try to take their framework of looking at things and place it on someone else. It's illogical. "If you don't believe in it, don't do it" is the logic.

It felt good knowing we were helping people. Even the daily aggravation of the picketers was almost like bonding as a group, because we all had to deal with those people, many of whom would use the clinic when it was convenient and then go back out picketing after their two-week check. It was amazing to me the hypocrisy of people. They'd have their abortion because they were God's only exception. It was OK for them. It was not OK for anyone else, but when they found themselves pregnant? More oftentimes than not, we would be serving former picketers or people who had become picketers. Those people just drive me crazy, but we'd still serve them and be compassionate. Either you believe people have that right to make the decision that's best for them or you don't. You don't get to classify or judge people based on whether they fit some certain mold or not.

For me, it's always been more important to be there helping the individual with that whole process rather than to be out on the streets howling for the whole. I find, a lot of times, people who are activists for the whole have lost sight of the individuals that are actually impacted. They don't really know the stories of the ones whose rights they're trying to enforce. And that's fine, because at a policy level the individual may not be as important. I've always been more about the individual.

It's only recently in my life where I have gotten to the point where I'm moving more into activism, because I use dialogue that's more about systemic oppression and racism and pulling those policies apart that have continued this racism. I think it's partly due to age. I'm forty-six now and I've been in a role now for a couple of years where I'm running things rather than representing or working with someone one-on-one. I'm getting further away from the individual people. And because of my participation in [the] NoVo [Foundation] process, I'm with a group of activists. I'm the only service provider within this Move to End Violence cohort. So I'm meeting people who use this dialogue just naturally. Ana is from Mexico. She lives in Chicago now but she frequently [would] talk about essentially dismantling the capitalistic patriarchal system. Hearing her talk about it is different than reading it. It absorbs, for me, better when I can hear it, ask questions, and help me put it into a context. I'm starting to see a shift.

Mostly recently, probably the biggest shift that happened is because I went to South Africa for two weeks as part of NoVo as a learning exchange. We spent a week in Cape Town and a week in Johannesburg. We started at Robben Island and we ended with the Apartheid Museum, and we met people, all these NGOs, in between. I remember apartheid. I remember it in the news and I heard people talking about it. While I was down there, I learned about the problems that the Africans were having with loss of language, loss of land, being removed and placed in these townships, the huge disparity between socioeconomic opportunity for indigenous people of Africa versus the settlers. And I realized this isn't about race at all; it has nothing to do with color. It is colonialism. This is the impact of colonialism. It's the same here as it is back home. For me it was a very profound experience. Prior to that experience I didn't get it. Almost all the languages, indigenous languages, have a word that essentially equates to "all my relatives."

The concept never really hit home until I went to South Africa, that we really are all relatives, particularly the indigenous people, regardless of where we are on this planet. It's not just Lakota or Ojibwa or indigenous people of the United States or the First Nations. Really it's all of us. [We've] had this same experience from colonization and no one talks about it.

I loved law school. It's all very logical and pragmatic; I love that about law. And it's subject to interpretation; I like that too. I never thought about Indian law or Indian tribal law. Never even considered that stuff. After graduating, I ended up clerking for a judge. He was one of the ICWA [Indian Child Welfare Act] specialty focus judges.[16] That's really where I started getting exposed. I really didn't even identify as a Native person until I got to Hamline [University], and then I started to kind of rediscover that.

For a year and a half, I did executive compensation and benefit analysis for nonprofit health systems. I've never been so miserable in my life. It was the worst job ever. You know, they paid me a lot. Benefits were great. I would walk to work every day: "I hate my job. I hate my job." And when I turned around to leave, I was dreading that I had to come back in a day. I was so unhappy. Maybe if I'd gone there right after law school I would have never seen court, seen the families, had that experience, but the shift between these families who are struggling with all this stuff and still doing a remarkable job and CEOs bitching because they don't get use of the corporate jet without claiming it as a benefit and wanting these golden parachutes even if they're fired—it was too much.

So the ICWA Law Center, which is still in town, called me out of the blue and said, "Listen, would you consider working for us?" And it took me, like, a second. There was no doubt. I gave one week's notice. I dropped projects. I was so glad to be out of there. I worked for the law center for almost four years. Direct representation of Indian families involved in child protection in state court and tribal courts.

Oh my God, I loved that job. Because I really felt like I was helping people. I was an advocate. A strong advocate. I rock in court. I just do, because I can be the reasonable one no matter what. I think because I'm so pragmatic and I'm so "it is what it is." People's situations didn't impact me at an emotional level. The fact that a mom had been house jumping or living out of a car or was prostituting herself to make ends meet, I had no emotional response to it. No judgment. It is what it is. But I could frame it in a way in court to be sympathetic or to be just matter-of-fact. "I mean, what else do you want her to do?"—I was good at that. I finally had one case happen—and I was already getting tired—but this case made me think, "It's futile." The futility of the child protection system and how totally dysfunctional and messed up it is. I don't know if it is that way everywhere, but it certainly is in Minnesota. I just decided not to do it anymore.

I wanted to try to get into a role where I was preventing. Here [at the Minnesota Indian Women's Resource Center], we are focused on healing whatever needs to be healed. We have a multitude of services. We have been in this space now—it will be twenty-five years in November, but we've been around for thirty-one. It was started by three Native women and a man. The oldest program is our training to help educate service providers who are working with Native communities to better understand the history, communication differences, cultures, stuff like that. We also have Nokomis Endaad, which is "Grandmother's House" in Ojibwa, and that is a co-occurring chemical dependency program, so all of our clients have both a mental health diagnosis—whether it's a chronic one or situational—and they have a chemical dependency problem. It's the only gender-specific—because it's only women—and culturally appropriate dual-diagnosis program in this federal region. They utilize an elder in residence. They do sweats. They go out ricing. They'll go out and gather sumac. They integrate culture. Even if I have clients who have not been raised traditionally, have never gone to the reservation, their families don't even really know where they're from or how to follow, when we start integrating ceremony and medicines, traditional medicine like sage, cedar, sweet grass, tobacco, it connects to them on a cellular level, and that helps programming stick in a way so the other stuff can work. We also do a lot of mind-body medicine work. Most of the things that these mind-body medicine groups do are actually historically traditional medicines and techniques that have been used by indigenous people forever.

We have our family stabilization work, which is child protection. We try to prevent [the need for child protection services] through parenting classes, life skills, one-on-one case management, and in-home parenting is what we're doing a lot now, because our clients are struggling so intensely with mental health issues they can't even function in a group. Our staff go out to their homes.

Then we have Sacred Journey. Sacred Journey is the second-oldest program. A healing journey. These are for our women twenty-one and older. It's a support group [that meets] twice a week. They do culture [and] tradition, but they also do curriculum on life skills. A lot of them, particularly if they've lived on the street quite a bit, don't know how to grocery shop or how to manage a budget or how to manage a house, and so they learn skills like that in there. Plus, it's not a dry program but they cannot be high when they come; however, the vast majority stay sober and keep sober throughout the time they're coming. Those ladies make beautiful quilts. They're constantly doing stuff. They're just amazing. Then we have an *Oshkiniiqikwe*—this is for women, girls really, under twenty-one—and Safe Harbor. This is a risk-reduction, harm-reduction program for trafficking, to work with victims or to work with kids who are at very high risk, which is all of them. If you're Native and a youth, you're at high risk, because the numbers there are hugely disparate. In 2013 one of the Minneapolis cops who does trafficking said 75 percent of his cases involve Native American kids, and we're less than 2 percent of the population. So, huge.

I think in some of the younger groups, *feminism* is a word that may come up more often. It's never been a word I've heard in my entire academic professional life up until fairly recently, when it kind of bubbled up to the surface again. What's interesting to me is even when I'd see it bubble up, it was still more of a negative. It was more like calling out people who say they're feminist and point out how they're not. I despise that kind of stuff. I disengage from it—in social media, in articles, on TV and the news reports. I've seen a few things recently—mostly because of my Move to End Violence colleague Jamia Wilson, who does a lot of work with online bullying and that women experience far more of that and how to legislate that too. How do we get antibullying, cyberbullying kind of stuff? But it's never been really in the framework of my thought process.

I don't see violence as solely a gender issue. I can empower women and children. I can. But "children"—there are boys in there too. I can empower women. Like, say she's in an abusive relationship. I can give her all the programming, empower her, get her to see what a healthy relationship is. She may leave him, but there's another one that takes her place, and I've done nothing to end violence against women and children. I'm still only saving them one at a time. So to me, the gender focus on ending violence is part of the problem. The men, at least in my community, and that's all I can speak to, also come from the same traumas that the women have: from the boarding schools, the sexual, the mental, the physical abuse, the trauma of not being able to be a man for your family, too, as child protection [services are] taking them away. Your kids are going to boarding school. Your women are being attacked. I can't imagine the impact because I'm not a man, but it's not a gender issue. It's a person—it's a trauma issue. We have to address the trauma. Not that I'm saying there aren't some evil people in the world. But I don't think there are all that many. It's so interesting to me. Empower women so we don't need men anymore? I just, no matter what, I can't. I can't embrace that thought process.

We do Two Spirit work. In Lakota and Sioux, the idea is that if an individual, a male, is born with female qualities, and vice versa, that's actually a blessing. They're a better person for it. Historically, they were seen as elders, teachers, wise men or women. And to be married to one was beyond awesome. Then Christianity came with colonial people and that shifted. And so we're really trying to turn the discussion back to traditional ways of thinking of it and respecting and honoring the family and however they identify.

The word *equality* is sometimes a struggle, too, because there isn't equality between genders anyway, just by virtue of nature. There is difference. Men are traditionally stronger because they have more dense muscles. There's a science to the differences too. So I think sometimes there's pushback, even in the community, that saying that we're equal is a lie from the beginning. But it's more about respect. Are women respected and are they held at a position of equal authority, equal decision-making, equal competence as men? That said, I would say yes! I don't want to be an equal with men. I don't. But I do want to be respected. I want my decisions to be heard, listened to.

PART TWO

Activists in Their Thirties

The women presented here were all between the ages of thirty and thirty-nine when we sat down for an interview. They include some who have appeared on national television and whose work has been covered in the national media, as well as others whose careers have attracted far less attention. These eleven women come from a wide variety of backgrounds—from the drug-ridden streets of 1990s north Minneapolis to immigrant communities in New York City and farming families in rural Wisconsin.

Taken together, these life narratives reveal a changing landscape of feminist activism. Compared to the women in the previous section, far more of the activists here were trained in women's studies programs, which by the late 1990s and early 2000s had become more prevalent in educational settings. One striking note in these stories is how deeply women's studies classes appealed not just to white, middle-class college students—as is sometimes assumed—but to working-class white women, such as labor rights proponent Trisha Harms and Erin Parrish, former director of the Minnesota Women's Consortium, and to women of color, including Samhita Mukhopadhyay, founding member of the blog *Feministing*, and Kwajelyn Jackson of Atlanta's Feminist Women's Health Center.

In another shift from the earlier decade, some of the women in this chapter had mothers who were feminist activists on issues such as reproductive rights. The focus of feminist activism has changed since their mothers' time, partly as a result of my interviewees' efforts. Jackson's interview reveals the complexities of reproductive justice frameworks that are starting to supplant a focus on reproductive rights. Hollaback! founder Emily May and her colleagues helped coin the term *street harassment*, which Holly Kearl then drew upon as well for her Stop Street Harassment campaign. Kearl also was an early activist in the realm of campus sexual assault, getting her alma mater to make information for victims more readily available and foreshadowing a focus of activism that would become far more familiar to the youngest women in this book.

Major events of the twenty-first century have indelibly affected the women in this section. When the planes crashed into the World Trade

Center on 9/11, these women were young adults, and several of them re-count specific ways in which that day changed the course of their lives, turn-ing them toward social justice activism in new ways and reshaping how they think about the world and the country in which they live. Their stories are also shaped by the economic crash of 2008. For example, Kwajelyn Jackson recounts how she was working in a bank at the time but could not stand the feeling of being one of the "bad guys" and turned to the world of nonprofits.

These women were in college in the 1990s to early 2000s, when email was becoming more popular (AOL was introduced in 1995) and the inter-net was starting to make its mark on the world. In their early work experi-ences they were more likely to use the World Wide Web than the women before them, but some, including Erin Parrish, remember the challenges their organizations faced adapting to this new world. They embrace the opportunities that online activism presents, although they also recognize the challenges it poses. As Dana Edell, founder of the SPARK Movement for girl activists, commented, "Online spaces open up the potential to work with thousands in one click." But, she noted, working only online leads to the loss of in-person connections and of a certain kind of energy. "There needs to be that combination, because you're not going to get that deep relationship reaching thousands online, but if you're only working on the ground you're not going to get a global movement. We need to find those ways that we're doing it all."[1]

Many of these women are also deeply concerned about the toxicity of the online world and its impact on face-to-face interactions. Emily May and Samhita Mukhopadhyay, among others, expressed deep dismay at the frac-tiousness of the online feminist community. Parrish reported seeing the kind of divisions she had once noticed only online showing up in commu-nity and political meetings in Minnesota as well.

Several of these women—Harms, Parrish, Kenya McKnight, founder of the Black Women's Wealth Alliance, and Kabo Yang, director of the Minnesota Women's Consortium—live in the Twin Cities, Saint Paul and Minneapolis, Minnesota, and their interlocking stories reveal both the con-nections and the fractures within that vibrant feminist community. Minne-sota boasts the Minnesota Women's Consortium, an umbrella organization for 150 women's nonprofits across the state that is unlike any organization found in other states. Parrish grew up in the organization, rising from col-lege intern to executive director before leaving for a new job just before our interview. Yang, the daughter of Hmong immigrants, is the new direc-tor; Harms serves on its board; and McKnight has been involved in several of its projects and programs. Their narratives reveal a long and organized history of feminist activism in the state as well as the challenges facing organizations that rely on older white activists but which also want to honor and meet the demands of newer, younger, more diverse communities. Minnesota passed the Women's Economic Security Act in 2014, and these women's recounting of that story and their reactions to it constitute a case study of the possibilities for and the barriers to making real progress in women's lives through legislation.

As this generation of activists seeks to make change, one theme that emerges in several of their stories is their sense that we need to change hearts and minds and behaviors, not just laws. This conviction was forged at least in part through the horrors of police violence unfolding during the time of these interviews and the Black Lives Matter movement that was taking shape in response.

Black Lives Matter echoes through many of these interviews, mentioned most often as a model for how to make change. But the violence and terror that spurred the movement also cast a long shadow and overwhelmed several of the interviewees who felt it most personally. The mood in these interviews was mixed. Asked whether they felt optimistic or pessimistic about the future, most gave conflicted answers. Samhita Mukhopadhyay revealed an ominous sense of foreboding—she worried that feminists were being distracted by online arguments with each other instead of focusing on major issues like attacks on women's access to abortion and health care. Kwajelyn Jackson felt depleted from dealing with the emotional costs of the wave of police killings and yet also cautiously optimistic about the potential for real progress.

Dana Edell

FOUNDING DIRECTOR, SPARK MOVEMENT, BROOKLYN, NEW YORK

I don't want to be running another girls' program. This is not a direct-service organization for girls. This is a movement, an intergenerational movement, where we work with girls as part of the solution.

Entering Dana Edell's apartment in Brooklyn, I was immediately struck by the artistry of the space: it was full of bold colors, dramatic patterns, and textured fabrics, a fitting home for a theatrical person. Clearly, Edell was a person whose life was full of flair and passionate engagement with the arts. As I learned in our interview, Edell's mother had yearned to be a concert pianist but was forbidden from pursuing her dream—in Edell's words, "That isn't what a nice Jewish girl did." Edell's mother promised herself then that she would never dash her own children's dreams.

Edell grew up in Wilmington, Delaware, and felt alienated at her private school because she could not find an artistic community there. One summer, when she was attending Interlochen, an arts camp in Michigan, she saw a sign for auditions for its renowned academy and signed up to audition on the spot. Before the age of cell phones, her mother knew what had happened only when she got an acceptance letter and a bill for tuition. She arrived at camp a few days later; after listening to her daughter express her desires, she agreed to support them.

Edell discovered feminism at the Interlochen Arts Academy. Devoted to the technical aspects of theater, including building sets and designing lighting, she always felt like she had to prove she could handle tools and climb ladders. She acted in *The Heidi Chronicles*, which she says taught her about the feminist movement, as it traces the main character's feminist awakening through the 1950s, 60s, 70s, and 80s.[2] Edell found it insulting to have male directors telling her "how a woman would walk" and decided to direct plays herself, starting with *Equus*, Peter Shaffer's adaptation of her favorite *The Bacchae*.

Wanting to follow her passions for theater, activism, and ancient Greek, she attended Brown University. There she joined a program founded by the playwright Paula Vogel, in which students facilitated theater and poetry workshops for women in prison. While in college, Edell cofounded a program for girls in juvenile prison, and after graduation she and a friend went to San Francisco, where they founded Inside/Out Performing Arts, serving girls in prison and homeless and domestic violence shelters.

Hungry for more academic grounding and training for her developing ideas about theater and activism, Edell enrolled at Columbia University to study directing. The program's focus on preprofessional training didn't fit her sense of how she wanted to use theater for activist purposes. It would take a national tragedy to help her find her purpose in New York: working with girls, supporting them as they learned to tell their own stories and to push back against the media's hypersexualization of their bodies.

M y second year [at Columbia], 9/11 happened the first week of school. That was a real catalyzing moment. I was directing *Miss Julie* at the time, which was this nineteenth-century Swedish play about a rich woman who has an affair with the stableboy. I was feeling disconnected making theater, and I was like, "Why am I making this play right now? Our city is on fire."

I really missed teenagers, hadn't worked with teenagers since I got to New York, and was feeling, particularly after 9/11, that I have to *do* something. All the activist energy in me was frustrated that I was in grad school and not actually serving the city in some way. A lot of people in my life, after living in New York through that—there was this sense of "What the fuck do we do? We can't go back how we were before. This has really changed us."

I found a high school in Harlem not far from Columbia, on 137th Street: A. Philip Randolph, a giant public high school on the top of this hill. I remember hearing that on 9/11 the students had run up to the roof after the first plane had hit, and they actually saw the second plane hit from the rooftop of their school. I got to pitch to this one English class: "I want to do a theater project. If you're interested, meet me after school today." There were twelve students who were really interested, so I ended up going to that school a few times a week after school and making a little theater piece with a group of students there. By the end of that semester we'd created this performance piece. There was a minifestival that somebody had produced that was theater by teenagers in response to 9/11. I started to see, "OK, I can be at Columbia and also do some of this work."

I met a woman who was an actor in my program, Chandra, and we immediately connected. We decided we were going to do a theater project with a group of girls from the neighborhood around Columbia, and we got the administration to give us the theater for free for the summer. We were putting flyers up and connecting with anyone we knew.

Somehow we got a group of eight girls that summer, and we made this play together that was called *Say It How It Is*, and it was just amazing. Chandra and I worked really well together, and we devised this whole play with the girls that they wrote, with scenes and monologues and stories that came from the girls' lives and experiences.

Kristin Marting, the artistic director of HERE, a downtown theater in New York, afterward was like, "We should talk, this is really incredible work." She basically offered us her theater. We very quickly incorporated as a nonprofit within a year of the show.

Our first year, Chandra and I each wrote a personal check for $500 and we opened a joint bank account, and we were like, "Now we have $1,000 for our first year." We produced three shows on $1,000 (plus lots of donated space and materials) that first year. We started building momentum, inviting funders, getting support through fundraising efforts through the performances. It was called viBe Theater Experience. I ran that for ten years. That was a huge part of my life in New York, building this nonprofit. We produced, in the ten years that I was there, over sixty shows that were all written and performed by girls.

I started reading about girls' psychology, and most of the girls' psychology books felt like it was about a lot of middle-class white girls. Ninety-nine percent of the girls in viBe were girls of color; almost all of them were from low-income communities in New York. I was feeling frustrated with the academic literature I was reading, and I was wanting to write. I started thinking about a PhD. Then I saw the NYU program in educational theater and I was like, "What?! I had no idea this even existed!"

I knew I wanted to write my dissertation about the girls' theater work, and I needed support and theory that could help me do this. I started taking classes in the applied psychology department. I immediately connected with Carol Gilligan, who was teaching at the law school. I had read her books and was very inspired by her work.[3] She was a huge mentor for me in terms of feminist psychology and theory around thinking about girls' voices. She totally provided the theoretical frame for my research.

During this time, I was still directing five shows a year with the girls. I was starting to get more and more frustrated with the ways that they were performing stories. I felt like it was dangerous, and we weren't really supporting them in the way that they needed to be supported. The lines between theater and therapy, drama therapy and performance, were getting too fuzzy for me, and I didn't feel like it was ethical.

I was also getting burned out on the stories of violence. Again and again and again. Every kind of violence. A lot of rape, a lot of sexual harassment and sexual violence and assault happening. I was getting to the edge of "What if instead of providing a space for girls who have suffered all of these things to make theater where they can heal, what if we just stopped that shit from the beginning? How do we do that?"

One of the professors I was working with at NYU was like, "Have you heard of the SPARK Summit that's happening in New York? Deb [Tolman] is a developmental psychologist who is planning this summit that's going to be about girls and sexualization and activism, and I know you're interested in these things. You should email Deb."

So I sent this cold email to Deb. I had never met her. I was like, "I'm a big fan of your work and I heard you're doing this summit, and if there's any way I can help I'd love to volunteer." She was part of the APA [American Psychological Association] task force on the sexualization of girls. They released this big report in 2007 on the sexualization of girls that had a huge, huge impact.[4] They were going to do this one-day summit to present the findings of the report and wanted the summit to also include girls and action stations where there were ways to take action to challenge sexualization. I became the coordinator of the action stations at the summit.

I had never been to that kind of academic/activist intergenerational space. This was in October of 2010. We had about 400 people. I felt, for the first time in a really long time, in a really positive activist space that was about strategizing solutions. I'd been feeling, after my dissertation research and my viBe work, "Wow, girls are in so much pain right now." The SPARK Summit felt like, "Oh, we can actually take action."

I got an email from the core planning committee for the summit a few months later. They were like, "We've got money and we really don't want to let this go. We're looking to hire somebody who wants to figure out what we can do. We want somebody who has a foot in academia and a foot in the girls' world. Would you like to be the executive director?" I was like, "Uh, yeah! Absolutely!"

The first thing I did at SPARK—that was super exciting about this whole new way of organizing—I was like, "I don't want to be running another girls' program. This is not a direct-service organization for girls. This is a movement, an intergenerational movement, where we work with girls as part of the solution. The first thing we need to do is get a team of girls that I'm working with so I'm not running a program for girls, but they're part of our organizing strategy if we're really going to challenge sexualization."

That first year we got, I think, about twelve girls on the SPARK team. We had sent out a call for girl activists through our social media and reached out to the dozens of girls' organizations we had partnered with in planning the summit. We got about fifty applications and had the resources to accept twelve girls. We brought them to New York in the fall of 2011 for a training retreat. The training was a whole combination of "history-feminism-activism 101." Some art-based training, some organizing training. Blogging, strategizing action, and strategizing campaigns. It was a really intense four days in New York. We built a private Facebook group with the girls, and the girls had to check in with Facebook every day. That's how we started organizing, through Facebook. The girls would identify something that was pissing them off or something that was in the media that we wanted to take action on. Then we would strategize on how to take action.

SPARK would not exist without social media. This organization, ten years ago we couldn't have done it at all. It would've been impossible, because what it allowed us to do was to work with girls in different cities and regions and countries. We had a girl in rural Ohio who was like, "I'm the only feminist in the state of Ohio!" By last year, we had girls in eight countries and all throughout the U.S. The relationships the girls built online could never have happened without the internet. It was also very intergenerational with the girls in the team. We had girls ages thirteen to twenty-two on the SPARK team, which is a huge, huge range. Being on the internet, you don't really know how old anybody is, so it doesn't really matter as much that a fourteen-year-old is pitching this to a twenty-one-year-old who's challenging the thirteen-year-old. We can forget those boundaries because we're not sitting in a room talking all the time.

We were able to build a much more diverse team because we were organizing online, and any girl with internet access had the ability to engage with SPARK. We didn't have to deal with transportation issues or schools or families, which allowed us to build a really socioeconomically and regionally diverse team. Their perception of feminism and organizing and what was important to them felt different—girls in Maine and girls in LA and girls in Chicago. It was very exciting. I feel like I was really understanding girls in the U.S., whereas the last ten years it had been girls in New York City. They are a very specific breed, girls who grow up in New York City.

Our retreat was in the fall of 2011, October, and it was Halloween season. There was a Halloween costume that was horribly offensive: A sexy skeleton costume, and the skeleton was wearing a yellow sash. It was a measuring tape, and she had a little button that said, "Hi I'm Anna Rexia." That was actually our first campaign; we started a petition on Change.org.[5] This is early Change.org days. We had 300 or 400 signatures on that petition, and we won. The company took it down. They sent us a letter saying they'd removed the costume and will never sell it again. It was very exciting. "Wow, what?

Did that just work?!" That was really exciting to me. The girls got pretty riled up, like, "Whoa, we can do something."

During the holiday season of toys, Lego had come out with their new Friends line with "Legos for girls," and it was super ridiculous. You can build a beauty salon! One of our girls, Stephanie, wrote a blog [post] that was like, "C'mon, Lego, really? Stop condescending to girls. I love Lego, and I'm a girl, and why do you have to resort to stereotyping? What you're doing is actually really dangerous and you're limiting the potential of what girls do." Some of the girls tweeted the blog at Lego and posted the blog on Lego's Facebook page. It got hundreds of comments on Lego's Facebook page. We wrote another petition on Change.org: "Lego, stop condescending to girls and make a commitment to more diversity in what girls can be in the Lego figurines." The petition exploded; within a few days, we got 20,000 signatures on this petition. We were suddenly getting media requests from all over the world. Tons of media requests. We started immediately media training all of our girls. The face of this campaign can't be an adult; it has to be the girls. The girls started doing all the interviews, and that was really exciting. It got really big, and then we got an email from the chief marketing director at Lego. We had a meeting with a bunch of the Lego corporate folks and some of the engineers. We presented a "gender audit" that the girls created that analyzed gender within the Lego company, from their board (all white men) to the gender breakdown of their toys and the ways they market to girls versus boys. We presented our ideas for how they can do better. They listened and defended their company, and we agreed to stay in touch. In their next season, they offered a new line of women scientists!

On the heels of that, we were like, "Now we have the attention of the media. Now suddenly there are all these journalists interested in SPARK and in 'What is SPARK? What are you doing, and are you just fighting toys?'" We knew we needed another campaign once the Lego was dying down a little bit. We had been talking about Photoshopping in teen magazines. That had emerged as an issue the girls were interested in. Julia, one of the girls, was like, "I'll write a petition." We got on the phone: "Let's choose *Seventeen*," because we wanted to choose a magazine that had been making efforts to do positive things for girls. You say you care about girls, you say, "Love your body the way it is," but you're Photoshopping girls' bodies?

That got a lot of media also. The petition got about 80,000 signatures on it, and it went global very quickly. We had a meeting with the editor of *Seventeen*, which was huge. So *Seventeen* ended up promising never to Photoshop ever. It was a huge win.

We started expanding the team. Over the next few years, we grew from twelve girls in that first team to thirty-seven girls last year. The team kept growing, and we kept deepening our mission and the kinds of campaigns we wanted to run.

We wanted to get a little bit away from just challenging corporations and into more systemic change and thinking about shifting rape culture ideas. We talk a lot about sexual violence prevention. The National Federation of [State] High School Associations [NFHS] is the certification agency which certifies over 1 million athletic coaches in public schools across the country, and we wanted to offer sexual consent education to coaches, who could then go talk to their athletes about violence prevention. It was a campaign that probably had more impact than anything else because we got these coaches—we got the NFHS to provide free resources for coaches on sexual consent and sexual violence prevention. It got no media attention, nobody really cared; it wasn't flashy. It was more a real partnering, communicating, working with the coaches.

About a year ago, we started getting over 200 applications when we would put out a call for more girl activists to join the SPARK team. We needed another space. There's so much hunger for girls to be connecting online as activists that we can't possibly work with all of them because we don't have the capacity at all. We have two staff members. So we created the SPARK Action Squad, which is an online space for girl activists globally, and we have about 400 folks on that squad right now. It's entirely online, and it's run by a leadership team of four girls from that squad. Right now, it's a private Facebook group and an email listserv and building toward using Slack, which is a new online platform we're moving toward right now. There's a "Take Action Tuesday," where every Tuesday they pitch an action for the girls to do. They have a book club; they have movie nights where they'll watch movies together. They're constantly posting links to issues, things that are erupting in the media that are connected to feminism in some way, or to girls' rights or women's rights. A lot of antiracist work also. That's become a political space online for a huge group of young folks. It's not actually just girls. There are a few boys in that space, which is cool, and a lot of folks who don't identify on a gender binary in that space as well.

The SPARK team has also shifted a lot over the past four years. We were entirely online, with the exception of the annual retreat, which kept growing. We had girls in eight countries, which was pretty wild. We had a girl in Indonesia and Jamaica, in Georgia, the country. We'd organize these campaigns and realize, "This issue is so different in Jamaica than it is in the Netherlands."

We made a specific, very deliberate choice that we wanted our team to be majority girls of color. It was significant and wasn't necessarily the number of girls applying, but it was important to us that SPARK was led by girls of color. I mean, it was frustrating—our staff is all white. We wanted to make sure that girls of color were the majority of the SPARK team and that they were taking more leadership roles in the work as well. Last year at the retreat, we did a day and a half of training around antiracism work. We brought in a facilitator, an incredible, incredible woman of color who was actually one of the leaders of the Black Lives Matter movement now. She was fantastic.

This past year, I started feeling really disconnected from a lot of the girls on the team. Especially because the retreat was so powerful, and we'd done some deeply personal work together. I feel like because we had that very intense experience and then went back to being online 100 percent, I was missing that personal connection with the girls. We lost a lot of girls. The team was too big. We realized with two staff members to try and manage these thirty-seven girls, that they were slipping through the cracks all the time. In an online space, you need daily accountability or they will disappear. We actually started talking with the girls about restructuring the whole organization. Those conversations started after the new year, around January or February of this past year, and started talking about "What is this work that we're doing? How do we make it as sustainable and as productive as possible? How do we use the tools we have online but also acknowledge the real challenges of organizing online?" I realized we have to have a hybrid on the ground/online. We had moved too much online, and we had lost some of the texture and relationship and energy of really working with girls.

What I've learned, and we at SPARK have learned, is that we cannot do this work entirely online. I also learned with viBe that you can't do it entirely on the ground. If it's entirely on the ground then you're only serving the bubble you're serving, which is useful in a lot of ways; you're planting deep roots, and I believe in the ten years that I was working with the girls at viBe we did amazing work with a few hundred girls. But online spaces open up the potential to work with thousands in one click. There needs to be that combination, because you're not going to get that deep relationship reaching thousands online, but if you're only working on the ground you're not going to get a global movement. We need to find those ways that we're doing it all.

Erin Parrish

NONPROFIT LEADER AND FORMER DIRECTOR,
MINNESOTA WOMEN'S CONSORTIUM, SAINT PAUL

It's almost like the definition of feminist leadership has changed and that
if you're not that professional feminist, then you're not seen as a leader in the
movement anymore.... Social justice used to be an outlier. And there's good
and bad things about it becoming more mainstream and becoming
more part of the public conversation.

Erin Parrish and I met in her dining room, where her new puppy insisted on joining the conversation from under the table, much to my amusement and Parrish's chagrin. Parrish worked for the Minnesota Women's Consortium for ten years, moving up from intern to executive director. As an umbrella group for nearly 150 women's nonprofits from across the state, the consortium is unique in the nation and gave Parrish a bird's-eye view of the shifting terrain of feminist activism in the first decades of the twenty-first century. Founded in the late 1970s, the consortium contributed centrally to many of the significant successes feminists have had in Minnesota, most recently including the passage of the Women's Economic Security Act in 2014. The bill, originally sponsored by state speaker of the house Paul Thissen, included important legislative changes such as doubling the pregnancy and parenting leave for state employees, expanding sick leave, and investing in getting women into higher-paid jobs and into entrepreneurship and business ownership.

But the consortium also struggled during the time Parrish was there. The economic crash of 2008 affected the organization's funding streams. It had to adjust to the growing importance of social media and the challenge of maintaining the support of older feminists while reaching out to younger women, women of color, and rural women, who brought new issues to the table.

Parrish's reflections on her years at the consortium and her views on the changing terrain of activism in the state and nation show a remarkably clear-eyed vision of the challenges facing older organizations as they confront new realities. She also carries a deep sense of understanding of activists on both sides of some debates. She worries about the lack of empathy she sees among activists and about what she describes as a problematic "attack mode" that she notices not just online but in face-to-face meetings. She is frustrated by those who say she has "left the movement" because the nonprofit organization where she now works does not have an explicitly feminist mission and by the assumption that one has to be a "professional feminist" in order to be a leader. At the same time, she is optimistic about the shifts she sees in rural communities like her family's, where she believes that feminist conversations have managed to go "mainstream" and are happening around kitchen tables, leading to significant change.

Parrish was born in Wisconsin, but her parents took over the family farm in rural Illinois when she was three. Parrish loved growing up on the farm, taking care of the chickens, calves, and pigs and hanging out at her grandmother's local hair salon. She maintains a strong connection to rural areas and people. An "underachiever" by her own standards, Parrish struggled in high school after her parents switched her from a tiny rural school to a much larger suburban school, which she found overwhelming. She started skipping classes and "hanging out with kids that maybe I shouldn't have been hanging out with." Concerned, her parents pulled her out, and she finished her degree by correspondence school—mailing all her assignments via the post office—while working full-time at a local chain restaurant. With little idea of what she wanted to do, she enrolled in cosmetology school but didn't like it and showed little talent for it. When she went to talk to the director of the institute about dropping out, that woman encouraged her to go to college and even helped her fill out her federal financial aid forms.

I started out at Columbia College, in Chicago. I had gone in with the intent of doing theatrical design and makeup and costumes. It was about a year and a half in that I took my first women's studies and gender class, and it changed everything for me. It was just like everything clicked and everything made sense. Everything that I had kind of been struggling with and trying to figure out just fell into place for me.

It helped me fully understand how religion can play a role in establishing what's right for each gender. And certainly, even thinking about where I grew up, and growing up on a farm, and thinking about the division of the chores on the farm and what chores I had and what chores my brother [had], where his was more with machinery and crops and mine was with animals, it just all really started to make sense to me about when I was sitting there saying, "Well, why do I have to do this, when the boys don't have to do that?" It was around the same time that I was taking a race and ethnicity sociology class, so all of these things just really started to fall into place for me.

Columbia College is a communications and performing arts school, so you can't major in history or traditional majors. I started looking at other schools. My husband, who was my boyfriend at the time, had family up here [in Minnesota]. And we had been up here to visit a couple of times. He said, "Well, let's look at some schools, while we're up here." Hamline just had the best program as well as the best financial aid package, which was really important because I was paying for college on my own.

I wasn't very active on campus. I was a little older than a lot of my peers in class. Also, being a transfer student, it's always a little harder to establish some networks when you didn't go through orientation there. I was also living with my boyfriend and working three to four nights a week waiting tables. That really hindered me in being able to be really active on campus. I found, through interning and volunteering at different organizations, I more established my presence within an activist community within those organizations versus campus.

The Minnesota Women's Consortium was the first place that I had ever volunteered, outside of the church. Any organization could be a member of the Women's Consortium, as long as they weren't actively working in opposition of any of the issues that we were advocating for, which was outlined by the Houston Plan of Action and the Beijing Platform.[6] But all of the organizations had some stake in those issues, and [we had] anywhere from 130 to 150 organizations. That's just incredible, to think that we even had that in the state.

The organization was founded in 1980, officially. There was a small group of women lobbyists at the [state] capitol, in the late 70s—they were the only women lobbyists at the capitol. And they just, after a particularly bad legislative session, had met and were talking about that there was no organized effort at the capitol for women's issues. And they just kind of pulled together a meeting of organizations and feminist activists as well as other advocates who were working on related issues. They thought that they were going to have a small meeting, in one of the founders' homes, and they ended up with about thirty women who showed up to gather in this living room to talk about these issues. And they decided to form the Minnesota Women's Consortium.

The organization started—I don't know if it's true or if it's an urban legend, but it started in the back of Grace Harkness's car. They had actually found a typewriter that was just kind of gathering dust in the back of a closet at the state legislature, in the Office on the Economic Status of Women. And as Grace says it, they "liberated" the typewriter. And they typed the first newsletters on that typewriter. That newsletter they did once a week, for years. When I started there in 2003, they had just stopped publishing once a week to publish every other week.

The organization was incorporated in 1980. They had a storefront on University Avenue for a number of years. Gloria Griffin had this vision of a building where women's organizations could gather together and support each other and network and share resources. They did this massive capital campaign to raise money for the building [and] purchased the Minnesota Women's Building. They purchased a foreclosed, condemned building from the city of Saint Paul. It had been a porno store, so their fundraising slogan was "From Porn to Power." The building came to be, and it was exactly that space: it was for women's organizations to grow.

Operationally, the organization had codirectors. It was their goal to have a balance across political ideology on the staff. So one codirector, Kay Taylor, was a Republican; the other, Gloria Griffin, was a Dem. After Gloria and Kay left, then Dede Wolfson was the Republican and Grace Harkness was the Dem. They operated that way until the late 80s, until you started to see some shifts in both parties. Some of the political divisiveness started. Dede, today, she's not a Republican. She says that the Republican Party left her, in just that it shifted so much, it no longer represented the values that she stood by. So it did become quite difficult, in the late 80s, to maintain that balance.

At its largest, the organization had about four full-time staff people and a part-time staff person. In 2008, things got tight financially for the organization. In terms of foundations, they were very much tightening their belts. There just also wasn't really funding for social justice work, especially advocacy. I think things have changed a little bit. But certainly there was very much a trend of foundations being afraid of the word *advocacy* and not wanting to fund organizations who did that kind of work. Is also was an election time, and the organization always took a financial hit whenever there was a major election. I think that that can be common for a lot of nonprofit organizations, but because we had so many donors who were also supporting women candidates, we certainly, I think, took a much larger hit at that time [when Hillary Clinton was running for president].

And then, just politically, things were tough in terms of getting any work done at the capitol. It wasn't a good time for reproductive rights. It wasn't a good time for trying to raise welfare grants and all of the things that we were working on. The Office on the Economic Status of Women—they're supposed to be there at the legislature to be monitoring legislation that's impacting women, and there were bills to sunset the commission. It was tough. It was definitely a tough time to be trying to do advocacy work on women's issues.

When I started [at the consortium] in 2005, social media was not an entity for nonprofits. There were nonprofits who were engaged, but it wasn't a necessary means of communication. At that time, the organization was actually switching its platform for email, and that was a really big deal because we were going from an ancient listserv that couldn't have any HTML—it was just text going out in email—to now, all of a sudden, we could have images. That was a huge deal for the organization.

In the time that I was there, [social media] completely changed how you communicated, how you engaged, and how you organized. If you weren't using social media, you weren't really a player. And as the organization was coming out of the second wave, I think it was very difficult for them, for all of us who had been used to operating a certain way, all of a sudden to have to think about a completely different way of engaging. For us doing the on-the-ground work, taking that off the ground into kind of this ominous space of online was strange. It didn't feel like we were doing the work—even though we were spreading the word.

We've seen how social media has completely changed the conversation around activism and feminism and what that means. It's been a fantastic tool. It's consciousness raising in a different sense. It's not women gathered around a coffee table in someone's living room; it's now consciousness raising online. But at that time, when I was there, it was a difficult shift for the organization to make. When I left, the organization looked very different. We all worked very hard to make that work and to make sure we were staying relevant. But it was not an easy transition. It was having to balance, basically, two generations and two different waves of feminism, which was hard. But it's manageable.

There's still certainly some tension there. I think some of the intersectional issues—race and gender and trans rights and all of those things—are starting to really be incorporated into the Women's Consortium. And that has come with many of the younger people who are engaged. But incorporating issues of race, issues of gender and identity into the organization, I would say, has led some of the older feminists to feel isolated and to feel like the issues that they worked on don't matter anymore, even though they're feeling like those issues haven't been solved. And many of them haven't. That continues to be a sore spot and a source of tension for a lot of people.

A really good example: There's a legislative race in the Cedar-Riverside area of Minneapolis. And it's Representative Phyllis Kahn, who's been in the legislature since [19]78 or [19]79. She's about to turn eighty. Phyllis has been an incredible champion for women's rights at the capitol. She is being challenged by a younger, Somalian woman from that community [Ilhan Omar, now a U.S. representative from Minnesota]. And there's some tension there, in terms of—they're both incredible women, doing incredible things, who have and will continue to fight for gender rights. But there's the tension around "It's time for new blood," "It's time for a fresh perspective." Those kinds of things can be hurtful for a lot of older people who have done really great, incredible work. And because it's hurtful, sometimes they say things that they didn't intend for it to come out the way that it did, but it does. When someone isn't ready to retire and isn't stepping down, and someone else and a whole group of people supporting them are coming in and saying, "It's time for you to go. It's time for someone new," I think that that can sometimes be the crux of some of the tension that happens between second-wave feminism, third-wave, and—I guess there's now a fourth wave coming in. There is ageism on both sides that can create some of that.

[The Women's Economic Security Act] would not have happened without the speaker of the house at the time, Representative Paul Thissen.[7] He really championed it and spearheaded it. This was really kind of his vision. I think he saw what happened in New York City. New York City tried to pass a women's economic security act. It failed because of a reproductive health provision that was in the bill. So Representative Paul Thissen had gone to Barbara Batiste, who's the current director of the Office on the Economic Status of Women, told her what he was thinking [which was to *not* include reproductive rights bills in the act], and asked her if she could get some advocacy groups on board. So Barbara came to the Women's Consortium and WomenVenture, that does a lot of economic development entrepreneurship stuff with women, to really talk about if this was something we could engage in, if this was something we could do.

From there, I had pulled in [the organization] Gender Justice. Barbara pulled in the Center on Women and Public Policy. And then AARP. Kind of pulled those groups together to start drafting what this bill would look like. The Women's Foundation was also pulled in. We started with an act that had thirteen bills in it. Through the legislative process, that got whittled down to nine.

I think that worked really well because the organizations that were around the table—you had the Women's Consortium that was able to convene the groups together, do the action alerts, organize the meetings, organize groups of people at the capitol. The Center on Women and Public Policy brought the policy analysis and expertise. Gender Justice brought the legal expertise. The Women's Foundation brought funding. WomenVenture brought the business perspective. We were able to kind of have all of the right components at the table in order to get the bill through.

It was just such an incredible project to be able to work on and to see that come to fruition. I don't want to make it sound easy, because it wasn't. It was late nights at the capitol pulling people off of the floor and having some very frank conversations with them and trying to counter every argument [from] the chamber [of commerce] and the [Minnesota] Business Partnership and the Federation of Independent Business Owners.

Part of the Women's Economic Security Act was [that] we introduced the bill at this massive summit prior to session starting. It was the worst snowstorm of the year; we still had 150 people in the room. One of our speakers got her car stuck in the parking lot and she just abandoned it and walked in. It was really incredible to see these people come out in this massive snowstorm to hear people talk about these issues and to be there for the launch of the bill.

[But] in the planning and the drafting of the bill, there weren't women of color or women from greater Minnesota included in the very beginning, because we had so little time to get things in place for the legislative session. We did the work and then we said, "Hey, we have this great bill and we want you to support it," which doesn't work well. So the second summit was very intentional that, from the beginning, it was going to be much more inclusive. It was very much more about bringing voices from across Minnesota to the table to say, "What are the issues impacting your communities?" and then intentionally developing a policy platform around that. So it's been interesting to see how those things have shifted. I think, as a coalition, we're starting to really address that inclusion-versus-representation issue that can be difficult to tackle, especially because that can mean very different things to a lot of different people. What does it mean to be represented versus included? Those are tough things within feminist organizations. I think many of those relationships were still so new and didn't have the history of trust that was really necessary to have communities of color and rural communities engage in that work and feel like they were going to be leading the work and not just [be] an add-on, but also that we weren't just going to get the bill through and then say, "Yay! We did it! Thanks for your help," and walk away, which happens for those communities a lot.

[In 2016] there were many more women of color around the table, [but] lumping everyone into "women of color" doesn't work when there's still a lot of tension between some of those communities, even within themselves. Historically marginalized groups in the U.S. can often feel overlooked in favor of new immigrant and refugee communities. So there's even that tension there. I think that Kabo [Yang] is the leader that was needed for the

[Minnesota Women's Consortium] at this time, not just as a Hmong woman but with her educational background, her work experience, her skill sets as well as her lived experience—[that] is what's needed for the organization right now.

I don't know where this is coming from, if it's coming from media or what, but all of a sudden, activist policing around who gets to be an activist and what is an activist and what does an activist look like—that seems very exclusionary, at times, where if you're not doing it the right way or you're not doing it the way I would do it, then you're wrong. There's a lot of divisiveness among activists who are doing similar work. And there doesn't seem to be, at times, a lot of room for understanding about why people do what they do, why they engage in certain types of activism and not others, trying to find out where they're coming from and then actually having a conversation. That's not happening. [We've been] seeing it on social media for a long time. And I feel like we are now starting to see that play out in actual meetings, in organizing. And it's not productive. The way that that conversation is happening is becoming divisive. And I think we're starting to see that kind of play out in politics, we're seeing it play out in political rallies. We're seeing it play out at the Capitol, where there's groups now that [are] on the same side of the table but they won't work with each other anymore. As you're seeing what's kind of playing out on the national stage, you're seeing that trickling down into the organizing work and the activist work that we're doing. Right now, I feel like it's damaging, especially when we know we're all working toward the same end goal. We just have different strategies of getting there. But there isn't room for those different strategies.

When I left [the Minnesota Women's Consortium] and didn't go to another women's organization, in conversations with people it was like, "Well, you're leaving the movement," or "Well, you're not getting paid for this anymore, so you're no longer part of the movement." It's almost like the definition of feminist leadership has changed and that if you're not that professional feminist, then you're not seen as a leader in the movement anymore. The activism has become more professionalized. Social justice kind of used to be an outlier. And there's good and bad things about it becoming more mainstream and becoming more part of the public conversation. The whole Black Lives Matter movement, for that to be the public media storm that it was, was incredible. I can remember being in high school and being like, "Why isn't there anything like the civil rights movement?" I think the Black Lives Matter movement, for me, was the first time that I felt like something's happening, real change is happening. I feel like feminism, much more than when I started at the Women's Consortium, is more of a mainstream topic. It's incorporated into the *New York Times* and the *Washington Post*. And there's more people talking about it.

There's good things and bad things about that, as things become more mainstream. There's a lot of research that shows, during the second wave, as many of those organizations became incorporated and became more professionalized, that that's really kind of where some of the conflicts within organizing started to happen, because as you become established and you become professional, then come "best practices" that are oftentimes very exclusive [of] people coming from nonprivileged backgrounds. You can see this next wave of organizations doing that.

But I'm just excited, even going back home to a rural area, to see those conversations happening with my family members and with friends and neighbors, and it's not always negative. I think some people think of feminism and social justice and they think urban areas. [But] those conversations are happening in rural America. And it's not in sort of the stereotypical sense that we think of rural America. They're real conversations. And it's getting people to think about what they believe and why they believe that. I think that's incredible. I have a lot of optimism around that. Because where that change starts to happen is around kitchen tables and that conversation that you're having. I've definitely started to see a change. I do think that's part of it becoming more of the mainstream, which is a really positive thing.

Kabo Yang

**EXECUTIVE DIRECTOR, MINNESOTA
WOMEN'S CONSORTIUM, SAINT PAUL**

*There are a lot of [Hmong] women who talk about lack of mentors because
they don't have access to women outside their family systems. Social media really
gives them access to perspectives that they otherwise wouldn't have.*

I met Kabo Yang in her spacious home in North Saint Paul, Minnesota. She was
looking forward to the spring when she could start entertaining in her large
yard again—she had taken over the role her father had played throughout her
life as the hub for many spokes of her extended family.

Yang was born in a refugee camp in Thailand, where her parents had fled
from Laos after the United States pulled out of Vietnam, because her father, who
had fought on behalf of the United States, would be in danger. Her older brother
was one of many children who were permanently disabled by what residents
believed were poisoned vegetables from the garden in the camp.

Along with many other Hmong, Yang's family moved to Saint Paul when
she was an infant. Like other immigrants, Yang chafed against the expectations of her traditional parents, particularly the strict gender roles. Along with
other Hmong girls, including her best friend, Dee, she started to articulate a
feminist perspective that, while shaped by American culture and schools, was
homegrown and concerned with race, class, and immigration status as well
as gender.

Married at eighteen, Yang went on to complete college and graduate school,
eventually obtaining a master's degree in organizational leadership. When I interviewed her, she was pursuing a PhD in human organizational systems. After
working in legal aid and then at United Way, she developed a business as a
consultant to small nonprofits and focused on women's issues. Not long before
our interview, Yang had become the new executive director of the Minnesota
Women's Consortium, as the thirty-six-year-old organization sought to serve
a broader, more diverse women's movement in the state. Her story illustrates
not only her own path but also how the Hmong community changed over
time in its relationship to feminism and how the mostly white, middle-class
feminist movement in Minnesota began to respond to the changing makeup
of the state.

W̲e came here because we had families that were here that were going to help us resettle. [My parents] had to learn how to flush the toilet and use the stove, refrigerator, and running water. We arrived in 1978, and by 1980 they both got full-time jobs. They were machine operators: my mom a sewing machine and my dad a fabric-cutting machine. She retired in 1998 and then my dad retired in 2003. When my mom retired, she was making $11.25 an hour, and when my dad retired, he was making $12.25 an hour; after twenty years, that's what they were making.

My dad became a spiritual healer as well—a shaman.[8] So I grew up with a lot of spiritual ceremonies taking place in our house, and for a long time, I didn't really—I didn't really get it and I wasn't really interested.

They were very family oriented. My dad, for the last four years of his life, was the only one remaining of his brothers. He felt like he had a big responsibility for my brothers and all my cousins, that he would have to really teach them the rituals and traditions of the family, but there wasn't as much interest from that generation. He was getting really concerned and sad that a lot of these traditions would probably disappear because the young—the next generation wasn't as interested in learning. Those were things that weighed heavily on his mind.

My mom was traditional in a sense that she knew what her role was as the wife and as the mother and often would support my dad and didn't challenge him. So they had pretty traditional roles in terms of gender roles in the Hmong community.

Growing up, I was always very independent in school, did well in school. My friend Dee, we became very close and we just did a lot of stuff together. You know, we were just these two little girls who thought that they could run the world. We remained best friends all the way through high school. Having her by my side kept me out of trouble because I grew up in a time where Hmong gangs were really strong. I think the response to bullying, to racism that they experienced was to form gangs for protection. Because I had her, we didn't feel like we needed to belong anywhere. She was the oldest of eight siblings and so she had a lot of responsibilities, you know, caregiver, babysitter. So when she was with me, we could talk about other stuff, about life and college. As Hmong girls, we're often not encouraged to think independently; we're often told, "You're going to be a good wife and a good daughter-in-law, and you're going to behave this way. You're going to have long, dark, black hair and no dark lipsticks, no makeup," all that stuff. With me and her, in school, teachers were really good to us and they would always encourage us to think about "What do you want to be when you grow up?" I have a very, very high respect for educators because of that.

There were cultural norms when it came to gender that we were experiencing. We couldn't go on dates. We couldn't stay after school and hang out with friends. As girls, we couldn't. We were very aware that we were treated differently because we were girls, and we didn't like that. So as we got into middle school and these terms came up—you know, sexism, racism, all these things—we were like, "Yeah, it is a sexist practice and that's not right."

Dee was always told to prepare to be a good daughter-in-law, prepare to be a good wife. She said, "Well, I don't want to—I want to be a marine biologist." "Oh, no, you're not going to be that." Dee's much more of a dreamer and I would say, at that time, much more ambitious than I was, and she was always much more of a fighter. She had cable television and I didn't, and so she watched more shows that gave her this vocabulary, so I would always learn a lot of vocabulary from her.

I remember in middle school, we were in music class and the teacher— we saw that he would only penalize the girls in the room. We walked to the counselor's office and we said, "We don't like the way he treats the girls. That's sexist. It's not fair." We actually said "sexist pig." Once we finished middle school, we went to Central [High School] in Saint Paul, where we became much more aware of our race and ethnicity. I think up to that point, we were just kind of like, you know, "We're different because we're girls." But once we went to Central, it was also because we're Hmong and we're Asian and we're refugees. Our identities became much more apparent because we would see the segregation in the school. But we'd see other students that had similar experiences and we could connect to them in terms of being a Hmong girl. I loved writing at that time, whether short stories or poetry; I would try to share experiences of being a Hmong girl and what that meant. So being around other Hmong students gave me confidence to be who I am as a Hmong girl but also as saying, "Some things aren't fair as a Hmong girl and I don't want it to be that way."

I got married in April of my senior year. He was older, and just being able to talk to him about what I'm going through—I wanted to go away to college and my parents wouldn't let me—was comforting. They'd say a young girl going off to college alone is really a bad thing. So he came at a time when I needed somebody that could be there for me, and he was there for me. He said, "Well, if we get married, you can do whatever you want." So in April of my senior year, I said, "Let's get married," and so we got married. I moved in with his family.

I ended up working full-time to pay for the rent and for the car and insurance and so only went to college part-time. After about two years, I had my son, and then a year later, I had my daughter, but I continued my undergraduate program until 2004.

My career began in legal aid and our practice was immigration law. I was in my early twenties, [and it was] probably my first realization of what it meant to be a refugee, an immigrant, and to really hear and see immigrants and the struggles that they go through in terms of resettling and learning a new language, a new culture, raising children in a new country. My parents rarely talked about their hardships. They just were trying to get through each day. They'd say, "We don't want you guys to be working labor jobs. We want you guys to be sitting in an office, using your mind. We don't want you to be treated differently because you can't speak the language. We don't want you to be struggling because you don't read and write well."

I think in their minds, if we knew what they were going through, we might get stressed out, and so they didn't really share their experiences. Working with immigrant families opened my eyes to see how much my parents went through and so really grew my respect for what they sacrificed for our sake and was really what pushed me to say, "I'm not going to just waste what they did for us. I'm going to really pursue education and career, make a difference for what they sacrificed for."

I [worked] at United Way for almost eight years. I tell people that I grew up at United Way because I really learned about leadership, about organizational politics, about all kinds of nonprofit functions like fundraising, marketing, communications, finance, and HR, and developed a wide network of nonprofit colleagues. I met a Hmong woman who was a consultant, and because we shared an interest in organizational leadership and organizational development, she subcontracted with me on some things and helped mentor me through the consulting process. So when I left United Way, I started consulting full-time. I was involved with a lot of boards of community groups—committees, task forces, roundtables, and nonprofit organizations. Oftentimes I was the only woman of color in the room and just being very aware that I'm the one that's different here. It made me always be mindful that my perspective was not going to be easily understood but it needed to be heard and eventually finding my voice and being able to share that voice in those spaces.

I was consulting and really enjoying being able to work with different organizations, understanding different leadership styles, exploring different organizational structures. I really liked it. I was keeping pretty busy. I had known the [Minnesota Women's] Consortium for several years. I was on the board of a member organization, Galore: Professional Hmong Women's Network. It was a nonprofit organization founded by Hmong women who were business owners. They began to come together as a group saying, "Yes, we need this; we can't go to [networking] happy hours because it's not culturally appropriate for us to go to happy hours with strangers and to do these things." So they began to come together on a monthly basis to support each other and to share resources.

So, when the position [at the Minnesota Women's Consortium] came up, the board of directors at that time was thinking about engaging a more diverse audience. The board was very aware that the organization had been doing quite a bit of work on women's issues but had been doing it through the lens of white women, and [they were] really saying, "How do we include women of color, immigrant women, low-income women, trans women?" They wanted to look for ways to engage and get more diverse perspectives in the work that they were doing. They understood that it wasn't going to be easy and that it was going to take time to build relationships, to build trust, to learn about communities, and to learn about what these issues look like in different communities. I appreciated the board being open to that.

Also, at that time, my son had started driving. The daughter was going to be driving soon. They don't need me at home as much anymore. I had split from my husband about two years ago. Also, I was doing quite a bit of individual organizing on women's issues and was thinking that I could probably do more with an organization that had a reputation for doing that. I could probably have more traction and have more resources.

I believe that issues and solutions are in the same place. So a big piece of what I wanted to do for myself but also for the consortium is to really get into communities, be invited in, be trusted, and to really see—what does violence against women look like in your community? How does unequal pay affect women in your community? Because it looks different in different cultural and ethnic communities. I wanted the consortium to really be much more research driven in terms of understanding and gathering [but also] creating research, as well, that's informed by and led by communities and [to] use that knowledge to then shape, form, and create policy to improve lives of women in the state.

I am somewhat new to social media. I primarily use Facebook. There are maybe two or three Hmong news channels that are run just primarily through YouTube, and they share news and current events but also what's happening in the Hmong community. There was one anchor, an older Hmong man, and last year he just went on a long rant about women, how women are bad, for fourteen minutes. Hmong women are bad: If they've divorced, it's their fault. If they're widowed, it's their fault. They need to bow down to their husbands. This video made its rounds on Facebook.

A lot of the time I don't pay attention to that stuff, but it was being shared on Facebook all day. I got messages from people who know that I am passionate about women's issues who said, "What are you going to do about this?" At first, I thought, "I'm not going to give him the attention that he doesn't need." But I was seeing so much emotion come out of it, really hurtful emotion. So I decided [that] instead of giving in to him, I'm going to divert the attention to positive images of Hmong women. The next day, I shared a selfie, which I rarely do, and I posted, "Let's plaster Facebook with positive images of Hmong women because he doesn't deserve the attention, we do." I didn't know what was going to happen. I hashtagged it #HmongWomen-Stand2Gether. A virtual organization called Hmong Women Today shared it on their Facebook page, and they have thousands in their network. Galore started to share it as well to their network, and so over the period of a week, we had hundreds of women just posting up their pictures and saying, "My name is so-and-so. I'm a married Hmong woman, divorced Hmong woman, single Hmong woman, here's what I do." Part of why he did what he did was because there were no positive images of Hmong women; there wasn't anything that was countering him, and so we're going to counter him. We had women who were physicians and state attorneys and county attorneys and then we had stay-at-home moms; we had just a wide range of women who said, "Yeah, this is why I do this. This is who I am and I love it." A lot of younger women said, "This really inspires me to do more. It's just great to have these images and these stories to inspire me."

This year we had a couple of domestic violence situations where women were killed. The perspectives on Facebook ranged from "Well, she cheated, so that's OK" to "That's no reason for someone to be killed. Who cares if she was cheating?" It was insightful to see the debates happening on these issues and seeing many, many more people speak up about it. There have been several key leaders over the last few years who've been very vocal about feminism and gender equity [so] that folks now have language to talk about it, to express how they feel about it. I do see, as there's language around it, as there are these spaces for perspectives to come out and to share our opinions, I do see that there's much more comfort with feminism.

Part of the challenge that I experienced working with Hmong women early on is that Hmong girls and Hmong women traditionally are not encouraged to network outside their family clan systems. It was believed that if they're not part of your clan, they will sabotage you. Especially for married women, it's looked down upon to be affiliating themselves with non-family members, and so they become isolated. And this includes young women too. There are a lot of Hmong women who talk about lack of mentors because they don't have access to women outside their family systems.

I do see on my [Facebook] feed a lot of women sharing articles about feminism, about women's issues. They'll say, "Wow, this is what I was feeling. This is what I was thinking. This is what I was doing all along and now I have language, so now I can talk about it this way." I think social media does give them a lot of access to data, to perspectives, that they otherwise wouldn't have.

My biggest hope is that we can really move forward in solidarity across racial and ethnic lines, across socioeconomic class. I do see a divide now between white feminism and women-of-color feminism and even within women of color, just all the different perspectives under that. So my hope is that we can find a way to really say, "Yes, we have all different perspectives and different experiences and we're affected differently by the paths that are there, but how do we learn about that, about each other? How do we look for ways to support each other, and how do we lift everybody up together?" That's my hope, that we can move forward with this movement in solidarity, and I know it's not going to be easy. It's not going to happen overnight, but we begin here.

Kenya McKnight

**FOUNDER AND PRESIDENT, BLACK WOMEN'S
WEALTH ALLIANCE, MINNEAPOLIS, MINNESOTA**

*I'm not just a woman. I'm not just a woman of color. I'm a
Black woman, and that means something different.*

Kenya McKnight and I met at the public library in Minneapolis. McKnight is well known among local activists in the Twin Cities; she has spoken out about a variety of issues facing the Black community in Minneapolis over the years, including housing, business, jobs, transportation, and police brutality. Her cousin Jamar Clark was shot by police in Minneapolis in November 2015, and his death was the focus of protests organized by the local chapter of Black Lives Matter and other community groups. In 2014 she founded the Black Women's Business Alliance, now called the Black Women's Wealth Alliance, which seeks to improve the economic status of Black women through home ownership, wealth education, and cooperative business ownership. Her perspective on the state of racial and gender equity work in Minnesota is different than Kabo Yang's or Erin Parrish's, profoundly shaped by her experience growing up Black with little wealth.

McKnight was born in Kankakee, Illinois, a small city about forty miles south of Chicago, where her great-grandmother was the matriarch of a sprawling, five-generation family based in a neighborhood called the Junction. Looking back, McKnight recalls Kankakee with great fondness and nostalgia. Because it was a deeply segregated town, in her community "it was just us. People there worked. They owned homes. They were the police officers, the doctors. They ran the schools. They owned their businesses: the corner stores, grocery stores." She credits her great-grandmother with giving her a solid foundation in moral values and entrepreneurial skills that helped her survive what came later—when her mother, without a high school education, moved her children to Minnesota and got entangled in the drug culture that devastated Minneapolis in the 1980s and 1990s. Surviving by her own hard work and ambition for a better life, McKnight says the Nation of Islam saved her from following her friends' routes to short lives marked by drugs, alcohol, and violent death.

Through the Black Muslim community, McKnight got herself back on a track to school, engagement in her community, and then fellowships in public policy and community development. She ran for public office and, although unsuccessful in her bid, came to the attention of Brittany Lewis, a PhD student in feminist studies at the University of Minnesota, who was studying politically engaged Black women in Minneapolis. Through conversations with Lewis about the history of Black feminism and her own interpretation of the Nation of Islam's emphasis on the role of Black women, McKnight began to focus on improving the economic status of Black women in Minnesota. She engaged with the broader women's movement in the state through discussions over the Women's Economic Security Act, but she is highly critical of white feminists for what she sees as their reluctance to address the differential impact of policies on women from different racial and ethnic backgrounds. McKnight opposes the use of the term *women of color* for organizing purposes. She is adamant that Black women's history of oppression is different from all others, and she wants to see policies and programs aimed at their specific experiences and realities.

I was born in Kankakee, Illinois. It's a small town south of Chicago, maybe forty minutes or so. My great-grandmother Memphis owned property. She worked to clean people's homes, but her husband, Ora, my great-grandfather, worked with the railroads. That was her primary source of income so she could take care of all of us. She owned a couple of properties. She ran a candy store out of her house. She was an entrepreneur. She ran her garden. She was also the woman in the community that everyone would come to for help with different things; if they needed clothing or a place to stay or some food, she was that woman. When I look back at some of the photos, I see that she was also an activist, a public housing activist. She was fighting for affordable housing, and she had us in protests. I learned about community, activism, collaboration, my humanity and spirituality, how to work hard, how to eat healthy, how to be yourself—all of that—from her.

My mother wanted us to have a better opportunity in life. Kankakee is also a place that isn't well resourced, being segregated. The things that Black people have there are the things that we created. She wanted more for us and so she thought Minnesota was that place. It was different. It was a big city. My mother did not work. I think she dropped out of the eighth grade or something. She did her best to take care of us, but I think she was struggling a lot with emotional—just the past pain and things that she'd experienced. We moved around a lot. I think it was tough for her to try to afford rent, and she didn't have a lot of skills. She was probably twenty-five at the time, with five children. I can imagine how tough it would be for her.

As a teenager I was thinking about surviving. At that time, our family had struggled so much that we were living in a crisis. We were living in a tsunami, a whirlwind, and the only thing I could think of was [that] life had to be better than what that experience was. We were introduced to the culture of gangs, drugs, violence at a level that we had not ever experienced, in our home and in our surroundings.

My mother began to live her life, and that really wasn't about us. I didn't come home for weeks or months. It was just—I don't know how to really explain it, but it got to the point where my house was just a place I could stop at, you know? And I don't want to be there because I didn't like what was happening. I was uncomfortable with it. It wasn't what I was used to. I didn't think it was right; I knew it was wrong.

I connected to the Cookie [Cart], a youth entrepreneurial program, if you will. They taught us how to make cookies and sell them. We'd go to the parks and stuff, and that was a thing because we needed money at this point. We needed to be able to get money. We needed to eat. I wanted to take care of my siblings because I had always taken on that responsibility since we moved to Minnesota. We're here by ourselves now and we've got to look out for each other. I was the person to do it. Working at the Cookie Cart helped me do that.

Between twelve and fifteen, I experienced so many things that by the time I turned sixteen I was super responsible. I latched on to a peer; her name was Denise. When I moved to the Northside [neighborhood], I latched on to another peer, Rachel. She became my first friend in North Minneapolis and we're still friends to this day. Rachel helped me navigate Northside. Denise came from a very similar family to mine, but she was the one who worked and was on this track to, really, "Let's go to school. Let's work a job. Here's this program, here's that program." We helped each other make it through.

The next youth thing that helped me was called Project Solo. It was in South Minneapolis; it was like a safe house. So you could go there anytime, cook anytime you like, and you can watch TV and wash clothes. You can get personal hygiene things. You had a workbook that you worked in at your pace. They taught you life skills. They taught you how to balance a checkbook, write a check, get your ID, your Social Security card. They teach you how to get jobs and internships. They take you on little trips, you know, the state fair. Teach you social skills. I really got some good development from them and that was one of my ways out. I stayed there a lot.

I was, at the time, in a gang. In a clique. Twenty-four girls who called ourselves the Dominators. We were getting into robbing people, stealing, doing all kinds of stuff as young people. It got real in the 90s when Minneapolis became "Murderapolis," and a lot of those people who died were my friends. I've seen a lot of people die. I found myself still working, still striving, but living between two worlds. One [world] was very much struggling with the oppression of the drugs, the low income, the concentration of poverty, and some of the results were gang violence, drugs. And in that, still striving to do good.

So that was the whirlwind I was in as a teenager. In a tsunami, I would say. The consistent thing throughout all of that was remembering what my great-grandmother taught us and showed us. Remembering our life in Kankakee. Remembering the good from my mom early on. I also was an entrepreneur; I was a neighborhood hair stylist. I made a lot of money doing hair. I found ways to hustle. I ran my business from about when I was thirteen until I was about twenty-three or twenty-four. I never lost focus of loving and taking care of my siblings throughout the process. I never lost focus of the foundation that I come from. And I never lost focus of my ambition, desire to want a better life. I could have easily ended up like some of my friends. They drugged out. They're alcoholics. Some of my friends were shot.

The real turn for me was I became Muslim. I worked cleaning homes, [in] nursing homes, fast food restaurants, all of that, growing up. I got my first job at a place called Allied Interstate as a medical debt collector. Then I became a student loan federal debt collector, collecting on default student loans, and I met some people at my workplace who were Muslim. They were talking to me about Black people. They were from the Nation of Islam. Brother Antonio Muhammad. And he began to talk about things that were interesting to me that I really didn't know much about. I was attracted to them because of where I come from. I come from a Black community that was rich in culture, that was all the things that are good for me. He was the first person to really connect to that culture. That's when I began to shift. I studied with the Nation of Islam for a couple of years and began to get some cultural knowledge and history. This was really a good, healthy foundation for me. It put a lot of stuff into perspective. I'm still Muslim today.

Once my grandmothers learned I was Muslim, my grandmother Beatrice said, "Girl, you need to take that scarf off your head and get you a man. Take that thing off your head!" And her mom (my great-grandmother) was like, "Well, that's what she's doing; that's OK. Long as you know that there's only one God." And I said OK. It was important for my great-grandmother to give me that blessing, because everything I knew about God was from her. Everything I knew about life, reality, from a good place of humanity, was from my great-grandma Memphis. I probably would still have done it whether she liked it or not, because Islam is very healing and helpful to me. It helped me think a lot clearer. It helped me heal from a lot of the trauma from our experiences. Yet my great-grandmother's opinion and blessing was important to me!

I would say that the Nation of Islam truly helped me begin to heal and understand the trauma I struggled with from my experiences growing up. I also, for the first time, learned about politics, and as my knowledge increased, I was able to better put the history of Black people into perspective. I didn't know that it was oppression. I didn't know any of those things. It helped me put all of that into a context I can understand, which eventually led me to forgive my mother and say, "Oh, this is what was going on. I didn't know."

[In the Nation of Islam] there's an emphasis on us as Black women, who we are, our history, what that means, our roles. I wanted to give back and help other Black women understand who we are, our position—that we're not a subset. We're original women of the planet. We are not isolated from humans; we are not trash; we are not lesser than white people. I started an organization called SPOKE, Sisters Proud of Knowledge Evolving. That was about intergenerational building of Black women—each one teach one—for us to reconnect to our history, our roots, our roles as mothers, as creators, as the real leaders of our communities. Like, the backbone. Everything we are and have been. At the time, I was nowhere near knowledgeable and skilled; I needed everything I was trying to create.

I was twenty-two years old when I created that. During this time, I met a sister named Clara, a community organizer working on social justice issues; she introduced me to community life. I knew nothing about it. [I was] working with her, going through trainings, even organizing trainings with her. Learning that whole community and political work. She took me to this alternative school called HandsOn Cedar Hill Academy. It doesn't exist anymore, but she brought me there to speak to young people. I had never spoken to anyone; I was very introverted, it's important to note, until I was about twenty-three. Never spoke to anyone. I spoke to those young girls, and whatever I said, the school wanted me to work there. So I became the leader of the girls' group and I taught then a group of mostly Black girls, taught them the very same things that I had learned from Project Solo and the Cookie [Cart].

I worked with that girls' group for a year and I gave those girls everything I had. After that I decided I wanted to go to school. I went to Metro Community [and] Technical College and ended up getting a Local Initiative Support Corporation [LISC] fellowship. That fellowship was about getting young people of color, young professionals of color, into [the] community development sector because the sector is predominantly white. There were about sixty fellows. At MCTC, I took an African American history class that opened my eyes to a history of Black economics that I had not heard of before such as the Black Wall Street, Jim Crow laws, economic segregation, and more about the Black economic history of America that I didn't know.

That history took me back to my great-grandmother: This economic, entrepreneurial business owner. I grew really passionate about that. Once I got the LISC fellowship, I started learning about economic history of my Northside community; I knew that was my passion, to be in that space. I got my first job in the economic development sector at a place called NEON, the Northside Economic Opportunity Network, in North Minneapolis. It's a microbusiness development. So you're teaching people how to start business, how to do business plans, how to do marketing plans, and we facilitate living. I did that for five years. I was excited to work in my community and do this fellowship at the same time.

I was upset at our city council person for the way he was representing Black people in our communities. So I ran for city council in 2009. At the time, I was the youngest candidate. I knew nothing about politics in that way. I just didn't know what I was doing, but I did it. I didn't win. It was really the first time that I experienced sexism when I ran for office. It was the first time that I experienced classism. There were times when I would be continuously asked by men, If they voted for me, what would I give them in exchange? I think the biggest adversaries to me were women, actually. According to them I was not good enough: I didn't have the education; I didn't have the skills; I didn't have the class. I was what they considered to be ghetto or uneducated and just not enough. That was part of my first personal level of consciousness about sexism but also classism. It was hurtful, but it is what it is. It taught me.

So how I got to feminism was Brittany Lewis. Dr. Goodman-Lewis is a Black feminist. She's done a lot of women's studies, and she learned about me running for office from her professor, and she came to me in 2010 or 2011. She wanted to study and work with me and learn about my work as a Black woman.[9] She got me to thinking about feminism. In my mind, what I'd learned about feminism prior to that is that it's a white woman's tool. It hasn't advanced our community. That's the general understanding in our community about what it is. Brittany was the first person that I met who was really building on Black feminism and what that really is and the history of it and capturing the importance of what it looks like today in this society. She studies the intersectionality—all these things I'm learning about, I'm like, "What's that?" But she really introduced me into all of that. I was curious about why she was curious to focus on our work as Black women.

I would often tell her, "Oh, I think it's divisive," but she was very persistent. So I learned a lot from her about the importance of Black women and the work we do. The reality is that feminism didn't start with white women.

In 2012 I ended up getting the Bush Fellowship, a two-year leadership program. I used the fellowship to learn about regional development and planning, and I got appointed to the Transportation Advisory Board as the first African American. I go to Oakland [California] for an internship for six months in the last year of my fellowship. I begin to research the economic status of Black women. It was wonderful, and I got to study about Black women, and I had never studied Black women before. I'd never looked at the movement, the suffrage movement. I didn't know Frederick Douglass was connected to it; I didn't know that Black women had been fighting for a long time. I didn't realize that when white women got their right to vote [in 1920], Black women still couldn't. I didn't realize there were income disparities between Black and white women. All these other things. I didn't know that Black women had been leading unemployment in America, as it is still today, for the last five years amongst women. Just all these things I began to discover. Black women leading entrepreneurship across America and Minnesota. Just phenomenal things but also devastating things.

Out of that, I was like, "OK. I really need to do something now with women." I came back to Minnesota and I worked with twenty women across the region to find out if the things that I found were very comparable to our everyday. And it really was. From there, I knew I had to do something. I wasn't interested in going back into all those other areas I'd worked in. Out of that, I created—at the time it was called Black Women's Business Alliance. It started with twenty women.

I began to get involved in the women's movement here in Minnesota through the Women's Economic Security Act. I heard about it a year before, but I didn't know much about it. So when I returned from Oakland I began to get involved with it to learn about it. I needed to know who the players were and what's the work of women being done in Minnesota. And so that's how I engaged. When I got there, it was all white women. The issues that were talked about were from a white woman's perspective. And I'm going, "Well, you're talking about being treated fairly in the workplace; we still struggle with people accepting us wearing Afros in the workplace and cornrows." There was a lot of differences. Some of them were not interested; some of them were. It didn't matter; I was there. I didn't see any other Black women. We weren't a part of the leadership or decision-making, and still that isn't true today. It's a struggle.

When the Women's Economic Security Act passed, who benefitted from that? The resources went to white women [and] organizations that serve white women. At the time, we were in the middle of our own research in Minnesota. Dr. Brittany Lewis worked with us to create a report on the economic status of Black women in Minnesota, which we just released a week ago. It's a starting place. It needs to be broader, but we focused on workforce, business, lending, business occupation/work occupation, and wages, income of Black women in the metro. That was going to be our foundation and justification for why we're here and why we need to push on this economic agenda for Black women.

I think we need to be very specific about ourselves. I don't think we need to be as general as being "women." White women are positioned differently than other women, particularly Black women. I would customize things specific to our community in that act. When you generalize it, it still advances white women. For instance, white women make more on the dollar than Black women. Black women in Minnesota—38 percent of our workforce numbers are concentrated in low-wage jobs, where white women are not even 15 percent. We talk about the child support. Well, child support also affects our community differently. A lot of our men are in prison, in jail. So we perhaps share the same issues, but the impact and outcomes are different. And that's what we need to recognize and understand. The policies and things that we put forth have to include and represent those realities.

We talk about the Women and Girls of Color act[10] that Obama put in place. That whole thing is, well, I'm not a Latino woman. I'm not an immigrant. I'm not an American Indian. My history is different. Black women are leading the number of women in prison. We're leading unemployment among women. We're leading new business starts in women, but we receive less money than everybody. We're the largest nonwhite ethnic cultural group in America, and our poverty, or situation, is deeper. It's generational and it's racial. Racism is between Black and white people. Politics are between Black and white people. Until we really address and respect and frame issues that include us not as just "people of color" but as Black people and that are very specific to who we are and how we function, then we can never get at inclusivity in a way that's meaningful. Because I'm not just a woman. I'm not just a woman of color. I'm a Black woman, and that means something different. I'm an indigenous Black woman of America, and my history is different than every other woman's on this planet. I need to be respected, supported, and seen through that.

I don't like how our community is compared to the Hispanic and other communities. We have similarities, but our histories are different in many ways that need to be respected. When we talk about feminism in "women of color," there's no woman in America who has the history that I do. Remember: We were working in the cornfields or the cotton fields having babies. And we couldn't feed our babies because we had to feed white babies our milk while our babies were starving. Being raped and everything else, and those things persist even today.

My great-grandmother worked until she was ninety-something cleaning a white woman's house. I can't say that anyone's history is or should be compared to us, and I don't want to be seen through a light of just "women of color." I'm a Black woman, and that means something different. We need to really understand that there are severe differences in our communities as people of color, whatever that is. What we see is a shift of resources, policies, and interests to new American communities that is needed but also at times comes at a disadvantage of us. We can talk about unity, and we do need to be more united across our communities, particularly people of color, but at the same time everybody ain't on board with our Black economic success and interests. And if they're not willing to partner in that, then I can't say that I'm willing to partner in this movement of feminism that includes everybody when no one is thinking of me.

If we believe so much in feminism and the movement of women and that all of us are valuable and important, why isn't anyone paying attention to what's happening with us? Who is talking about these issues in a culturally specific way? Why are we not talking about the fact that Black women are leading unemployment among women in America? Why are we not talking about the mass incarceration of Black girls and Black women that's at a higher rate than every community, if we care about our feminism? Why aren't these the conversations? Why are we not talking about or acknowledging the history of Black women in America? I argue that we are the first ladies of America in the sense that we have helped white women develop their courage and perspective about even fighting for what should be naturally OK for them. Why isn't that homage paid? Why does Harriet Tubman—she got to be on the twenty-dollar bill, but the white man is still on the back? Why is that? There's a lot of questions that need to be answered among the community of feminism.

The Black Women's Wealth Alliance is unapologetically interested in advancing the economic issues and interests of Black women because we believe and know that the well-being of Black women is greatly, greatly beneficial to the salvation and the future of the Black community. A nation cannot and will not rise any higher than its women. We are here to stake our claim about who we are, where we are, and take complete control of our future forward. We know that that starts with us as women and girls, and creating clear pathways to our success is extremely important, which is why we're doing the research to track ourselves. We're also setting up strategies such as procurement that will help us learn how to get into these businesses, private- and public-sector contract opportunities to do racial equity and other work. And we're also looking at youth entrepreneurship, teaching our youth wealth-building skills, teaching Black girls responsible spending, and all these other things that are important. Those are just some of the things that we're doing and will continue to do forward.

Emily May

**FOUNDER AND EXECUTIVE DIRECTOR,
HOLLABACK!, BROOKLYN, NEW YORK**

*My critique of where the feminist movement is today . . . is that, because
we saw so many great academic institutions build up these women's studies and
gender studies portfolios, so many people who are feminists today came up through
that, myself included. But academic institutions are very much about
critiquing things. They are not about creating things.*

Emily May was pregnant when I interviewed her in her un-air-conditioned
Brooklyn office; a fan blew directly at her desk to help disperse some of the
oppressive summer heat. May is the cofounder and executive director of Hollaback!, which she defines as "a movement to end harassment, powered by a
network of local activists around the world." Originally focused on street harassment, a term the organization helped bring to life, Hollaback! has now broad-
ened its mission to include fighting back against online bullying as well. Only
twenty-four when she founded the organization, May has received multiple
awards and significant media recognition. While May's approach depends on
social media for its impact, she is well aware of the challenges as well as the
promise of online feminist activism. She feels strongly about the damage that
harsh, public critique can do to individuals and to the movement as a whole,
and she lays some of the blame on the academic field of women's studies and
how it trains its students. But May is also hopeful, believing that while earlier
generations of activists focused on changing laws, this generation is focused on
changing culture, and she argues that online social media is playing a central
role in that fight.

I was very ambitious from a young age and, honestly, I don't know where
it exactly came from. I think my mom was constantly always in shock.
She was very much a B/C-type student and just wanted to raise a kid
who was nice and confident and cared about people and the world. The
fact that I pushed myself hard to try and get good grades and had big dreams
for my future was always a little bit of a surprise to her. I was actually president of the Future Homemakers of America for my seventh-grade class,
which meant that I made giant ghosts out of cheesecloth for Halloween

and I cooked things like monkey bread after school.[11] I also had this dream, at the same time, that I was going to be the CEO of Pepsi—Pepsi, of course, because I liked to drink Pepsi—and thought there was really nothing that stood in my way. I even had this blue suit that I called a power suit. I don't know where I got the terminology from. I would put it on with my button-down white-collared shirt, and I would prance around in what I would now call my executive director drag. But at the time I was just trying to get ready for my future as the CEO of Pepsi.

I was raised with this belief that I could do anything that I wanted to do. It wasn't that I had no insight into sexism, because my mom was a feminist and we certainly did have those conversations about how the world is differ-ent for girls. But it was almost like, "Because the world is different for girls, it's going to be harder for you. You're going to have to work harder but that's even more reason why you should do it anyways."

My aunt, when I was seven or eight, bought me the autobiography of Susan B. Anthony. I was so taken by the idea that you could spend your whole life being persecuted for an idea that history would play out to be so obvious. And still am really taken by that idea. I think that basic concept is what has led me to want to work on street harassment and to now want to work on online harassment as well. Because these are ideas that are very, very much movements that are in their infancy. The ideas that street ha-rassment isn't OK [or] that you can't just say whatever you want to people on the internet are very, very nascent in their historical development—not new but, from a movement standpoint, still very young and shocking to people. And there's so much hope there, that we'll get there, right? There's plenty of historical precedence for it, and there's historical precedence for the fact that it'll be really, really hard and that we'll face a lot of persecution for having this idea. And that we'll make mistakes and screw up and go from being, at one point, perhaps, in our lives, an obvious feminist champion to history looking back and being [like], "Oooh, maybe not."

I, being a girl, was very outwardly feminist. And very much identified as a feminist activist and went to the Southern Girls' [Convention] when I was eighteen, which is a conference for young, ragtag feminists in the south. Fighting systems of patriarchy, learn how to say no really loud. Learn how to sew my own maxi pads. Anyway, [I] was really into all that stuff and moved by all that stuff. In high school, I sort of am embarrassed to say at this point, but I was doing a lot of activist-inspired artwork, most of which was totally over the frickin' top. It was so over the top that it ceased to be art but was like "I have something to say and I'm seventeen." My friend and I made this shirt that said "Dead men don't rape," which I wore to school, and my teacher was like, "Not appropriate," and I said, "It's just a fact" in that way that high schoolers can rationalize things. That is not something I would do now. But, you know, I was pissed off.

I think my twenties was largely about crossing things off my list in terms of "Could I be good at this? Am I good at this? I'm all right but I'm not great; cross it off. Could I be good at this? Is this interesting to me? Eh, not so much; cross it off." So being a case manager and outreach worker was one of those things; working in schools as a teacher was one of those things. I was good, but I wasn't great. And political campaigns were one of those things. I was good and I didn't want to be great, because the people who were great at it were not my kind of people.

Hollaback! actually [was] started back in 2005 by myself and six other folks between the ages of about twenty and twenty-four. There were three men and four women, and we'd recently heard the story of a young woman named Thao Nguyen, who was riding the subway when an older man sat down across from her and started to publicly masturbate. Thao took his picture with the idea of taking it to the police. The police ignored her, and she put it on Flickr, where it went viral. It made it to the front cover of the *New York Daily News*, and it ignited this citywide conversation about public masturbation.

At the same time, we were sharing our own experiences with street harassment, of which we had had hundreds, individually, at that point. What was interesting about that was that I went through all those women's studies classes—nobody ever gave me the language to call what was happening to me street harassment, nobody ever contextualized it as a form of sexism. Sexism was the wage gap; sexism was reproductive justice; sexism was gender-based violence. But this thing that happened to me on this day-to-day basis wasn't sexism. And so in my own mind, I thought about it like it was just something—I was a feminist, I thought of myself as quite tough—and I thought about it as some sort of weakness on my part that it hurt to the degree to which it did. Because I didn't have that context, that framework, to understand it as something that felt like it was about me, but it wasn't really about me. It was about the more messed-up world that we lived in. And that sucked.

But there we were, and we were like, "This is messed up," and at the time we were like, "What do we call it?" We just referred to it as "the crap guys would say to us on the street." P.S.: these are all people with very academic backgrounds; none of us are dumb cookies, right? And so we were like, "We can't just call it catcalling, because that diminishes what it is and language is important. What is it?" My friend Kaya was like, "It's harassment." And we were like, "It is harassment! It's totally harassment! What kind of harassment? We can't just call it sexual harassment because then people think about the workplace." Then she was like, "Let's call it street harassment."

We went with it and Hollaback! took off, and it was just a local project here in New York City. From the beginning it resonated with people. And within a year, we were doing *Good Morning America* and the *Today* show talking about this issue of street harassment, which we literally had to make ourselves experts in. Because there were no other experts to be the experts in this thing, because people just weren't talking about it but everyone was experiencing it. It just really hit this nerve.

It was all a side project. All during that, I was working other jobs. I think when we launched it, I was the director of development for the Northern Manhattan Improvement Corporation. I traveled around Central America for a while. Then I came back and was special projects coordinator for Opportunities for a Better Tomorrow. It wasn't until 2009 when I started to really realize that the impact we'd made with Hollaback! felt greater to me than any impact I'd been able to make professionally.

I quit my full-time well-paying senior management job on May 1st of 2010. I had been rejected at that point by eight foundations and two fellowships and was stark raving mad that nobody would fund this. I was just like, "Screw you, I'm going to do it anyway." I did it, and we ran a Kickstarter campaign and we raised $12,000, $13,000, and then the Ms. Foundation showed up and they helped us out a little bit. The first six to nine months I wasn't paid, but then finally I was.

It was a really, really intense time. A lot of people look at that story and the success of Hollaback! and the trajectory of Hollaback! and they're like, "Oh, you know, I want to do that too." Do you really? Do you really? Because I worked nonstop. I had to almost completely stop hanging out with my friends. I saw very little of my boyfriend at the time, gained fifteen pounds eating rice and beans because I wasn't making any money. I would shoot up out of bed at 7:00 A.M. like my butt was on fire, would work straight through to midnight, go to sleep, do it again. I knew that if I just input enough, that out the other end would come this movement. I knew it, and I was right, but it was a really significant personal sacrifice that I cannot in good faith advise people to do. I think the only reason you should is if you can't do anything else. And that was how I felt at that point. I knew that I was standing in the way of the movement unfolding completely, and more specific than me—my ability to get stuff done and to create these pathways for people all around the world to do this and to get stuff done. People just needed a little bit of loving, and they would be able to make this happen in their communities and to scale that out. It was intense but it worked.

The power of it is that with the internet, we've been able to take this thing that otherwise would've stayed local, right? We were able to use the internet as a communication tool to scale it out. The ability to communicate those tools and share those tools with people so that they could do it and could do it in conversation with hundreds of other people around the world that were also doing it.

I think some people are very thoughtful and nuanced in their understanding of how to use online feminism, and some people just are holy terrors. My critique of where the feminist movement is today and the challenges is that, because we saw so many great academic institutions build up these women's studies and gender studies portfolios, so many people who are feminists today came up through that, myself included. But academic institutions are very much about critiquing things. They are not about creating things. And so as these young feminists have grown up through that, they have taken that love of critique—and I think it's an incredibly useful skill if paired with the ability to create things. I think the challenge now is that we are doing a few things: First of all—a lot of online feminism is being gatekeepers to, What is feminism? Who is feminist? How are they feminist? If you don't have this academic, intersectional analysis—and even the word *intersectionality* is not accessible to so many people who are otherwise quite feminist; they're on our team, right?—that somehow you're not enough.

Even the articles—"Is this TV show feminist?"—I'm like, "What? What kind of question is that? That's a ridiculous question. Who are you to be the gatekeepers to feminism?" But I think the other piece of that, other than the incredibly exclusionary part of it, is that when you do see people creating things, feminists love to critique them. And I'm like, "Hello! Go spend some time with Rush Limbaugh, critique what he's doing." But nobody wants to touch that. They just dismiss it. They'd so much rather critique whatever the hell Hollaback!'s doing, or some other awesome feminist activist organization is doing, than they would critique and play ball with some of these big players that are destroying women's lives on a massive scale. A massive scale—and are being left relatively untouched by online feminism. I personally would love to see a rule enacted where you have to go after two out-and-out big-boy jerks before you can critique another feminist.

I have a rule where I do not ever publicly critique other feminists. I will call them. I will be like, "Hey, you should work on this thing." Certainly I will have private conversations about things as a way of learning and parsing out why are they doing this and how are they doing this and what's the impact on the movement. But I will never do it publicly. I think it's terrible for movement building. I think critiquing any feminist initiative is a useful academic construct, but it's not useful in movement building. There's a huge divide there that has burned out and tortured so many incredible feminists, and they don't talk about it publicly. They just leave. They slowly leave the field, and that's the result. I want to build a movement that's inclusive and welcoming. I'm not saying we can't critique each other, but coming out of the antipoverty movement, talking to friends in other related movements, it's not the same intense focus on critique as it is in feminism, and I think that that has allowed those movements to accelerate much, much faster than ours.

I'd just like to broadly see more of a gear toward action. It's not that I want the critique to go away, because I think the critique is useful, but how do you present the critique in a way that is useful and it's not just you sounding off on Twitter? How do you give that feedback so that you can work together in a movement? Or how do you write an op-ed that shifts the public's thinking, not just skewers the individual who you're going after who is, P.S., your friend the feminist? I think that's the kind of stuff that people just aren't taught to do. We see people coming in with these amazing intersectional analyses but without any sort of framework on how to really get shit done. And that's all it is. A movement building is 99 percent mucking through the muckety muck. Yeah, occasionally you'll get an award or get something published, and that's when everyone will cheer, but that's not the actual work. The work is having a million doors slammed in your face and being told that what you're trying to do is impossible. That nobody will ever care, that nobody will ever fund it, that people in the United States don't even experience street harassment. I've been told all kinds of crazy stuff, right? I think that it's a detriment to other young feminists because they feel like if they're not writing the article or having the tweet that's retweeted 500 million times or winning the award, that somehow they're not doing the work, when the work is work. It's mostly muck—muckety muck, you know?

I think what's happening in the racial justice movement in America's awesome, and I think that we can't move forward with the antisexism movement or the antihomophobia movement without also moving forward on the racial justice movement, and it's so cool to see that history happening. Globally, I think that race means wildly different things in different cultures. What it means to be a person of color in India, for example, is different than what it means to be a person of color in the United States. Oftentimes I think that there is this desire from an American standpoint to think about race playing out the same in all cultures everywhere, and it just doesn't.

I think that's why it's so critical to have this leader-full movement. Because I am who I am, I'm a white woman, I'm cisgendered; I don't represent the movement. I think that it was almost my discomfort with representing the movement that led to the structure of Hollaback!, where we do have all these site leaders all around the world that are representing their communities and their identities, and I think that ultimately it's the strength of these leaders that helps to navigate this. I'm not going to get it right every time; I'm not going to have every answer. I certainly can't have a different life experience than the one that I've had. And I don't think anybody can, and that's cool. As long as there's a bunch of us. [*Laughter.*]

Where I find hope in what's happening right now with Black Lives Matter, and the horrific, horrific instances of violence that have happened particularly against African Americans, is that stuff has always happened and now people are paying attention to it. It's the same thing we see with street harassment. It's always happened, and then all of a sudden there's an infrastructure with which people can start to think about these issues, and then you start seeing everything get bubbled up in a way where it used to just be ignored and pushed to the bottom of the pile. That is a testament to years and years and years of movement building on the racial justice front. The organizers have been laying that groundwork for people to finally pay attention, and now that people are paying attention, America's kind of waking up to what it's like to be Black in America. I find so much hope in that; however, I do know that a lot of my African Americans friends are just like, "It's so depressing." It's so depressing. Obviously the instances of violence are so depressing, but you combine that with study after study coming out about the systemic oppression that black people face. It's so hard on a personal level to be on a team that's just getting battered and bruised. But frankly—what I tell myself anyways, so I don't slit my wrists at night—it's always happened, but now people are paying attention, and it's because of those stories that we have an opportunity for change.

I think that from a movement trajectory, movements start because people tell their stories. They grow with diverse decentralized leadership. People start to pay attention with research, and then you see some policy change start to happen. And then I think cultural change is the web that connects all those four things. We are very squarely in the storytelling-and-decentralized-leadership part of the street harassment movement. Starting to edge into the research stuff. We really need to see the government showing up and doing that kind of stuff.

What we need is that culture change, which is really a financial investment from governments. It's investing in PSAs, it's investing in education, it's investing in the research, all that prevention work that goes into prevent-ing this from happening to begin with instead of just playing Whack-a-mole with the people who've perpetrated street harassment later. That work isn't just hard to fund because of street harassment; that work is hard to fund, period. Governments want to provide services to people afterwards, when there is a quote-unquote demonstrated need. The prevention work—there's a movement to start to fund it, but it's really hard to measure. How do you measure something that doesn't happen? And there's not a lot of money around that.

I think that what's interesting from a bird's-eye view is that this genera-tion of online feminism is largely looking for cultural change, not political change. I think that our parents' generation did a bang-up job of getting a lot of those structural pieces in place and a lot of those laws in place. Cer-tainly not all of them, there's certainly improvements to be done—yay, gay marriage—but a lot of them were in place so that this generation has really been able to walk in and say, "OK, shit's still happening, so what else can we fix?" And I think there's a ton of energy around day-to-day instances of racism and sexism and homophobia, which tend to bubble up in the media in these more extreme, like, Charleston massacres, but the organizers on the ground are not just seeing the massacre.[12] They're seeing that entire spec-trum of violence against people, and they're seeing it as part of a culture that's racist, part of a culture that's sexist, not necessarily part of a problem like a policy. I think that that's where our generation is going to push a lot of change and has pushed a lot of change, is on that changing-hearts-and-minds piece. And I think that's where, when we've seen movements that have sort of waned, it's because they lost that hearts-and-minds messaging in the same way, and I think at the end of the day that's—it's God-awful im-possible to fund, it's terrible to try and measure, but that's the engine that fuels everything else. That's the work that we need to be doing, and that's why online feminism is having a great impact. Because it's getting those voices out there to change those hearts and minds, not just going to work at a domestic violence shelter.

Holly Kearl

FOUNDER, STOP STREET HARASSMENT,
WASHINGTON, D.C.

If I feel like I'm useful, I find meaning in my life.... I think
activism has become a way to feel useful.

During our interview, Holly Kearl and I and her dogs all sat together comfortably in the lower level of her townhouse in a suburb of Washington, D.C. Kearl works as a consultant to a variety of nonprofit organizations, but she is best known for her research and activism on street harassment. She founded a nonprofit organization called Stop Street Harassment after writing her master's thesis at George Washington University on the topic and has published three books: *Stop Street Harassment: Making Public Places Safe and Welcoming for Women*; *Stop Global Street Harassment: Growing Activism around the World*; and *50 Stories about Stopping Street Harassers*. Her writing has appeared in the *New York Times*, *Washington Post*, CNN, the *Guardian*, Forbes.com, *Huffington Post*, *Christian Science Monitor*, and the *Ms.* magazine blog, and she is a highly sought-after speaker, both in the United States and abroad.

Kearl is part of the cohort of women who took women's studies courses and even attained graduate degrees in the subject, a possibility that was becoming more widely available in the early 2000s. In addition to her education, family experiences also shaped Kearl's decision to focus her energies on activism. Like Soraya Chemaly in the previous section, Kearl started her interview with a family story of sexual violence that indelibly shaped her own understanding of the issue and its impact on generations of women and men. Kearl's family was strictly Mormon, and her mother's mother had nine children in quick succession—including two sets of twins and a set of triplets. As adults, those children recalled her as a "robotic" mother who seemed to take little pleasure in parenting. Kearl attributed this at least in part to the fact that her grandmother had been the victim of incest by her own father and had also been raped by "multiple people before she was in her late teens." Although the grandmother had repressed the story for decades, she had an "emotional mental breakdown and was really sick for a year, and it all sort of came out and resurfaced" when Kearl was a child. Kearl calls her grandmother a "primary person" in shaping her activism. Kearl's development was also profoundly influenced by other family realities and tragedies that hit closer to home. Due to her father's work at Proctor & Gamble, Kearl's family moved repeatedly during her childhood, and by the time she reached high school, she had lived in seven different states. More devastating was the loss of her older sister, Heidi, who had been born with severe disabilities. Kearl's childhood role, freely chosen, had been as a helper to Heidi and their mother; when Heidi died, Kearl's ten-year-old world changed drastically.

T he loss of Heidi, I mean, twenty-two years later, I still sometimes feel like I can't cope. Every day it's hard. I feel like she was such a big part of me. I don't have a twin, but I can imagine it would be similar. We were so interconnected; I would take care of her, and she was there for me. I feel like I'm always trying to find a way to fill that gap, and I think sometimes activism is that way, because I feel like I'm helping someone. I find a lot of meaning [in activism]. If I feel like I'm useful, I find meaning in my life. I was always useful for Heidi, and then when she was gone, I can look back and see that I was sort of floundering like, "How am I useful now? What can I do?" I think activism has become a way to feel useful.

My junior year of high school, I left Mormonism. Boys and girls in Mormonism are raised similarly until age twelve, and then boys get a lot more responsibility and privileges, and you just start to go different ways. I was like, "What is going on?" I did have some sense of gender equality and of thinking women can do things. So when there started to be this difference, I started questioning that too. I guess my first kind of pushback on the Mormon Church was "Why can't I do this too? I'm perfectly capable."

My junior year, I took a philosophy class, and that completely changed my world view, and I realized that I was atheist by the end of the semester. It completely changed how I thought, and that gave me the freedom to question some of the stuff that had bothered me in Mormonism. I started reading feminist literature, and I started to pay more attention to LGBTQ issues because around then it was the first time the California Mormons were lobbying against a same-sex marriage bill. It was fortunate that most of my good friends weren't Mormon, because it's a very bad thing to leave the church—like, you're going to hell. I have over fifty cousins, and it was hard to lose that closeness and those relationships, but I don't regret it. It's one of the best decisions I made, to walk away from all of that, because I felt a lot of pressure to be "perfect" and follow the church's doctrine.

It takes so much time and energy to be Mormon. You have to read your scriptures every day and pray multiple times a day, and you have to go to church multiple times a week, and Sundays were off-limits. I couldn't do homework or go out with friends or exercise. I just had to be at home or at church. It was such a relief to let it all go. And it gave me more space to explore feminism, because feminists are not welcome in the church. You can get excommunicated if you speak out. I almost never tell anyone that I was raised Mormon, because it feels so shameful and against what I believe now.

Santa Clara isn't the prestigious university I had hoped to go to, but I think it turned out well anyway. I joined the cross-country team. One morning, September 11 [2001], we just happened to be driving to a park instead of running nearby, and someone else had the radio on in their car and told us when we got out, and we were just stunned. I was the only one from the East Coast. My next-door neighbor worked in the Pentagon in Virginia. One of my uncles works for NSA [National Security Agency]. I had family and friends in New York City, and I was immediately, for that reason, like, "What?" No one else had that, and they were just kind of, I don't know, oblivious, and it really soured me to cross-country right away. There were a lot of things running through my head without a lot of information, and I just was appalled that most of the teammates didn't care at all. I think September 11th kind of shook me out of this complacency about not reading the news, not caring about what was happening, not paying attention to anything about politics. Outside my dorm, they had the *New York Times*, the *Washington Post*, and, I think, the *San Jose Mercury*, and so I began reading newspapers every day for the first time, and I started looking at *BBC News* just to get the world perspective. So it really did shift me to start to become more of a global citizen, I hope, and to just be paying attention to politics and things.

Santa Clara's a very social justice–focused university, and they have a volunteer organization called Santa Clara Community Action Program, SCCAP. I began volunteering at a domestic violence shelter as soon as I finished the cross-country season. At one point, I think I was volunteering at four shelters a week. I became more aware of my privilege for the first time and just the opportunities I had and that I needed to do something more. I became friends with a lot of activists. I started going to more social justice events and speak-outs and rallies, and when the Iraq War was being considered, I was going to all these protests in San Francisco. One of the only classes I missed all of college was to go protest when George Bush was coming to a defense plant a couple miles from campus.

I declared a major in history, and when I took a women's history course, I was like, "Here's where the women are!" It inspired me to add a second major in women's studies. I studied abroad my whole junior year in the UK, and I went to Lancaster University, which has the oldest women's studies program in that country and one of the oldest in the world. So I took mostly women's studies courses while I was there.

My sophomore year I was just talking with a friend—I had gone to a Take Back the Night march, and we were talking about sexual violence on campus. We're like, "What would we do if something happened to us or one of our friends?" So we began looking to find information, and we went to the health center, the counseling center. We went on the school website. We looked a couple other places, and there was nothing. Finally, we pulled out our campus handbook that we got as first-year students, and there was one paragraph about it hidden in this book. And we're like, "OK, you're in crisis mode. How are you going to sit there and remember that in this handbook that maybe you don't have anymore, there's this one paragraph that tells you what your rights are and what to do?" Our hypothesis [was] that this was ineffective and no one knew what to do. We wrote up a survey and went dorm room to dorm room. We had a table in the cafeteria area. We would do shifts, and we ended up surveying about a tenth of the student body, a pretty close number for each grade, and it did turn out that almost no one knew what to do. It was alarming that by senior year, most people knew someone who had been sexually assaulted, or they had been. The education level did not increase, their awareness of what to do did not increase by grade at all.

We worked with a sociology professor to analyze the data, and we took it to the dean of student life, and we had some suggestions and they agreed to do everything. They were grateful to us and said, "Wow, we're so impressed by students here who are taking initiative." I studied abroad the next year, but my senior year I came back. Every bathroom stall on campus had pamphlets. Every bathroom had an informational thing as soon as you walked in. Every student got a magnet. The counseling center and the health center now had information about that, which you would've thought they would have already. I think a lot of the department heads had information too. Doing that survey, getting that research, and getting the results has really influenced my activism and trying to do my own surveys on different things and document things and just be like, "Here are the data." So that was influential for me.

My whole senior year I just had this major conflict: I knew I wanted to go to graduate school, but did I want to study history or women's issues, activism? I went to [George Washington University] and met with someone there about the women's studies and public policy program they had, so that's what I ended up doing. I had been very involved in activism, feminism, women's studies major in college, and I didn't know the term [*street harassment*]. I didn't know how to deal with it; I didn't know what to do. I was grabbed, followed, had so many bad experiences, but it wasn't until I had to think of a thesis for my master's and was researching and came across the Street Harassment Project and Hollaback!, I was like, "There's a name for it! There's something I can do; I don't have to be alone." My thesis focused on how people were using websites to cope and find resources and share ideas [about street harassment].

Then, when I finished graduate school, within the same month I got a job at AAUW, the American Association of University Women, and I was there for almost six years doing feminist activism. I started off doing web design at AAUW because this was 2007; it was a hard job market. Not as bad as it was going to get, but it was harder, and I was only getting responses for jobs that I applied to doing web stuff. [Then] the Legal Advocacy Fund department ended up needing a manager, and so I got that job. I got to help coauthor a national study on sexual harassment in schools, so that was my highlight of my time at AAUW, getting to work on that from beginning to end, to really think about who's on our advisory group, how do we craft the questions, who are we targeting, the whole process.

I was the one who got AAUW to start a blog and to start getting on social media, and it was hard. I did a lot of research to see what other organizations were doing and so—I can't remember, maybe the National Women's Law Center, the Ms. Foundation, or Feminist Majority— if they blogged, it was once a month, and it was, like, a letter from the president. I'm like, "That's not a blog." Trying to explain what a blog is and why it's useful and has purpose was hard. Now AAUW's blog has won awards, and it's really read by a lot of people, [but] it was hard to get them to recognize its worth then.

Part of the issue is it's a lot of older women who are leaders of established women's organizations like AAUW, a lot of older white women in leadership positions who maybe aren't always open to new ideas. And then, also, there can be conflict with younger people who don't recognize the importance of having an established organization who can have sway in Congress, who gets invited to the White House, who gets invited to the Department of Ed to talk about Title IX issues in a way that maybe regular activists don't have that access. I came away really appreciating both sides and how important they are, and together they can try to make progress happen.

After I did my master's thesis on street harassment at G[eorge] W[ashington University], reporters started finding research that I put on my website, and one of them was for CNN. That was a shift for me, because I hadn't intended to keep doing street harassment activism. I had this full-time job;

I was already doing feminist activism. I was good, I was covered. Once it was on CNN, people started emailing me and it just blew up online, and I was like, "Oh, maybe there's more need for conversation and dialogue." My parents suggested I write a book because I had so much knowledge from my thesis and I do such thorough research. So I thought about it for a few months and then ended up starting to do research on that. I had a lot of free time at AAUW, where I could kind of overlap and do street harassment activism there. I started a website in 2008 called Stop Street Harassment, which became a nonprofit in 2012.[13]

I think I had the courage to do what I was doing around street harassment because other people had already done it. I mean, I generally don't have new ideas. Because of my focus on history and what has come before, I know that it's very hard to invent new ideas. You're just recreating or improving or adapting what has been done before, generally, and so that's what I often do, especially, and I look globally. What are other people doing? What's working? I think it's better to learn from that than to start from scratch.

Social media, and Twitter in particular, has been a huge resource for me as far as finding people to connect with. And for awareness around this issue, it's helped a lot because anyone who's on Twitter can share their story when it happens, any day. I'm often organizing or part of TweetChats with people all over the world, and so that has really helped put the issue out there more and connected us.

That CNN article that I was interviewed for in 2008, the headline was "Catcalling: Creepy or a Compliment?"[14] That's how the issue was framed, that maybe it's a compliment. Generally, outlets are not going to do that framing anymore; it's more recognized that this is a serious issue. So I think that's been an important shift, and the awareness of governments has been really big. There are so many more that are taking this issue seriously, passing laws, policies.

Here, in D.C., we've seen this shift. In 2012, I was a board member of Collective Action for Safe Spaces, which does street harassment activism only in D.C., and we were trying to work with the Washington Metropolitan Area Transit Authority on addressing harassment on their system and couldn't get a response. So we recruited people to share their stories about harassment at a D.C. city council hearing focused on the transit system. I was an expert witness. The *Washington Post* did an article right before it happened. This was Metro's party line for the article: "One person's harassment is another person's flirting. It's not a problem in our system," which was repeated by the leaders at the hearing. Council member Muriel Bowser, who's now the mayor of D.C., was chairing it, and after the men—all four men—gave their "Rah-rah-rah! Here's how Metro's doing," she said, "Well, do you have anything to say about what the members of the public brought up?" They gave the same party line, and—I was so proud of her and so happy—she said, "As a woman, I feel differently, and you need to do something about this issue." And within three weeks, Metro had completely changed: They had a sexual harassment task force; they created an online reporting form; they've been working to train all of their frontline employees on this issue so they know how to respond appropriately; they're now tracking all types of incidents of harassment. We're working with them to survey a representative sample of transit riders about the experiences of harassment. Have they seen the ads? What do they think, are they helping? That'll help inform us for the next round of ads. Almost no transit systems have had surveys, so this is going to be big. At this point, basically, anything that we ask them to do, they will do. So that was a huge shift since we testified in February 2012.

I think online activism is useful in that I can connect with people all over the world, and almost wherever I travel, I can find someone that I know or I've met online, and I can connect with them, and I love it. But I also sometimes feel—especially working remotely, mostly—I can feel really isolated, too, and that my only interactions are online or by phone. I've also experienced a lot of [online] harassment over the years, and I think that's horrible. Why are you arguing with me about rape? Why are you arguing with me about feeling unsafe in public spaces? That is a harmful indicator of our culture that people feel comfortable openly criticizing someone and harassing them. Then, if you feel unsafe to share your views, certain views are going to be dominant and can help inform culture.

Online is a public space, and there's going to be people who only read the headline and start lashing out at you, or they do read the whole piece and they start lashing out at you. And then there are people who are thoughtful and have meaningful back-and-forths. Those kinds of responses make me think more about who might be upset by what I am saying or who am I excluding, so then I try not to exclude them. I have had a lot of education along the way. When I started off, I was very focused only on women, but I don't anymore just focus on that, and I am posting things about the backlash [to] Muslim-looking people in public spaces right now, for example, or the Black Lives Matter movement, with police brutality and harassment. I am trying to broaden to those issues, and I think I've been strengthened, and I'm appreciative of people who point those things out, but it can be hard when people don't do it in a nurturing or loving or understanding way. I mean, I also know it's not people's job to do that though. It's not, for example, a black woman's job to be like, "Oh, Holly, I think maybe you should do this."

I understand if they're angry or upset; they've faced so much discrimination and marginalization. I've hopefully gotten a little bit over myself in a way in knowing that if someone lashes out, it's not necessarily personal to me, but it's because of the systems of oppression that they face and that I am part of that, whether I want to be or not.

I went through a one-day seminar with the OpEd Project in early 2010, just about six months before my first book came out. I had never written for anything except academic writing for school and then blog posts on my own blog or AAUW. I didn't even know that you could write opinion articles. I got obsessed with it and wrote my own, and that really springboarded me and helped me have a platform on this issue. Since I did that training, I've published seventy articles and done 250, maybe closer to 300, media interviews now and close to 150 speaking engagements. You have to get good about making a compelling argument in a short amount of time and really being persuasive and being timely and showing "Why does this matter?"

For me, the most influential part of the training was a game that you play, which helps you realize that your voice matters, what you know matters, and that you can make a difference by sharing it. For me, that's key to what motivates me, is trying to make a difference and be useful. So with that framing, I felt more confident to be able to speak out, even though it scared me. That's something that I try to pay forward. I work as a consultant for the OpEd Project now, mentoring people as they write op-eds. Last year I co-led an [OpEd Project] fellowship at Northwestern University with twenty faculty. People got policies changed because of their op-eds. One woman got a book deal; people got radio show interview requests, speaking engagements. One woman went on CNN. The outcomes can be really big. Not every op-ed that I have written has led to something, but continuing to have a voice and being relevant has helped establish me as a leader on the topic and helped keep the issue in the public conversation.

Trisha Harms

UNION COMMUNICATIONS OFFICER, MINNEAPOLIS, MINNESOTA

*[A union] protects women from not getting paid as much, from being
passed over for promotion, from not being taken seriously and gives them a place to
have their voice heard about issues that impact them. I think the women's movement
and the labor movement would do well to work together more closely.*

I had not heard of Trisha Harms (or most of the women I interviewed in Minne-sota) before I started researching the Twin Cities feminist community. Several people mentioned her to me—she served on the board of the Minnesota Wom-en's Consortium, the umbrella organization for all of the women's nonprofits in the state; she is a feminist labor organizer; and she had a blog, most notably about her decision to have bariatric surgery despite years as a "fat-positive fem-inist." I did not realize until after we finished our interview that she had also recently started a feminist podcast, *Head Bitch in Training*—the name perfectly encapsulating Harms's quirky, salty persona.

Harms identifies as a queer third-wave feminist—one of the only women I interviewed who wholeheartedly embraced a particular "wave" of feminism. I met Harms and her wife, who makes her living as a sailor in Canada and is gone for months at a time, in the small house they shared with Harms's younger brother and a cat. They live in the working-class neighborhood in North Minneapolis where Harms grew up. She worked for many years at a nearby coffee shop, where she said there were still pictures of her making funny faces hanging in the bathroom. Over time, though, through community college, a bachelor's degree at Hamline University, and then a master's degree, Harms developed skills and a large network and deepened her knowledge of intersectional feminism. She applied them all to her work in communications for the union representing state and county employees and in her role on the board for the Women's Consortium. Harms's embrace of labor unionism and its relevance to feminism is notable and clearly related to her working-class background as the daughter of a single working mother.

I was born to a single mom. She was eighteen when I was born, so we lived with [my maternal grandparents] when I was a baby. They're both from rural North Dakota. My grandma was a schoolteacher in a one-room schoolhouse, and they met at the schoolroom when he went to pick up his little sister from school one day. I think they had just dated a couple of times, and they ended up having to get married because they were naughty. My grandpa was being scouted for minor-league baseball, and he ended up having to give that up because my grandma got knocked up. They were both German. My grandma's parents were second-generation and my grandpa's parents were first-generation immigrants. They were both farm kids from out in the sticks, Midwestern farm kids.

My mom's an incredible woman. We lived with my grandparents for a little while, and then she sort of struck out on her own. She went to tech school for a while and ended up building a pretty decent career for herself. I was always really impressed that she was able to take care of me and be a professional and command respect. When I was a baby, she was cleaning motel rooms and working at Kentucky Fried Chicken. We lived in a little apartment upstairs from a Chinese food, hole-in-the-wall restaurant. Every day, all she could afford to eat was an egg roll from the restaurant down-stairs until when we moved to Minneapolis and she had a good job working at a law firm doing accounting. She didn't go to school for it; she just figured it out.

My mom always just did everything: She cooked, she cleaned, she worked, she paid for everything. She was the disciplinarian, and she was also the comforter. In that sense, I learned there's not really a specific role that women have to take, because I grew up with a woman who didn't put up with—am I allowed to swear?—shit from anybody. When my dad moved into the house, he definitely took on more of the traditional male roles: He did the lawn things and he had a manly job and he didn't clean. He took out the garbage. He became more of the disciplinarian. But I never was directly told by either of them or ever felt pushed into a specific gender expression or gender role.

I was the most awkward high school person. I didn't know my identity. I had my hands in all these different pots: "I want to be an artist," "I want to be a musician," "I want to be super goth," "I want to be punk rock," "I want to be a feminist," "I want to wear overalls," "I want to wear fancy dresses all the time." I just did not know what to do with myself. It didn't help—I was a fat kid. It's really hard to be a fat kid, and I think it's even harder if you're a girl. And I was also struggling with my sexuality, so I was just the most awkward creature you could encounter in the world. I feel like if I met myself now as that person I would be really uncomfortable but also "I feel so bad for you." I was just a super awkward weirdo. I also really wanted to be a badass, but I was such a Goody Two-shoes my whole life. I had a lot of conflicting identities inside myself. I had short hair. I had green hair. I was really uncomfortable with my body and tried to hide it, but I also adopted this sort of, like, "I don't give a shit if I'm fat" persona, which I held on to for a very long time. High school was rough. It was rough.

The first thing I really associated with feminism was being pro-choice. I didn't know a lot of history of the women's movement or what it really meant to be a feminist. I just knew I had had a conversation with my mom where we were both, "Well, it's fucked up if people are saying women can't have abortions." And I was, "Absolutely! That's something I want to do something about."

When I was in high school, it was the blooming of the internet. I found a couple of message boards. The one that I was most active on was the *BUST* magazine message board. The women that I encountered on there were so inspiring in how confident and true to themselves they were and how outspoken they were on issues that mattered to them. They were able to take the feminist mentality and apply it to their own lives and just live their lives in a feminist, pro-woman, "I want to do what I want to do and fuck everybody else" kind of way. So to me, in high school, that's what it was. I just want to be a bad bitch who crusades for women.

I'd started doing college in high school. I did the PSEO program, Post-secondary [Enrollment] Options. It's basically where your high school pays for you to go to college classes. I took German because I was super nerdy, and I spoke German better than anyone at the school. They sent me to the U[niversity of Minnesota] for German and some other classes. I stayed at the U for one semester, and then I met a guy on the internet and decided to move to Chicago and go to college in Chicago for fashion design because that's where he lived. The boy was a secret. [My parents] thought I was just going to go to college. I dropped out of college pretty quickly; I think I went for a year. I didn't know what I was doing. And I wasn't really happy in that relationship anyway so I moved back. I moved back in with my mom for six months, and then I got an apartment here in North Minneapolis.

I started working at a coffee shop and really focusing on paying down all of this debt that I had racked up so I could go back to school, and trying to figure out what the hell I wanted to do with my life. I was working super hard. I didn't really have a goal or an ambition or a passion. I just partied and worked, partied and worked, partied and worked. It's a blur. I finally went back to school. I went to Minneapolis Community and Technical

College and I ended up doing business management. I still didn't really have a clear idea of what I was doing, and I had this weird associate's degree that I didn't really know what to do with. One of my English teachers at MCTC had [said], "You have a lot more in you than just being a manager somewhere or working at a coffee shop." I think her exact words were "You are a scholar. You belong at a real college." So I was like, "I guess I'm going to go to real college. I don't know what else to do." By that time, I was twenty-six. I ended up going to Hamline to get my bachelor's, and I did women's studies and English. I didn't know a whole lot about women's studies, but I knew that I was passionate about women's rights and I love history and, obviously, women are underrepresented in history. So women's studies seemed like a good fit.

I studied with Kristin Mapel Bloomberg.[15] She was probably one of my first real mentors. She's great and really helps you figure out what to do with the knowledge that you've gained and helps you find a path and helps you apply it. She really sparked this sort of motivation to create change in the world and not just be an academic. I had another really great advisor in my English program. Her name was Veena Deo; she was amazing. They both encouraged me to go on to graduate school, so I did, still not knowing what the hell I was going to do with my life. I was like, "What the hell am I going to do? I gotta go to grad school before I have to start paying back those other loans." Erin Parrish from the Women's Consortium sent me a message saying, "I just heard about this really cool program that is up in Duluth; you should look at it." It was the Master of Advocacy and Political Leadership program. So two weeks before the semester started, I called the MAPL people, and then two weeks later I was in a van of random people driving up to Duluth together to start grad school.

The program is focused on how to create change in the areas that you want to work in. So you can focus on nonprofit work. You can focus on running for public office or what you do when you are in office, how does the legislature work, how to run campaigns. You can concentrate on the organized labor sector. I ended up doing the nonprofit concentration just because it made the most sense to me. I learned how to start a nonprofit, run a nonprofit, do taxes for a nonprofit, run a board, be effective.

Most of my big projects in grad school were focused on reproductive health, reproductive health care access. I got my job at the union [the American Federation of State, County and Municipal Employees] halfway through the program. It started to really come together how all those things sort of mesh together to form a "This is where I fit into this, where my passion is and the work that I've been given to do and the work that I'm capable of doing."

Right now my focus is reproductive justice and women's economic security. What I'm focused on right now is economic security for women of color. I think in the women's movement in general we have been, unfortunately, a white women's movement for a very long time. I think that that is really terrible in a lot of ways, but also we can't continue to call this a women's movement or a feminist movement if we're not being inclusive. So right now, particularly at the Women's Consortium, I'm doing a lot of work on equity and inclusivity and making sure that the policy work we do doesn't impact groups that are silenced differently than it impacts the white ladies that are at the table talking about these issues.

I'm not really sure where [I] made the connection. I think part of it was I did a project on food security and it was "How does this specifically impact women? Why is food security a women's issue? Why is racial justice a women's issue? Why is the minimum wage important to women?" It became clear to me that every social justice issue impacts women in a myriad of different ways, and those consequences are overshadowed all of the time.

I think that Minnesota is unique. I don't really know how to articulate that, but we're the home of [former senator] Paul Wellstone.[16] We have a lot of people who still cling to that era and those values. I think a lot of people think of his slogan as the Minnesota slogan: "We all do better when we all do better." We've always been a progressive state even when we haven't necessarily elected progressives. Huge voter turnout and huge involvement, huge civic involvement. It is unique.

This year, we have another women's economic security act [in the Minnesota legislature]. It's the Women of Color Opportunities Act. I'm really excited about that. It has not gotten as much traction as I was hoping for. It's a package of bills that invest in economic opportunity specifically geared for women of color. My understanding is a lot of them are also geared toward neighborhoods where there's a lack of economic opportunities, North Minneapolis, where we are right now, being one of them. There's not a whole lot of job opportunities around here. There's also not a whole lot of access to resources or basic needs. This is a food desert by technical terms. There's no grocery store within walkable distance here; there's convenience stores with junk food, that's it. There's also nowhere to have a job over here. If you don't have a job, you can't afford a car. If you don't have a car, you can't drive to a job. If you don't have a grocery store you can walk to, you end up feeding your family junk food from the convenience store, which happens to also be four times more expensive. How do we expect anybody to climb that ladder?

What I love about working for unions, about the labor movement, is that women who are in unions always do better. Women in communities where there's strong union membership, even if they're not in a union, also do better. I also really love that unions are willing to stand up for economic legislation that helps people who aren't their members. My biggest example on this is raising the minimum wage. State employees don't make minimum wage. County employees don't make minimum wage. None of our members make minimum wage. We spent a whole year putting all of our force behind getting Minnesota's minimum wage lifted by two dollars because we care about helping everyone out.

I feel very strongly that unions are one of the last major forces holding the line for letting people even get into the middle class or helping people climb out of that hole just a little bit. The middle class doesn't even exist anymore. On paper, sure, I'm middle-class, but I still fucking live paycheck to paycheck. The opportunity for anyone to move up in the world is so small. I think for women, specifically, having a union there to back you up is one of the best—I don't want to call it a back-up plan, but it's a good support system. It protects women from not getting paid as much, from being passed over for promotion, from not being taken seriously and gives them a place to have their voice heard about issues that impact them. I think the women's movement and the labor movement would do well to work together more closely.

I represent the union in my role on the Women's Consortium board. The union supports the work financially and by giving my time. We also always stand up for issues of choice. When Planned Parenthood is under attack, we speak up for them; we're there for them. Unfortunately, organized labor is being attacked from every aspect just as much as reproductive health. We just barely survived the Supreme Court case where—I don't wish to speak ill of the dead, but if Antonin Scalia had not passed away when he did, the labor movement would have been crushed. There's five more Supreme Court cases just like that in the pipeline.[17] Just like there's seventeen Supreme Court cases trying to defund Planned Parenthood or take away access to any sort of reproductive health care for women or ban transgender people from using the bathroom they want to use. We're so preoccupied with not letting ALEC destroy organized labor and turn America into a "right to work" country that we don't have the capacity to focus on issues that our members really do care about.[18] That's the strategy, right? If we're always on defense, we can't help our allies. It's fucking divide and conquer. It works.

I was not active in the gay marriage campaigning. My take on it is that it was totally a white man's gay marriage movement. Poor queer people are not concerned about having the right to get married. They're concerned about having the right to not get fired for being gay on the job. Or having the right to not get beat up for being gay. Trans queer people of color, specifically, are worried about not getting stabbed on the street. This is super weird for me to say because two years after it passed, I totally got gay married. I loved it and it was great, but I wrote a blog [post] for the Women's Consortium when I was interning there that was "You know what? This is not the fight that we need to be fighting. And all of you people who have the time and resources to be fighting for permission to get married better not turn around and walk away from this fight when you get this, because there is so much more work to be done." Unfortunately, I don't know how much of that work is getting done. And I don't know how much that big group of gay-identified people with time and resources to put into that campaign have stuck around to help the people that still got left behind.

I used to identify more as a radical feminist. Radical feminists, now I think of them more as second wave and [they tend to] be very trans exclusionary. Third wave to me is more of this whole "Do your own thing, speak up for yourself, and speak up for other women. Be a slut if you want to be a slut. Do what empowers you, and encourage everybody else to live that life too. Stand up and speak out when people are hurting other people." I definitely identify with that.

Feminism cannot be a white movement. That means we're obsolete. Feminism needs to be not just speaking for other people but creating space for women who have been silenced to be heard finally. I think the feminist movement has a PR problem, as a PR person, and I think it's coming from a lot of directions. There's men's rights activists; there's people like the podcaster Milo Yiannopoulos, who travels the world holding town halls about how feminism is unnecessary and the oppression of women is a myth. And then we've got another group of people who need feminism, who have not been represented by feminism, and who feel alienated by it. At the consortium, we've really been focused on not just being inclusive but on lifting up voices and actively working on policy issues that target underrepresented groups of women. But it's a long road for sure. If women still agree that we still need feminism, which I do, this is something we're all going to need to work very hard on together. It's going to be difficult and painful and complicated and slow.

Soledad Antelada

FOUNDER, GIRLS CAN HACK, SAN FRANCISCO, CALIFORNIA

*I always felt that I had to do something. I always had this thought: If I don't
do it, who's going to do it? Because I'm the only one here.*

I first met Soledad Antelada, thirty-nine, when I visited my cousin in San Francisco, because Soledad rented a room in the duplex and would often join us for
dinner. I knew she worked in cybersecurity—we always laughed about how we
couldn't ask her about her job—but later I discovered that she had founded
Girls Can Hack, an organization to help other women move into the field. Born
in 1977 in Argentina to teenage parents, Antelada moved with her mother to
Spain when she was four after her parents split up. Her maternal ancestors were
Sephardic Jews from Spain, and many of her family returned to Spain after generations in Argentina to escape the dictatorship there.

Antelada explains that she never felt completely at home in Spain—she always felt that something was missing. She struggled in school with humanities
classes but thrived in the sciences. She studied computer science in college, but
it was in the workforce—beginning with a programming internship—where she
really found her strengths. At age thirty-one she moved to San Francisco and
found her way into cybersecurity—in part because she thought it would be the
most challenging thing she could do. She now hopes to encourage more women
to enter cybersecurity jobs and to change the culture of the field. In addition to
offering a compelling account of her own life in the field of computer science,
Antelada's interview reveals how feminist activism is unfolding in new realms
like cybersecurity that didn't exist a few decades ago.

I think I always felt I was different. Like something was missing, maybe
because I came from another culture; I grew up in Spain where I was
very integrated, but my whole family was from Argentina. So it was a
different culture at home and outside. And also a big part of my family
was in Argentina, and I lost contact with them. I always felt that there was
something else I had to do, or [some place] I had to go, or I don't know.

My family was very male dominated, and as a Latin family that's how it
is. But at the same time I had a lot of support from my stepfather. I was an
only child too. So, I don't know, maybe if I had a brother it would have been

different. But I think I had a lot of support from my stepfather actually. In a way, at the end of the day, you need somebody that tells you, "You can do this. Go for it." And that happened to me. When I decided, for example, to come to the United States, he really supported me and pushed me, and that really helped me to move forward.

I was very good with math, and I was very science oriented. And I have a sense of curiosity that goes beyond anything, that is very strong in me, for everything I do in life. I think that's a part of the good scientist and researcher. I was in school, and I was doing good with those courses. It's like, it came natural to me. I was always struggling in other fields like history, for example, or literature, languages. But math and biology or those kinds, physics, I did very well. They came easy to me.

Some situations made me look back and say, "Well, that was because I was a girl." But I think when you are young and you are just going and you're struggling, growing up, and you're focusing your mind on other things, you don't get that.

I remember one story that happened to my roommate at that time. She was studying computer science with me. And she was turning in a project and it was almost perfect. So she turned in the project and the professor, the first thing the professor said to her was, like, "You didn't do this alone. I think you copied it or somebody helped you." And in that time I remember she came home and told me the story and was like, "Wow, that's not right." We forgot about it. But that got stuck in my brain. And I think that was, that was part of a bias against women.

I had a course that—it was called AI here, artificial intelligence, and I didn't pass one test. So you can go and talk to your teacher after the exam and go over the test to see what did you fail. So I got in one of those evaluations, and there were two teachers, and they were laughing at me all the time because—I don't think it was on purpose, but they thought I was funny. But I don't think that's the right context to laugh about a student. And that bothered me a lot and actually undermined me a lot for continuing studying that course, actually.

In the [computer science] class of maybe 100 people, we were, I don't know, maybe five girls. I was living with three of them. We stuck, we got stuck and stayed together.

I started working second year in college or third year. Working a lot and doing very good and better and better every year. And that was very good for me, because I didn't have a great time when I was in college because I thought that wasn't for me. And when I started working, I realized I was very good at that. And I think that's part of why I did so well, like, on the workforce. That was a huge difference. Once I started working, the way I was learning fast and advancing in my career was very different from me starting at college. It was very different. I was working in a company that was a contractor for the government for the health care system, and I was a programmer there. I was starting my career. I was learning as much as I could, but I realized that was going to be a limit of growth. The way I was seeing management behaving wasn't a way that a woman can fit in, for example. There was a lot of meetings at bars or going out at night, having drinks. So I don't think I would have fit in [in] that kind of situation.

I came here first in 1999, when I was in college, to visit a friend that was living here from Spain. I came with my boyfriend at the time, and we were computer science students, and we decided, "OK, after college we're going to live there because it's San Francisco." Ten years passed, and I didn't do it. So I talked to my father and I was thinking that it was time to do that; I was already thirty-one. I wasn't going to do it when I was forty, that's for sure.

I moved here alone. I came here to try for one year. I got enrolled in a program at City College of San Francisco in network security. And after a year I got an internship—that's the story of my life repeating again—I got an internship at Lawrence Berkeley National Laboratory, where I still am. After the internship they hired me. So I stayed here and I'm currently working there [in cybersecurity].

I decided to study computer science because it was the most difficult thing to do. When I started my career in computer science, I didn't even have a computer. But I was sure I wasn't going to be a math teacher or a science teacher. I wanted to do something else and something that was challenging to me. And I said, "Oh, computer science. I have no idea what is that. That's why I'm going to do it." And then for security, it was the same. I was tired of being a programmer because, I think, a developer, that wasn't for me, in a way. That is very static and I needed a little bit of a more dynamic job. Security, like, you don't stop. You don't stop learning, and there is no one day that is the same as the other days. So it's perfect, and also I thought it was the most difficult thing to do and [I] started studying and realized I could do it.

In technology we [women] are a minority, but the cybertechnology, cybersecurity field is the worst for diversity. It's the worst. There's a lot more developers, women developers, probably now than before and user designers or web developers, that kind of stuff, but in cyber, there's no women at all. It was hard. It was hard. I was used to the fact that I am the only woman in the room. But definitely was harder than ever because the stereotypes of a person working in security are very strong. First of all, to be a man. And then a little bit obsessed with computers and spending nights without sleeping, trying to hack into systems, maybe not very healthy, not interested in social life. I think that's the stereotype. It's changing though. It's changing, and I hope I'm contributing to that.

I think there wasn't resistance but a sense of, really, "Do you want to be here? Why?" I noticed that a lot. Like, "Are you sure you want to be a computer and cybersecurity engineer?" And I was pretty sure.

I never thought of myself as a feminist when I was young. But again, it's like I said before, when you are younger you don't realize actually what is going on. It's like you're building your life and your character. I always admire strong women that will go out in the world and do their thing and succeed in their careers or whatever they were doing as women, especially the ones that didn't have much help, like, they weren't coming up from rich families or they didn't have, like, support. You're going to laugh at me, but I always looked up to Madonna, for example. I thought that she was great; I think that way now, and I thought that way when I was ten years old. I don't know if that means something. I always admired that strength in [a] woman, like, taking the world and doing whatever. And I also always missed those kind of role models. I mean, there were not much that I could look up to. Like, not even in my family or in my environment or in the newspaper. Now, I think, especially in the last few years, you can see that a lot more, which is awesome. But back in the day you couldn't.

I started Girls Can Hack two years ago. I always felt that I had to do something. I always had this thought: If I don't do it, who's going to do it? Because I'm the only one here. I don't see anyone around, like, any other woman. So that's why I decided to do that. I don't have much time, but I'm going to try to do something at least. And I put together a group that is called Girls Can Hack and is trying to support women that want to go in the technology field, especially in cybersecurity. I missed that when I was growing up as a computer scientist. I hope if I had that, my life will have been much more, much easier. I have a sense of duty to do it in a way. And I know that it's very beneficial to have role models and people to look up to and to have a sense of belonging in this life. In this field and this career, that's very difficult to achieve for a woman. So I mean, I'm just only hoping that I can do something for it to change and the next generation can have, like, a more, a smooth path to choose this as a career.

I try to bring the cybersecurity world down to earth so people, so women, see that it's not actually that difficult and especially [that] if I can do it, they can do it. It's just "Go ahead and do it and study and work." I do meetings that talk to women about that, how is it to be a woman in the field, that especially I put an emphasis on the fact that there's a lot of jobs right now, there's a lot of demand, and women are missing out on it. It's like there's a gold mine over here. Come get it. And then I go to panels, and I represent Girls Can Hack, and I'm very happy [that] this past year, the last couple panels I've been in there were a lot more women there.

I have noticed in the last couple years, especially the last year, in cybersecurity, first of all, it's like a sexy field now because it's all over the news. People are more and more curious, and they want to get into the field. So there's more women because of that. Second of all, there's a lot of women doing great things for women. I don't think I have seen that in my life before in the media. So that's a lot of support for all kinds of movements about women. So I think that it's making a difference. The fact that Hillary Clinton is a presidential candidate, I think that's having a lot of weight, like, on the world focusing more on women and noticing us and, like, taking us into account. I really have felt that way this last year. I have noticed that—I work for the government and I think there's a shift toward women that I haven't seen before. I think there's a lot more support, and I really feel that it's a great time to be a woman right now.

I hope my organization grows and somebody takes over, it takes off and gets its own life as an entity. I would love to get more and more women interested in what I am doing because it's a great career. And I really, really believe that women are great for that because cybersecurity, you have to have a lot of technical skills, but there's a lot of intuition in it too, and you have to apply your smarts in a way that sometimes women do very well. I think women are great cyberengineers.

At the last [panel] I did, there were 100 and something men and women. We were talking about cybersecurity, and I got to the place and I thought there were going to be ten people, and then I saw those many people and the organization started to pull out chairs from other places because people were standing up. And I was happy. There were a lot of women in the room. So yeah, I think it's changing.

Kate Farrar

**POLITICAL CONSULTANT, K. C. FARRAR CONSULTING,
WASHINGTON, D.C.**

*My perspective always is, you can be upset and annoyed and pessimistic
about it all—and there's plenty of others that feel the same way—and at the end of
the day, if you aren't going to try to be an individual to change it from the outside or
the inside, then unfortunately we're just all going to have a lot more to complain
about and be pessimistic about and hit our head against the walls about.*

When I interviewed Kate Farrar in her apartment in D.C., she had just left her
job as vice president for campus leadership programs at the American Association of University Women (AAUW), where she had been working for more
than seven years overseeing leadership development programs for college-
aged women. She was getting ready to move from Washington back to Connecticut, where she had started her career working as a lobbyist on behalf of
nonprofits at the state capitol. Farrar had recently launched her own consulting business, and her goal was to reestablish her residency in the state and
run for political office.

Farrar had grown up in rural Connecticut. She was an only child and as a
young girl found creative ways to entertain herself, whether through calligra-
phy, needlepoint, or building her own library in her home, complete with cata-
log and checkout system. An excellent student, she was not excited about the
college at which she ended up—the University of Connecticut—but soon fell in
love with the campus and discovered a passion for political science. In her interview she describes how, over years of working as a lobbyist and in leadership
development, she developed a desire to run for office herself and discusses her
hopes for the role that female politicians, especially at the state level, might
play in making change.

I grew up in a very small rural town called Norfolk, Connecticut, way in
the northwest corner of the state: 2,000 people, no stoplights, not really
many neighbors. In my graduating class, which was four towns, about
100 kids, there were probably three to four nonwhite students. My mom
her whole professional life has been a nurse practitioner, and she was a
part of the first wave in the 60s and 70s to be trained specifically around

women's reproductive health care. She worked at several Planned Parent-hoods around the state, but she also worked at several city health clinics. Some people have conversations once with their kids about sex, and in my house and in my experience growing up, it was, like, I just wanted her to shut up about it.

When I was in college I secured an internship at NARAL in Connecti-cut, and I was suddenly advocating for reproductive rights and abortion.[19] I was having this moment with my mom where we suddenly knew all of these same people. When I was at NARAL of Connecticut is when I think I first had this recognition of how much my parents' views on feminism had really influenced me without me even knowing. I wrote an article for the newsletter that summer where I really pointed out my mom in particular as fighting for these issues, working on these issues through many years, and empowering me with this feminism ideal I didn't even really consider was different. I remember quite poignantly that after that—because I had told them that they were going to have this article in the newsletter, and she read it, and she said, "I'm really glad that you have reflected on this and you realize all these things, but it's not just me, you know. It's your dad too. He's a feminist too. It wasn't just me who wanted to make sure that this was how you thought and saw the world."

I went to the University of Connecticut very disgruntledly. My plan had been to transfer, but by the end of my first year, I knew that I wasn't going to go anywhere. I had just really fallen in love with being there and my friends and how I was being challenged at such a large and different place. I kept taking these political science classes because I just liked them; I never really thought about what you did with them. But what really directed me was I had a class junior year, it was called Women in Politics, and in that class we had to interview a woman in politics, which was a very novel idea for me because I'd never even met a politician. I'm a junior political science major, and I've never even met a politician in my life. My parents vote and talk about politics, but they never volunteered anywhere. I never went to an event of any sort.

I reached out to a woman politician that was recommended to me, who was the state representative for UConn at the time, that region, Denise Merrill. I interviewed her, and there were several things that really changed my perspective. One, I thought all politicians, that's what they did, that was their whole lives, and that's entirely not who she was. She was someone who had been a concert pianist; she'd been an educator. She had run a nonprofit, and then, later in life, she decided to run for office. So that really changed my perspective on who politicians were.

Secondly, I really had no concept of how few women there were in politics. Because I was raised in this feminist household, I just thought everyone was a feminist, and why wouldn't you be? So I didn't have a sense of how few there were of her, even in what I considered a progressive state of Connecticut.

After that interview, she said to me, "You should come intern for me." I went to intern for her at the state capitol, and it was the first time that I had any sense of how the political system worked without reading it in a book. What really drove me is that I saw her advocating on all of these issues that I really cared about and that there were all of these other people really trying to make change through the political system. She was the one who introduced me to a small network of nonprofit advocates in the state of Connecticut who really embraced me. It was through her that I got my first internship at NARAL. It was through that internship that I met who would be my first boss and significant mentor, a woman named Judy Blei, who is a lobbyist for nonprofits in the state.

After college, Judy offered me a job working for her. And it just seemed like a fabulous job to get paid to advocate on issues that you care about. But right after college, I really had the urge to run away. I hadn't studied abroad in college and I really wanted to go away, out of the country. So right after college, I actually secured a work visa for six months through a great program called BUNAC, and I flew to London on September 10, 2001.[20] And I woke up in London on September 11, 2001.

There were a few things that I remember very clearly. One was that I woke up in this new city, this very foreign place, and we had an orientation that day at what were the BUNAC offices. During that orientation, because of the time difference, was when the planes were crashing into the World Trade Center. So they said, "We need to stop this orientation. What we know is there are planes crashing into the World Trade Center. We don't know any more, and we're sending you back to the hostel." I remember I took the subway back to the hostel and there was just one communal room where the television was, and we all were sitting there just watching the coverage, stunned just like anyone else and trying to make sense of it. And what I remember clearly is trying to figure out how I could get in touch with my parents. I had to get a calling card and use the pay phone. I remember I kept trying to call them, but all the circuits were busy. It was many, many hours on that day before I was able to get in touch with them.

What I remember next was when people around the world were gathering together in memoriam. A whole group of us went to St. Paul's [Cathedral] that had this significant memorial for all of those that had passed, and everyone had American flags, and they were playing "The Star-Spangled Banner" here in this foreign country, and everyone there was supportive of America and our loss. It was a time during those first six months after 9/11 that you really felt this strong sense of international unity.

I came home January 2002 to start my job [as a lobbyist in Connecticut], and it was very weird because I felt like I had missed this shared experience, and I couldn't relate to it or understand it in the same way that everyone else did. I almost had a delayed grieving. When I came back and saw how it had changed people and how it had changed people's view of the world—I couldn't understand that until I came back to the United States. People's sense of security and American dominance, too, and just how it changed how you go to the airport, and how it changed people's view on war. I think there was this very unique time period that America was viewed so positively right after 9/11. And so I was there during that time when that seemed like a true hope and reality, and when I came back, there had already started to be that shift.

I came back, and I lobbied for Judy. Judy Blei had at that time, I want to say, twenty different nonprofits that were clients, ranging from Planned Parenthood, NARAL of Connecticut to hunger organizations to the League of Women Voters to social workers. It was her, another colleague of mine, Carolyn Treiss, and myself, and we were the threesome. For me, because I was the youngest and most junior, I was taking direction from Judy, and it was really a trial by fire.

I saw that the majority of legislators, of staff, of people that I worked with, they really wanted to do the right thing. They really weren't there for the wrong reasons. That was even somewhat surprising, I would say, to me. Another really strong takeaway was how much you can influence the process just by showing up. One of the reasons I felt so strongly about advocating for our clients is that they had so little resources and, often, so few volunteers to step up and speak up for them, whereas you could say other interests had a lot of money to put against that. It really was us finding a legislator at the last minute and saying, "These constituents, this is what they're really feeling about this particular bill," and unless they heard that from you, that would not have occurred to them.

I worked for [Blei] for two sessions—the first session was when we got the smoking ban passed in Connecticut. Connecticut was one of the first states to do that. Not surprisingly, we were up against significant resources and other lobbyists to make that happen. I was one piece of probably a twenty-five-person team. It was probably one of the first times

I saw a significant coalition build around one legislative effort. I remember every step the bill would take, counting votes and going to hearings and trying to track down legislators, and then you'd get to the next committee, and getting to the point where the bill had passed both the house and senate, and you were up late because, like many legislatures across the country, you do things at the very last-minute session. So you're up there at midnight, 2:00 A.M. on these session nights. And then it passed, and the governor signed it, and there was this significant celebration. It really was nuts to bolts, me seeing how years of work could coalesce into one legislative session of getting it done and getting a significant piece of legislation passed that would make the difference in the health of so many of our citizens.

Between the legislative sessions, I went out and worked in Yellowstone National Park as a hostess at the Old Faithful Inn. So it was a whole other realm of people that I was introduced to when I was out there. I was trying to figure out what I really did want to do. I didn't imagine being a lobbyist forever, even though it was great work. I just didn't feel satisfied that that was going to be it for me. So when I was in Yellowstone, I hadn't had a single political conversation in months; it just wasn't a topic of people I worked with. But I remember, actually, there was one night about three months into me being there that I got into a significant political debate with three other coworkers, and I felt so alive. It just really hit me that that's who I was, and I was really missing that. It really convinced me that I was on the right track, but I needed to go a route that I was learning more and getting more skills to be more effective in the political realm. I narrowed in on public administration and specifically going to the Maxwell School at Syracuse [because] it was this year-long program, and it was this mixture of policy and politics and management.

So, in that spring, I was applying to jobs all over the country, really, a whole litany of nonprofits, mainly in the fields of health care, anti-obesity work—because that had been some policy work I had done in Connecticut—and then women's rights. I wasn't really getting anywhere, and so after graduation in May, myself and several other graduates, we were unemployed and like, "How did this happen? We went to graduate school, we were supposed to get jobs, and now we don't have any jobs." This was 2004. I had a friend who had been on [the John] Kerry [presidential] campaign from the beginning, and she connected me with an opening that they had in Wisconsin. So I packed up the car, I drove out to Sheboygan, Wisconsin, and showed up and started working there. I had this idea of "We're going to win this campaign, and then I'm going to go to D.C. with all these other Kerry staffers." So when we didn't win, it was like, "What do I do now?" So I took the jump anyway and moved to D.C. without a job, like many people here do, and really, within a month of me being here, I found a job. That was at this small women's organization called Wider Opportunities for Women.

So that role was great, but it was one of those places, because it was small, there was very little mobility after a few years of me being there. I had a friend who told me about a job she knew of that was at this organization AAUW, and I was like, "I've heard of them." What caught my eye is she told me that one of the responsibilities would be running a conference that they had, called the National Conference for College Women Student Leaders. It sounded very familiar, and that's because I went to it in college. I went to it between my junior and senior year, and it was one of those experiences that you go home and you're, like, seventeen, and you tell your parents, "My life has changed." That's how I had felt about that conference.

So I had two lunches, and then I was hired. I started in January of '08. It ended up turning into way more than I could ever imagine. What I was given, which was this one conference and no staff, turned into, seven years later, seven national programs and a team of ten and impacting now tens of thousands of women and girls a year versus a few hundred when we started. For me, what became extremely powerful about the position was I started to recognize [that] all of the advocacy that I had done, absolutely it was so important, but I realized over time that I also had an opportunity to impact who those decision-makers were, and if there weren't women decision-makers at the table, how could we really make long-term substantial change? So for me, getting to come at making a difference in a very different way and trying to build up and encourage women's leadership was very fulfilling because I felt like it was really getting at the root of what I saw, so many of these issues we were fighting against.

I was able to really connect the dots of what I was trying to change in the political system and these collegiate women, that I just saw so much potential in, changing their views of themselves in politics. When you're able to do that in an intense one-day experience and then support them along the way, it really allows you to feel like you're making change at all these different levels. And for me, it became very personal because, over time, me spewing this message of "You need to run not just for student government, but we want you to really see yourself as a politic leader"—for me personally it just really started to make me question when I was going to take that advice. That's why, in June, I left AAUW, because I'm moving my life back to Connecticut, actually, with the goal of running for the state legislature in two to three years. That program and all the programs in which I got to really build up and develop women's leadership was an opportunity for me to feel like I was making a change in their lives, but just like anything, it really helps you reflect on what you care about and how you want to make a difference, too, and why you're telling others to take risks and leaps but you're not taking one yourself. So that has really come to fruition for me now.

I have always felt this particular responsibility to make a difference, and it's just there. I can't get rid of it. I almost wish sometimes that I could get rid of it. And not just to make a difference, but to feel like I'm that stone that's thrown in the pond, and I get to make bigger and bigger ripples of a difference. I'm always driven by "How can I fulfill that purpose?" I had often thought about wanting to run for office, but I kept putting it off.

So in thinking about it now, it's kind of like, "What am I waiting for?" It took me a little while to even tell my family or friends that I was thinking about this. Because I knew, once I said it, it was real, and they were going to be all for it, and that was really scary. It has really meant just starting to think about what I want to run for, when that might be, and it's great because everyone in my life is like, "Just tell me when and where, and I'll be there and I'll knock doors and I'll give you money." I'm like, "That's great, but there's so much that I need to figure out in my life to get to that point." I don't know what that's going to look like, and I don't know if I'll be successful, but that is really the essence of taking a chance and trying to be a leader in a new way. Honestly, I don't know how I'm going to feel when and if I'm a legislator. I might go down that path and run and win as a legislator and be like, "This is horrible." My perspective always is, you can be upset and annoyed and pessimistic about it all—and there's plenty of others that feel the same way—and at the end of the day, if you aren't going to try to be an individual to change it from the outside or the inside, then unfortunately we're just all going to have a lot more to complain about and be pessimistic about and hit our head against the walls about.

From my perspective, there's so much more opportunity for policy making at the state level than at the federal level, and that's really because of the stalemate that we've had at the federal level for so long now. So I am somewhat pessimistic about what can happen at the federal level. I have become somewhat pessimistic and impatient about the federal political prospects. You tend to grow up thinking that D.C. is where it happens, but I don't believe that.

I'm inspired by women. I think that's what every woman who runs really does if she knows it or not: she inspires other women as a role model. I think what I've been exposed to in the last ten years of being in D.C. is more women than I ever was prior to that who have run, have lost, have run again. That inspires me, every single one that I meet. So in that way, it's like a domino effect for me. Absolutely each and every woman that runs, when I see that, it's never old to me yet. It still feels so new and groundbreaking when these women are running. That's why I really feel like I need to follow in their footsteps.

Samhita Mukhopadhyay

AUTHOR, COMMUNICATIONS SPECIALIST, AND EXECUTIVE
EDITOR OF *FEMINISTING*, NEW YORK, NEW YORK

You can look at history and you know that blogs changed the game.

Samhita Mukhopadhyay and I met in her New York City apartment, where her collection of shoes lined the small hallway. She chuckled telling me how some people assumed that, with a popular book published, she had a much cushier life than the reality her cramped rooms belied. But her laughter had an edge to it, because some of those people were her online critics, who, according to her analysis, were frustrated in part by their lack of ability to get to the level of media attention and economic security that she had attained.

The daughter of Indian immigrants to New York, Mukhopadhyay earned her living as an editor, writer, public speaker, and communications specialist for organizations such as the National Women's Business Council. She is a long-time writer for and executive editor of *Feministing*, one of the first and most important feminist blogs, founded by her college friend Jessica Valenti. Mukhopadhyay's 2011 book, *Outdated: Why Dating Is Ruining Your Love Life*, sought to answer the question of how women might apply feminism to their own personal lives. Recently, she became executive editor of *Teen Vogue*.

Mukhopadhyay is proud of the role that blogs have played in the feminist movement of the twenty-first century. But she also suggests that a new level of attention needs to be turned on major issues facing the movement that primarily affect activists like her—those whose efforts are focused online, where the caustic tone of many interactions takes a heavy toll.

My paternal grandfather was a very successful businessman in colonial and postcolonial India. My grandmother was a child bride—but they didn't call it that then—at thirteen years old and had nine children and lived to 102. My parents were arranged into marriage in 1972. They settled in New York.

I was a rebellious teenager. The thought of an arranged marriage made me really upset. I was born and raised in the U.S. I have gone to India many times, but I am very American. There was always a disconnect between myself and my parents. I felt from a very young age, "Marriage is slavery! I am not doing that!"

I was very frustrated; I had a lot of anger. Looking back, partially it was gender with my family, partially it was that I was one of the only people of color where I was growing up. My parents moved to the suburbs when I was about five; I grew up in Northern Westchester. We were the first South Asian family on the block; obviously, it's the 80s. So all that anger manifested for me in really just being rebellious. I shaved my head when I was fifteen, or most of it, because it was the 90s, and had a lot of earrings. I was like, "I'm punk rock" and riot grrrl and all that stuff. My parents were really unhappy about that; they were like, "Why did we move to this country if our kids are going to be like this?" I was an angry teenager for sure. I was the kid that would get up and storm out of Thanksgiving dinner because my cousin was a Republican. I would be like, "I can't stand for this!" I would get up and start crying and walk out of the room.

I wasn't a very good student in high school—I may have had an undiagnosed learning disability or ADD, I don't know. I had a pretty hard time in school, and my grades weren't really great, but I was really good on the debate team. So I was shocked when I was accepted to [SUNY] Albany. I did very poorly my first two years, really struggled through my classes. I didn't feel like I fit. I had the fortune of taking a sociology class that led me to gender studies, and I met a professor who saw something in me. She said, "You have really strong perspectives, you're really stubborn, I think you have potential. Consider taking some women's studies classes." It was completely game changing; all of a sudden I was a straight-A student.

I was finally able to articulate the rage. I think the people that are attuned to gender studies or activism have a temperature gauge sometimes, and they have a sensitivity. I had never had an opportunity to channel that sensitivity. I had thought it was something I had to overcome so I could be a normal person, not that it was something that I should actually centralize and would end up becoming the core of who I am. Just reading things like bell hooks and Audre Lorde and being like, "Wow, I didn't imagine this stuff; other people have had this experience, and other people dealt with this rage or this feeling of not belonging and have been able to rewrite their own stories." So I got really interested in that, in having a vocabulary to describe these experiences that had led to depression and rage and all of these things. All of a sudden, I had the space to talk about these things and it was OK.

That was the moment in women's studies when people were like, "Wait, we actually need to centralize the voices of women of color," because it was the late 90s and third wave was in the mix. I was still taking classes that were like, "Global feminisms: this is what women in India do." We still hadn't incorporated intersectional feminism in a real way.

The women's studies students really hung out together all the time. It was a part of our broader activist community. The women's studies program at SUNY Albany also has this thing called a feminist collective, where they trained students to teach Feminism 101. That was where I met Jessica Valenti; we were in the same feminist collective. That was kind of our community, I would say.

After I graduated I did AmeriCorps like every other humanities major. I lived on a boat on the Hudson River, Pete Seeger's boat, and taught inner-city kids about environmental education.[21] I taught in public schools for five years. At that point I moved to San Francisco.

Jessica [Valenti], who founded *Feministing*—we were great friends, but this was before the days of social media, so we lost touch. Then I happened to be visiting New York and I bumped into her at a coffee shop. She was like, "I'm working on a project, and I really want you to be involved." Her and her sister had started this blog. It was 2004; I was like, "What's a blog?" At the time I thought, "Why am I going to get up at a nine on a Sunday to write about feminist stuff in the Middle East for some blog? I don't even know who's reading it." I had another friend who was a writer and she said, "No, dude, you have to do this. This sounds really cool. It is a really cool opportunity." We were all a bunch of nobodies at the time.

I was not that committed for a long time. I would just write one day a week. But then I would write something on a Tuesday, and by Wednesday morning there would be 400 comments. It becomes a cycle; it really feeds you, that excitement, to see how much it was impacting young women across the country. When I started speaking on panels, even for people to come up to me, or other writers that I had respected for so long, to be like, "I really like your writing," it was just so reinforcing and such positive kind of feedback.

I had always been an activist. That is what I identified the most with. Whatever it was, I was there protesting or organizing or at a meeting or working or interning at an organization that was fighting for rights in some way. I think that blogging linked for me that I was actually a writer; I was a writer in an activist's body. Once I realized the power of that tool both in how much writing and my voice were impacting other people—but also what it was doing for me, and this feeling of being able to articulate and imagine what a world with gender justice could look like or a world with racial justice could look like—it, to me, became unparalleled in my life. Power was a piece of it. Blogging was a place that I could be free.

But *free* is the operative word; I was not paid. So that freedom came at a cost. I had to do it in my spare time, as a hobby; it was not a full-time endeavor for me. For a year, student loans supported me. And then I started working at a place called the Center for Media Justice, which is a nonprofit in Oakland that does media training and campaigning and strategy for grassroots organizing groups. The executive director for the Center for Media Justice is this amazing woman, Malkia Cyril, who has been the executive director now for maybe fifteen years. She was the child of Black Panthers and felt that the news and the people who controlled the media controlled our lives. So her life's work has been to change and push the dial on media representation and coverage of the issues that we care about. It was really through her that I understood the language of intervention. I didn't realize that *Feministing* was interrupting the status quo. Looking back, obviously it did, because all of a sudden the news cares about gender. I do think that is due in part to feminist blogs from ten years ago. So it really gave me the language to talk about how *Feministing* was a strategy; it was a tool to push the mainstream narrative on how we were talking about a lot of these issues.

I currently work for the National Women's Business Council as their director of engagement and communications. I would say my work is mainly focused on pushing for coverage of women as innovators and founders and entrepreneurs and really looking at the way that we talk about business and the way that we talk about the workplace and how we decentralize women. My interest in this has been, How do we take a lot of the language that is flourishing and amazing in the activist communities and actually bringing it to the beast? How do we get *Fortune* to actually write about women CEOs [in a way] that is not just like, "And she has a family! Can you believe it?" On a high level, that's what I'm hoping to do with this job. It's been interesting. I think feminist communications—there's this space that we don't know yet. Everyone is really excited about hashtag campaigning, but it's going to be a long process to get that to decentralize actual power in media—who has the power and who is in charge of coverage and who gets the money and who gets the articles and all that stuff. I don't think that the rights that we benefit from have come because people were polite. I struggle with this a lot in my day job, where I have to use a certain language because I'm dealing with a certain age of people that aren't as comfortable with the language of gender justice as I am. I respect that, and I think you find opportunities to intervene anyway. But I do think that ultimately what makes the impact—we can soften the ground, but we also need a vision and we need to take some people somewhere. It is in those moments it behooves us to be as courageous as possible in our thinking and in our words. I think that's what Black Lives Matter has done. And that's why it's been so powerful.

I think that they have articulated a vision that is not reactionary. "Kill the police" would be reactionary, right? But instead it's "We are going to elevate this kind of experience that society is telling us black lives don't matter, and we are saying we do." It's a simple message that people can get behind. It is an intervention because, still today, in 2015, black lives don't matter. So we actually have to have a movement called Black Lives Matter. It's a rallying cry and it elevates an issue in a way that's very elegant, I think. But it also pushes against; it's not being nice about it either. It's not saying that *all* lives matter. You know? Even having *black* in the title brings a discomfort for most people. That is exactly right; I think it is exactly the kind of friction you need to really push people.

I was asked to write a book about transnational feminist theory, and I said I didn't think I was the appropriate person to write that. I had written a lot about international feminism, but there are people who have like eighteen PhDs on the topic and they should write it. But I was going through a breakup. It was like my come-to-Jesus moment with feminism: If I am a feminist, this relationship doesn't feel feminist, and what does that mean? And that started me on this journey of really reflecting on cultures of shame and expectations. Going back to the arranged marriage stuff, where every woman in my family for the last five generations has been arranged into marriage, against their will often—what does that mean? What does it mean for us as leaders, as feminists, as thinkers if our house is not in order? If in our own personal lives, we don't have the space or the political power to be our most feminist selves?

So I got really interested in this question of "What does it mean?" What does it mean to be a woman who has multiple sexual partners? What does it mean to be a woman who refuses to get married? Also just seeing so many of my friends struggle with it, as well, made me want to write something about it. The review that *Salon* gave [my book] is my favorite because "it's like *Chicken Soup for the Dating Feminist Soul.*" I didn't have the answers, and I knew I didn't have the answers; I wanted to try something. What would feminism look like if we applied it to our dating lives?

The response was amazing—how many women engaged with it and really how many letters I got from women being like, "You articulated this thing that I've always felt but thought I was imagining, and I was wondering why no one's ever written about it." It is usually young women of color, which means everything to me.

Obviously feminist blogging and access to online tools completely changed my life. I'm a protechnology person. I think that the access and the way broad groups of people have become engaged in political issues through online technology is amazing. Twitter did what democracy failed to do, which is engage the masses in any serious way. I genuinely believe that the reason why so many people were marching [after] the death of Freddie Gray and for Eric Garner and all that stuff is because Twitter and Facebook had a huge role to play in that.[22] So I do think there is this tremendous and exciting potential, and we've seen it. It will only continue to grow as the best leaders strategize around it.

I guess what I worry about is that sometimes things get so insular, and the constant culture of criticism that is also on the internet. I have been critiqued a lot, to the point where I almost don't engage online as much as I used to. I should have ten times more Twitter followers than I do, but I just cannot bring myself to tweet. Because you get sick of being criticized all the time. It's something that women do to each other. I feel frustrated in the way that the conversation is so polarizing and that you can get torn down for one thing that's not feminist enough. I have literally committed my life to this work. You know, frankly, I am comfortable saying that I deserve some credit for that too. I think that women are expected to be really humble about the contributions they've made, but you can look at history and you know that blogs changed the game. Rather than maybe tearing us all down, a thank you would be nice, too, every now and then. Even from early on, just the fact that I wrote for *Feministing*, people criticized me for being in cahoots with white feminists. This constant accusation and tearing down—like, what do you want me to say? Would it be better that I don't write at all? Because that's what it sounds like.

I think it's hard. A lot of us are burned out from that kind of energy. That polarization is just frustrating, and it feels defeating to at least the promise of women's voices online. Toxicity really flourishes on Twitter. It really does. So many young women I hear from are afraid because they are not going to be perfect in their politics. I'm really interested in messiness; I'm really interested in how we apply our lofty ideas about feminism to the messiness of our regular lives. What do we do when we mess up? How do we forgive ourselves? How do we still build a community rather than brand each other like "you've done this thing or you've done this thing"? Because that's a distraction. I know a lot of people think the infighting is good, voices are being heard; I don't see productive things coming out of it. I don't see strategies that are sustainable in a real way. That's what I don't see. I could get killed for saying all of that, but I don't care.

We can kind of spend all of our time trying to figure out all the divisions of feminism and being as inclusive as possible, but then an armed gunman can still walk into a church and kill nine people because they're black. There are certain things that are just like they were fifty years ago. In some ways, I'm so inspired that Obama was elected because, like, "Wait, we can pull it out. We can do this. The kids are all right." But I don't know that we have a cohesive sense of where the fights should be all the time. I think reproductive rights is a great example of that; we're, as feminists, fighting for all these different types of identity, and that's so important, but I do think we have lost sight of some of the bigger fights that we have not won: equal pay, sick leave, access to reproductive health care. It's hard to build a movement around that because not everybody has a shared sense of the strategy and the tactics to do it effectively, which has been true since feminist organizing started, but it's really bad right now. The attacks are the worst we've seen in twenty years. Literally, I don't think the people that work at NARAL even saw this coming ten years ago. And it's easy to lose sight of that when we're in New York and we're in California and we're like, "We just need inclusiveness," where in other parts of the country, that is just not the case. I'm really worried. I'm worried about access to abortion. That is a real thing we have to worry about right now. I don't think we have the infrastructure, the support, to really fight it, in a way. Not that Planned Parenthood isn't amazing and the ACLU and all of the organizations that are doing it, but I don't think there is a broader consensus that it is an important issue the way gay marriage was. I do worry about that, and that is why I am voting for Hillary Clinton. Because I don't even care if we don't have the same politics; I just know that she's pro-choice and I'm like, "Yes, that is what we need." Not to oversimplify it, I just think it's a balance. We need to figure out how we are going to move forward and create some sense of consensus around these issues.

I worked with the ACLU for a year at my last job before this one, working on their reproductive rights campaign. I actually didn't know how bad it was until I was in those rooms, in those strategy meetings. And I was like, "They did what? Missouri did what?" Then you realize, "Why are we wasting our time talking about 'this person's book is sexist' when literally women's lives do not matter at all in five states, legally?" So that was just very eye-opening. We might need a Supreme Court decision. Another one.

I feel like we are distracted a little bit. I do think that rape culture, college sexual assault—there are so many issues that are not going well. They're not going well, and I just don't see our organizing energy going to them. I want to research the intersection of these two things: How do we take this momentum we have online and this anger and this rage and actually do targeted, impact-driven work with it? We need a Black Lives Matter for abortion. We just do.

Kwajelyn Jackson

COMMUNITY EDUCATION AND ADVOCACY
MANAGER, FEMINIST WOMEN'S HEALTH CENTER,
ATLANTA, GEORGIA

*If you live in an environment in which you know that it is not safe
for young people growing up, how might that impact your decisions
about whether or not you choose to have children?*

In order to interview Kwajelyn Jackson, community education and advocacy manager at the Feminist Women's Health Center in Atlanta, my graduate assistant Rachel Gelfand walked past a protest at the clinic. Feminist Women's Health Center, or "Feminist," as Jackson calls it, is unusual in that it provides both reproductive health services, including abortions, and advocacy and programming initiatives for the wider community, such as the Lifting Latinx Voices Initiative and the Black Women's Wellness program. Jackson, who recently became codirector, is focused on trying to make sure that the two arms of the organization serve each other; she wants her programming initiatives to help grow new leadership for the reproductive justice and abortion rights movement, and she wants her volunteers and program participants to understand how state and local politics affect the choices they can and can't make about their own bodies and to feel empowered to make political change.

Jackson's is a deeply intersectional approach, one that embraces a broad understanding of reproductive justice. She was profoundly affected by the waves of police violence against black men and women and by the Black Lives Matter movement. The eighth woman in her family to graduate from Spelman College, she roots herself in black feminist thought but also worries about the level of conflict she sees within the feminist community. In this interview, she was worn down from the personal costs of her commitment to activism and yet also guardedly optimistic about the future.

I was born in Kansas, but I was raised mostly in Saint Louis, Missouri. I came to Atlanta for college, to attend Spelman. I was the eighth woman in my family to go to Spelman, including my grandmother. Spelman is a historically black, all-women's institution. So it's really very rooted and connected to the kind of formations of my feminism and what really connects me to the work that I do now.

My mom also went to Spelman, and she worked in social justice for most of my childhood. She worked for an organization called the National Conference for Community and Justice and did youth programming around anti-oppression. Then she transitioned from there to working at Planned Parenthood and was their vice president of education and diversity in Saint Louis as well. So that was also another connection to reproductive justice and using that sort of intersectional lens of looking at gender and race at the same time.

For all freshmen who go through Spelman there is a required course called ADW, which is African Diaspora in the World. A lot of it is centered in black feminist thought, talking about the ways in which women of color function in society depending on all of these other kinds of layered identities, how class and education and sexual orientation and all of these different things impact the way that we're able to navigate through the world. And then looking at that across history, so looking at slave narratives and then looking at theory and then looking at literature and taking all of those things together to sort of get some context for where we fit in the world. And it was really, really powerful to me, just going through that class.

A lot of people like to think about historically black colleges and universities in particular, or single-gender institutions, as this homogenous blob, like you go there to escape from all the other people in the world. But to me it was really revealing about how much diversity there is within black women, how many different kinds of black women there are and how many different ways there are to be a black woman. That was really something that was big for me at that period of time. It started to reveal to me that there was not a singular way of performing womanhood or blackness or those two together. That kind of spurred me to continue to want to be thinking about those things, the ways that we perform gender and the ways in which we're conditioned to think different things about people and the way they should behave and all that kind of stuff. So I give Spelman a lot of credit for helping me to understand those pieces.

I majored in economics and I minored in dance. A lot of my peers who were studying economics or business management or something like that had dreams of going to New York and going to Wall Street, and that was the plan for a lot of folks. But 9/11 happened my senior year. And so that changed a lot for people who thought they were going to New York.

I had an internship with what was First Union Bank at the time. I had rotated through several departments at the bank, and the only one that I really had any interest in was community development, which was centered around low-income communities and reinvesting and revitalizing neglected city centers, and it seemed like the most helping-people part of the bank, because banks exist to make money, and so it felt the most mission centered. That seemed like something I could do and not feel icky every day. So I just called them and asked if there were any openings. I took a chance because I had interned with one woman and connected with her, and I gave her a call and said, "If there's anything that comes up let me know," and then they hired me. I didn't interview or anything. It was awesome. And then I sort of grew in that department. I worked for the bank for eight years through several mergers. It was fine. I didn't love it. I didn't feel like it really fed anything in me.

Over time it became more and more profit centered. When I first joined that part of the bank, they used to call it the double bottom line: we have to try to make a little bit of money, but our real goal is to try to impact communities. Slowly but surely that other bottom line started to get a little more weight. I felt like we're just trying to make the bank money; it doesn't really matter what happens to the people, and I didn't feel good about that.

Then 2008 happened, and all of a sudden there was this shift where we're foreclosing on all these places and displacing people, and it just felt horrible to come to work every day because it's like we're the bad guy all of a sudden. So I decided that I wanted to move into nonprofit work. I decided that I really wanted to do social justice work.

The thing that's really hard right now because of this internet age we're in, where we have so much access to so much information so quickly all the time, [is] it can feel very overwhelming to get bombarded with all of the tragic, just heartbreaking, things that are happening here and in Nigeria and in Jordan and all around the world and all around the country. And it is really, really exhausting to feel that way all the time and to feel buried by it. I mean, I think that's something that is really hard with the shooting, with Michael Brown, in Saint Louis. I mean, Ferguson is literally four miles away from where I lived. And so that has been really, really hard to manage through and to be able to care for yourself in such a way that you can keep doing the work at the same time, because it's just depleting, I guess, for lack of a better word. And so that Black Lives Matter movement, alongside thinking about how that's impacted with the gender lens and how black women or black trans women are having this simultaneous moment but not getting some of the same recognition, has also been really hard.

And then again, taking all of those racial dynamics to the reproductive justice movement and looking at those simultaneously, too, to say we can't just be singularly focused on abortion rights; we also need to be thinking about what it means to live in the world and how this moment is a part of reproductive justice—it's not separate from [it]. So all of those are the things that make it really, really difficult to rest easy and to take care of yourself and to feel settled. It's fuel, to a point, to keep doing the work. But it's also depleting.

When things happened in Saint Louis, I was really messed up for a while. It was hard to do my work, and I told folks here that I would not be comfortable with us as an organization being silent on these issues. And so at that point we put out a statement and a letter. I have tried to make it really clear that we have to be a part of these conversations and we have to continue to make the case for why this state violence is a reproductive justice issue. The way I like to think about it is that because we use a reproductive justice framework, we're thinking about not only the right to decide whether or not to have children but also to decide when and with whom. I mean, to have the ability to have safe and healthy relationships and families and to also have healthy pregnancies and healthy children. All of those things are connected to each other and having full bodily autonomy. All of those things are a part of this bigger reproductive justice movement. If you live in an environment in which you know that it is not safe for young people growing up, how might that impact your decisions about whether or not you choose to have children or have more children? How might the police state or the interactions with law enforcement with your community impact your ability to parent with dignity and have all the resources you need to care for the children that you already have? How are women dealing with issues of pregnancy, delivery, abortion access, gynecological care within the prison systems? How are incarcerated mothers able to have connections with their families and children? All of those things all wrap up together, and that's why issues of reproductive justice are complicated, and that's why abortion rights are complicated. It's not cut-and-dried "People get abortions because they hate kids."

I think that [homosexual] marriage bans being lifted is amazing. It's a huge accomplishment, and it took a long time. But it's really hard to just count that as "We've done it," because there's so many other things that are left undone around LGBTQ rights. When you think about how many queer youth and queer youth of color don't have a place to live or are facing threats of violence every time they walk outside, getting married is really far removed from their actual lived reality. So I think that there's a challenge to try to celebrate the small victories, not get stuck there, and continue to do more of the work. Georgia is a state that doesn't have any protections around discrimination against orientation or identity. So you can get married, but you can get fired the next day.

LGBTQ issues are really central to our work. We have a lot of work that we're still trying to do and that we are trying to partner with other LGBTQ-centered organizations to sort of push a little bit so that it's not a very white, cis male gay movement. Lots of nonprofits that we work with value us as a partner but sometimes will lose political will by aligning with us very publicly. So sometimes we have to just step back. Sometimes we're fine with that; I mean, it's like, if it's going to get the job done, we'll do it. But at the same time, we want to try to work in the progressive movement to try to build an environment where people will go to bat for us in the same way that we'll go to bat for them, and not be scared. There are plenty of queer people who need abortion access. And we need to be able to be working together all the time.

What we're seeing around LGBTQ issues is, to a point, they are becoming less and less controversial. I mean, it's not a challenge to get big corporations to come out in front around queer issues. It's not even for some conservative legislators—they're feeling more and more safe to be vocal about their opinions. We don't see as much of that around reproductive rights. What can we do to address some of that stigma so that people can talk about it?

At the federal level, things are interesting. We've seen some very brave and outspoken legislators who are pushing to end the Hyde Amendment and to add additional protections to prevent states from eroding away women's access to care on the basis of not medically sound information.[23] Locally, in Georgia, it's a really difficult political environment. I feel like a lot of what progressive organizations and legislators are doing is trying to maintain, as opposed to really push more proactive stuff. It's more stopping bad stuff before it happens. But we know that it's going to be necessary to have real change for us to be able to do progressive stuff.

We've introduced a resolution that kind of talks to some of these things. It's an intersectional approach to talking about health care access and workplace issues and racial disparity and all different kinds of family formations, and trying to take back the language of family from those who might use it as a weapon against our issues, to say [that] if we really care about families, working families, and making sure that they have everything they need, then we have to be considering all these things at the same time when making policy. You can't make policies that only work for two-parent households with 2.5 kids. We have to think that sometimes a family might look very drastically different; probably the majority of the time it's going to look drastically different. It's our way to try to bring a lot of folks to the table at the same time. Because it's not abortion-centric, it allows for people who are working on minimum wage and equal pay and those kinds of things to come in. It makes room for advocates around workplace discrimination to come in, and people who are thinking about the ACA [Affordable Care Act] and closing the coverage gaps to come in, and us all to talk about these things at the same time and hopefully to have a platform to have some more proactive legislation to come out of it. It's called the Strong Families Resolution, and in 2016 we're hopeful that we'll be able to get some movement around it and get it passed.

We've been doing a lot throughout this year working with different legislators on it and trying to get some grassroots support in Atlanta and in other cities around the state, trying to get people talking about the issues that impact them, regular everyday issues that folks are facing. Like "My job is here and I live here, and transportation issues are a barrier for me to be able to support my family." Or "I take care of an elderly parent, and my job won't let me take time off to care for my parents." There's all kinds of little things that are really impacting people, and we want to give them an opportunity to start to talk about them and see how that fits in with state policy. We hope that will be a way to encourage people to get more engaged in politics, to vote more, to really see the president is important but your state rep is the one who is calling a lot of the shots around your life, and your city council person is calling a lot and your school superintendent and your police chief—and how all those pieces fit in with the way that people live, so hopefully they will speak up more.

I identify as feminist, and I know that sometimes there are people who find just the term *feminist* a little bit problematic and not sufficient for them. But I do. But I also identify as a black feminist, and that part of my identity is really important and really informs the way that I think about feminism. I think feminism is really something that is defined by people's perspective and lived experience and informed by history and theory. And we get into so much of a frenzy trying to police the way people live their feminism that it becomes more harm than good to me sometimes. People pitting people who consider themselves a Beyoncé feminist and saying that that's not real. Or "Is there space in white feminism for people of color?" Or "Is your feminism trans exclusive?" All of this stuff. I mean, I think it's important to keep having the conversations, but I think we have to keep open to having our views shifted over time. None of this stuff is static. Our feminism is constantly developing and redefining itself inside of us. I feel like that's a perspective that I sit in most of the time. But I'm excited about the fact that a lot of conversations are happening around how people live their version of womanhood, their version of feminism, their version of this sort of gender identity and how it interacts with other people.

I really hope that more people who don't identify as women can start to really talk about the issues of feminism and the ways that sexism and patriarchy play out in the world. I hope that people can learn to apply the gender lens; there's so many of these issues that have implications across gender identity that are not seen that way. Think about something like having conversations about minimum wage. Somewhere like 60–70 percent of [people earning the minimum wage] are women and are likely parents. A good portion of those are likely women of color, so let's talk about that.

If folks had a real understanding about what feminism is about, that could create the entry point for a lot of change. It's not going to fix everything, but it at least gets people thinking differently about how to address some of these really, really big problems. I feel like we really are on the cusp of some major change, and there is sort of a tipping point looming, where things are going to start to really shift. I think that marriage equality is just the beginning of these major changes. I don't know exactly what it's going to look like, but I do think that there's going to be a leveling out in some ways of some of the social inequality that we're constantly fighting against. I don't think it's going to be quick, and I don't think it's going to be easy. But I do think that we're kind of on the precipice of the beginnings of that.

PART THREE

Activists in Their Twenties

The six women and one trans man in this chapter were all under thirty years old when I interviewed them, at the beginning of their adult lives. Their stories, though, are not ones of pure youthful optimism. They have been active in feminist causes for years—some of them since they were preteens—and they have a clear-eyed sense of both the possibilities for and the obstacles to change. Like the women in the first two parts of this book, they search for ways to balance their passion and commitment to making a difference in the world with the need to earn a living, maintain their health, and craft lives that include time for friends and families.

The events of September 11, 2001, happened when these activists were children, and their lives were shaped by the events of that day. Noorjahan Akbar, a young Afghan woman, had fled with her family to Pakistan six years earlier to escape the Taliban; after the American intervention following 9/11, she and her family returned to a devastated but optimistic homeland. Akbar later left her country; when I met her in Washington, D.C., in 2015, she yearned to return home but could not, fearing for her life. Rye Young points to 9/11 as a turning point in his own coming-of-age story in suburban New York, affecting the issues that interested him in school and the way he viewed the world. Park Cannon posits that as a youngster who had moved from the south to the north, 9/11 refashioned her understanding of race and her position as a black person in the United States.

These young people came of age during and after the Great Recession of 2008, and it, like 9/11, had a profound impact on most of them. The economic collapse shaped the way they thought about the choice to be a "professional" activist and whether or not that would remain an option for them. Ho Nguyen of Minneapolis noted that because of the crash,

> 75 percent of my friends are not working in our field. We couldn't find jobs in our field, and we're all insanely in debt. You know, it's been almost ten years since we graduated and we're all still paying off our student loans. A lot of my friends who were doing activism with me all

left. I'm probably one of the last of my friends that is doing activism for pay. You know, a lot of my friends, when we talk about it now, they say, "Oh, you know, I sold out," and I say, "Well, you didn't sell out; you did what you had to do." Activism is broad. I'm a gay for pay. You know, you don't have to do those things. You don't have to—your job doesn't actually have to reflect your personal identity for it to be legit, right? This is just the path that I chose.[1]

Alice Wilder, at nineteen the youngest person I interviewed, recalled how during the recession "there were all these news stories about young people and unemployment. It changed my perception of possible career paths. Especially now that a lot of my friends have graduated college and are underemployed or unemployed, my thought right now is just 'How can I put myself in the very best position by the time I've graduated, where I can have skills that are marketable and enough of a cushion that I feel like I can pay my rent?' And activist work just is not really going to be able to provide that for me."[2]

Like their elders, these activists tackle a variety of issues. For them, *intersectionality* rolls naturally off the tongue and inherently defines the way most of them think and talk about their views of feminism. Although some of them focus on a particular issue, most of them see interconnections between issues—whether reproductive justice, police brutality, Black Lives Matter, transgender experiences, or housing and economic development—as key to making progress.

Their activism, fueled by youthful energy, is not necessarily joyful. Andrea Pino, whose journey as an activist fighting sexual assault on university campuses has been featured in the documentary *The Hunting Ground*, took up activism to save her own sanity after a brutal assault but nearly lost everything in the effort. Noorjahan Akbar aches to join her family in Afghanistan but does not want to be a "sacrificial lamb." Former girl activist Alice Wilder was burned out by the time she got to college. Who Needs Feminism founder Ivanna Gonzalez felt motivated to keep going to a large degree because she didn't want to abandon new online activists who might feel all alone. "It's really scary, and I know how scary it is."[3]

These young activists display remarkable ingenuity, an ability to tap into local and international networks and to connect theory to practice. Their wealth of experience and knowledge promises that feminism will remain a vital, evolving, and exciting movement.

Noorjahan Akbar

FOUNDER, FREE WOMEN WRITERS,
WASHINGTON, D.C.

Feminism and women's rights and equality are not Western inventions.
The West does not have a monopoly on freedom. Women have been singing about
freedom in every little village you can find in Afghanistan for centuries. Women have
been writing about it, if they could. They have been teaching their daughters.
That is an act of protest in a country where people think that women's
voices are a sin to be heard, to be spoken loudly.

When I arrived at Noorjahan Akbar's apartment building on Connecticut Avenue in Washington, D.C., there were fire trucks with running engines and flashing lights parked at the curb and scores of residents—apparently from dozens of different countries—milling about outside. There was no real emergency; someone had burned her dinner and set off a smoke alarm. Once we were able to get into Akbar's apartment, I noticed the folding chairs stacked around the spare living room. She revealed that her father had recently died in Afghanistan, and since she was unable to go home, a group of friends had come over to eat with and comfort her earlier in the week. Akbar's father was a critical figure in her upbringing, and his death was clearly a source of pain, but she insisted on carrying on with the interview.

Only twenty-four, Akbar was already a well-known figure here and abroad. She was one of *Glamour* magazine's College Women of the Year in 2013 and was named one of *Forbes*'s World's 100 Most Powerful Women, the American Association of University Women's Woman of Distinction, and one of the *Daily Beast*'s Women Who Shake the World. She has appeared on Al Jazeera, CNN, ABC, and Fox News to discuss Afghan women's issues, and her writing has appeared in many outlets including the *New York Times*. She cofounded Young Women for Change, an organization for Afghan women, when she was in college, and when I interviewed her she was actively engaged in a new endeavor, a blog and website for women writers in her home country called Free Women Writers.

Raised in Afghanistan and Pakistan, the daughter of progressive activists and teachers, Akbar came to America through family connections to attend her last two years of high school at the George School in Pennsylvania, and then received a BA in sociology from Dickinson College. She earned a master's degree from American University and was working in D.C. and running her blog on the side. She worried about the safety of her siblings and her mother in Afghanistan and felt deeply torn because she ached to help her country on the ground but recognized that to do so would mean putting her life directly in danger. Her powerful story points toward the international dimensions of feminist activism and highlights how the internet makes new forms of engagement possible.

My best memories from growing up with my family was my mom helping us with schoolwork and our dad giving us extracurricular books to read because he loved books. Even when we were poor and could barely afford food, he somehow found ways to buy us books. For as long as I can remember, we have had a library of thousands of books always in our basement. It's always been a part of my life. I think that he looked at books as a window to an outside world. When I came to the United States to go to school, I had read more Charles Dickens than any of my American friends. I had read more Jane Austen than any of my American friends, and it was because my father, somebody who never lived outside Afghanistan and Pakistan, had this vision that we didn't have to limit ourselves to a geographical boundary. I think that had great impact on me. My dad also loved poetry, and I remember [that in] winter we would sit around reading poetry. It wouldn't just be Afghan poetry. I read Langston Hughes, I read Bertolt Brecht. I grew up with literature that had a cause; literature that had passion. He never learned English, so all his books were translated in either Pakistan or Iran by authors who changed it from English to Farsi. But his love for poetry, I think, is sort of an Afghan trait. Afghans love poetry.

My mom is incredibly resilient. I do not know how she does it. She has seven children, she teaches, she has been a teacher for over seventeen years. She has arthritis right now but she doesn't want to stop teaching, so she goes to school despite the fact that she's in pain, there are security threats, there's street harassment, there's so many obstacles for women who work outside the home in Afghanistan. And she does more than that. On several occasions, she has volunteered with me; she has participated in the protests I have organized; she has written for my blog that I run for women's issues; once she ran a creative writing project with me for girls in an orphanage. So she's incredibly passionate about women's rights, and I think she takes pride in the fact that so many of her daughters also have taken on that cause.

It was 1996, I was five years old, when the Taliban took over Mazar-i-Sharif, which is where we were living then. This is in the Balkh Province in the north. We moved because my father was a teacher and my sisters went to school, my older sisters, and with the Taliban coming, they couldn't do that anymore. In addition, it was well known that my father was very progressive and he would bring students over to our house and he would have poetry readings. Women and men would sit together and learn about poetry, and my father would teach them at our house. This was not something that the Taliban under any circumstance, even now, would accept. So we moved to Pakistan and we were there for six years.

We first lived in Peshawar and then we lived in Attock, another city close by. When we were in Attock, we actually ran a learning center for other refugees, so we taught about 700 Afghans. My entire family was teachers. I was around twelve, and there's a photo of me teaching. We had a huge population of refugees who went there, and especially important, there were a lot of refugee girls who came to the school. That was something that my father always was a proponent of.

In 2001, the Taliban fell out of power. When they lost power with the United States' intervention, we went back to Afghanistan and we opened a school, a learning center, again. And we had about 300 women that we taught. This one was just for women because they had lost the opportunity to go to school for six years because the Taliban did not allow it. In Pakistan we had had the chance to learn English and computer skills, something that most Afghan women, they don't have the chance to do, so we were able to teach those skills to Afghan women. My father also taught literature class, because that's one of his passions, and my mom taught a variety of school subjects for people who needed to catch up so that they could go back to school.

This was a time when Afghans were very, very hopeful. If you look at surveys, it's like a skyrocket, the amount of hopefulness and passion and people returning to the country. The numbers are just staggering compared to now, thirteen, fourteen years later. I remember going to the local school—the first day was my first day in school back in my own country—and there were so many students and it was a big chaos because so many girls had returned to school. I was supposed to be [in] sixth grade, but there was literally no space left in sixth grade, so I repeated a grade. But it was never something that I thought of as a negative thing, because in my mind it was always equated with "Look at this movement! Look at this life growing in Afghanistan," and that was really beautiful. I remember the first few weeks—this was right after the Taliban had left, so the city had been shelled completely by air strikes and, of course, fighting on the ground against the Taliban. You could see bullet holes on the streets and buildings that had fallen apart, and it was such a stark contrast to see these girls dressed in uniforms, full of laughter and energy and excitement that they could have a normal life again. So that really stuck with me. It's one of my favorite memories of Afghanistan.

I never felt like a victim growing up. I, of course, living in Afghanistan faced discrimination; living in Pakistan I was a refugee—that's never easy. And, of course, there was war and, of course, we lost our house and we lived in poverty—I lived in poverty for most of my life. But I never felt like a victim. And it was because my parents found this little haven in our house where we could be ourselves, where we could express our feelings, where gender would not be a means to control us. Gender rules were not implemented the way they were in the general society. So I always felt free growing up. And it also gave me the tools to deal with my oppression.

When I was twelve, my father [said], "If poverty makes you so upset, you should do something about it. Why don't you start a magazine with your classmates?" And I did. They always made me feel like I had agency. I think that served me very, very well when I came to the United States [to go to the George School in Pennsylvania]. Because when other people looked at me like a victim, I would be like, "What are you talking about? Yes, of course my life was tough, but that's not all that I am. I also have these skills; I also have these good experiences; I also have all of these things that I can bring. I don't need your pity."

That pity is never a solution to creating a global feminist movement, or a global anything, or any kind of human connection. The moment that you pity someone you dehumanize them, and I never wanted that. And I never do that to women I work with, regardless of what their experience has been.

I took a class on African American history my junior year in high school. I realized that I knew more about discrimination against black people in the United States than most of my American classmates because my father gave me a copy of *Roots*; I had already read Angela Davis, I had already read Audre Lorde. I had read it all in Farsi. Separately from my own oppression as an Afghan woman, and as a brown woman in America, I first got to know oppression through learning about slavery in America. And one of the things that stuck with me most was that slaves were told to not read, were told to not write. This was so striking to me because I had moved from Afghanistan to Pakistan because the Taliban had told me that I couldn't read and that I couldn't write and I couldn't go to school. At the heart of it—I'm not original in thinking this, Edward Said has, for example, written a lot about this—is that power is basically knowledge. Who gets to create knowledge? Who gets to create information, create terminology, create language? It's the same person who creates power. The fact that men have had the monopoly on power to call forced marriages "marriages" instead of slavery is very telling to me. It's because of our language and the ways that it's created.

So, for me, oppression—language can be a force of oppression, but it can also be a very incredible force for change and for fighting back oppression and for taking back terms and for taking back history. I think it is a universal thing that women's literature is always looked at as secondary, as less important, as less critical or even less academic, less valuable. Women's words are considered less valuable. There's the words of a Palestinian poet [Suheir Hammad] who says, "I have stories to tell you. Listen to me."

I think about this a lot in terms of women, because we have so much to say and literature is such a powerful tool for us to say them. So it's important to create those platforms where women can speak, because it doesn't just benefit us. Men could learn a lot from shutting up and listening to us once in a while. They don't have to do it every day. Just once in a blue moon would be very nice. Literature has the power to change minds. It's tough in a country like Afghanistan, where only less than 30 percent of the population are literate, but what gives me hope is that also in Afghanistan around 67 percent of our population is under the age of thirty. Which means that they have more chances and time to get an education, a chance to at least learn how to read and write, and they're the future. If we want to target anyone, we should be targeting them with our literature, with our writing, with our poetry.

I've seen it make a difference. I have done a lot of creative writing projects in Afghanistan. I worked in two different orphanages, with children—girls and boys—to help them write their stories. That was something that I began in 2008 or 2009 or 2010, very early on when I had started working on this. I worked later with an organization called Young Women for Change, and we had a huge effort toward writing women's stories and getting international and national media to pay attention to it. We would literally write media updates and we had dozens of media contacts, and we actually created a lot of stories by writing about street harassment for the first time in decades. It had never been talked about in Afghanistan in this way before: that street harassment is an issue, that street harassment causes women to stay at home and not participate in the society, street harassment causes social and economic and political marginalization.

In 2008, I traveled to Afghanistan and I collected women's stories, women's songs, and traditional folk songs. Because—actually, I didn't know why

I was doing it; I found out later. I went, and I thought most of the songs would be about love, but I found out that a lot of them were actually about women's issues. They were about early and forced marriages; they were about not being able to go to school. That was really a wake-up call to me, because I had seen this top-down approach of feminism and women's rights in Kabul, where I lived, where an educated woman would come to the grassroots women of the poor neighborhoods and tell them about their rights. But I was like, "What? Let's wait a second, let's listen to them and see what they have to say."

They were actually singing what they had been singing for decades, for centuries, about these issues, and we just didn't want to listen to them. So I've recently begun publishing those on the website and on the social media pages that I run. So right now I'm working on a blog that has about 114 contributors from inside the country. They mostly write in Farsi and in Pashtu. We have 26,000 readers, and I just started translating the stuff into English. This is a one-woman project; I do all the editing, I do all the photography, I make all the posters, and I do social media, and I connect with the writers and follow up with them.[4] So it's exhausting. And it's not my day job; I have another day job. So it's taken me a while to translate the stuff into English, but I've translated about thirty of them and try to do at least one or two a week. I try to put them in English as well because I think there's a void in American media of real voices, authentic voices, of Afghan women and men. Because we are so often, especially women, are so often talked about and rarely listened to. We're the subject of so many conversations, we're looked at from afar, but we are silent. But these stories of women writing bring a new voice and create a new narrative for Afghan women. I don't necessarily think that the more educated class of women who are working for women's rights are ignorant or are not connected with the real issues, but the real stories and the narratives of rural women could really enrich those experiences and those stories and our activism.

But another, bigger part of it, to me on a personal level, was realizing that feminism and women's rights and equality are not Western inventions. The West does not have a monopoly on freedom. Women have been singing about freedom in every little village you can find in Afghanistan for centuries. Women have been writing about it, if they could. They have been teaching their daughters. That is an act of protest in a country where people think that women's voices are a sin to be heard, to be spoken loudly. So it gives me this perspective to never look at women as helpless and to never give both the Islamists who say, "No, feminism, women's rights are all Western propaganda," and the bigots and racists in the United States and Europe who are like, "Oh, those backwards Afghans. What do they know about women's rights? This is our—we are the flag bearers of democracy and progress and freedom"—no. You're both wrong. The need to be free is a human need.

I want to contribute to change in Afghanistan. I think it's best then when you're on the ground. But I'm also aware that the security situation is not really great, and I want to go back, I want to help; my entire family is there, so I want to see them and spend time with them. But I don't think a Noorjahan who's dead is very helpful for Afghanistan. I've been threatened a lot before for my work, and I've never taken it seriously. Dozens of women's rights activists have been killed, and [in] the recent attack in Kunduz, the Women for Afghan Women organization office was threatened. So I want to contribute to the change in Afghanistan, but I want the Afghan government to know that it has a responsibility toward our security. I hear this so often from governmental officials who say, "Oh, all the Afghans who are outside the country should return. You're betraying the country, you're betraying Afghanistan." No, a country that can't give at least the basic services of security—we don't even want paved roads, we just want to live there without getting killed—doesn't have the right to tell us. We can't be sacrificial lambs for a corrupt government. If the government cleans up its act, I will be the first to join them. But I don't see it coming. So I'm stuck. I don't know. I fight with it, with myself, so many times. Every day I'm thinking, "I could be writing so much better if I was there. I could be gathering women's stories; I could be running a print journal for women, a magazine for women, using the stories that they contribute to the blog." I want to do all that, and even if I don't have the money for it, I'm happy to fundraise for it and get it done. But I don't think I should be a sacrificial lamb.

Afghan women have been killed for so many different reasons. We have been sacrificial lambs for the socialist Soviet movement in the country. We have been sacrificial lambs for the Taliban's Islamist movement, for ISIS. Generation after generation of politicians has profited off of our bodies—off of our dead bodies. And I don't want to be another dead body.

I've been able to create a safe space for the women to come and write their views, knowing that I won't call them an infidel and kick them out or run a smear campaign or anything like that, while the vast majority of internet platforms will do that to them in Afghanistan. They won't be harassed, because literally anyone who threatens or harasses a woman is immediately blocked off my page. Because my priority is not talking to men; my priority is talking to women to create these systems of support, to create the means of advocacy, and to raise the awareness of women, as well, about their own issues. Because we haven't had a chance to do that yet—self-realization and getting over our inferiority complex. All of this needs some interconnection. That's what I'm trying to do. Literally, I think if women have the power to speak up their voices and realize their own power, we don't need to beg for our rights from men.

Ivanna Gonzalez

COFOUNDER, WHO NEEDS FEMINISM,
CHAPEL HILL, NORTH CAROLINA

*It just was a social media campaign that was run by a bunch of
college kids and got really big, and I think that was exciting to a lot of people.
I think the story of how it happened really captured people's imagination and
made them think, "Wow, I can make a difference," as cheesy as that sounds.*

I first met Ivanna Gonzalez when she took a course on poverty in North Carolina
at Duke University that I cotaught. Since both of us were returning to Chapel
Hill, twenty minutes down the road, I often gave her a ride after class and enjoyed our long conversations. She later took another course I taught at Duke,
Women in the Public Sphere: History, Theory, and Practice, and was instrumental
in developing the Who Needs Feminism social media campaign that emerged
as the final project in that class. The campaign showcased images from people
across the globe holding up signs explaining why they needed feminism. When I
interviewed Gonzalez, long after her graduation, she was continuing to monitor
the Who Needs Feminism web page and email inbox on her own time, communicating with other young activists around the world.[5]

Gonzalez is the daughter of Venezuelan immigrants to the United States
and grew up in Miami. Her father is an entrepreneur whose life was turned
upside down when one of his business partners was caught committing fraud.
Her mother, trained as a doctor in Venezuela, never practiced professionally in
the States, but her skills were widely valued in the community. Gonzalez was an
activist even in high school, where she organized a protest against the firing of
a beloved local teacher.

Coming to the University of North Carolina on a prestigious Robertson Scholarship, Gonzalez originally planned to major in journalism but later switched to
political science. She became active in student government, and through a variety of campaigns, classes, and experiences developed a sophisticated approach
to her ongoing activism centered around labor organizing.

In the following excerpt, Gonzalez reflects on her development as an organizer and on the role she sees for online campaigns in the wider landscape of
social justice activism.

One of the things I remember about growing up is my mother was a doctor, and people in the community that I grew up in—this little suburb-y part of Miami, it's called Doral, it's kind of this little enclave of Venezuelan people, mostly middle- and upper-class Venezuelans. It's grown now, but it was a pretty tight-knit, small community when I was really young. My mom was like the town doctor. She would get calls in the middle of the night: "So-and-so's coughing, we don't know what it is." "So-and-so has a mysterious bump on their shoulder. We don't know what it is." My mom would just go wherever she needed to go. [She] would just herd all the kids in the car, my little sister and I, whatever time it was, could've been midnight, could've been one in the morning, and off we were, wherever we were needed, and my little sister and I would be asleep in the car. So I think that was just a part of the culture in my house. My dad was always really out of the picture, because he was not emotionally there, always financially supportive but not present in other ways. So I always kind of think that my mom raised me and my little sister, and that's what she was like. The impulse to help came from that, and I think that's what put me on this path to where I am now. It starts with this kind of very naïve, almost paternalistic "I need to help everybody"-type thing. Thankfully I got the opportunity to be challenged by people here at UNC and took a lot of really important classes that took that energy and turned it into something that isn't just an impulse to help but is part of bigger movement building and working *with* people as opposed to *for* people. I think I trace that back to my mom.

That [History of Poverty in North Carolina] class was the class—it's really cheesy, but I think it just kind of turned my life upside down. I remember somebody [in that class] saying something to the effect of "Anybody can go to Harvard. Anybody can apply and you can just get a scholarship. Or you can just get financial aid and then you can go to Harvard." I was like, "No, that's not true." I had perfect grades in high school; I did all of the things and had really supportive parents, but I wouldn't have been able to go to Harvard. I think that was just the first time that I learned about privilege, essentially, and the fact that not everybody starts in the same place. I think something as basic and fundamental as that is what I got out of that class.

I went to London, I studied abroad there. And while I was in London, there was going to be the biggest public sector strike that there had been in the UK since the [19]60s. I was bored out of my mind so I was just trying to find random things to do. I found that there was a women's committee of the big labor union, and the meetings were open to the public. I showed up, just sat there, and listened and watched these women have a conversation about how these public nurses wanted to stand in solidarity with all the other workers, but they weren't willing to leave their patients because if they didn't show up to work their patients would die. I had also started dating somebody whose family was really involved in the labor movement. That was the first thing that made sense and captured my imagination and was at least theoretically rooted in letting the people who were affected be the ones calling the shots in making change for themselves and for their families and their communities.

So when I came back I started to get involved [in] Student Action with Workers. We were trying to do this housekeeper bill of rights thing. We were hosting small group discussions with housekeepers that we knew and trying to get more people involved in trying to collectively write this housekeeper bill of rights document, which is something that had been tried in the early 90s when there was a housekeeper association that was worker led at UNC. But while we were kind of wrapped up in trying to collectively write this document, somebody from the employee forum at UNC came and told us that the legislature was considering a bill that would have eliminated the State Personnel Act, which is essentially the only labor protections for public workers at UNC. And that became our campaign, to make sure that this bill [SB 575] did not get passed. That just consumed my life the second semester of my junior year. We were having three or four meetings a week, because we would have internal meetings among ourselves, we would have the coalition meetings with community members and some members of the labor unions, and we were having separate meetings with campus workers to keep them informed.

We were planning actions that culminated in the disruption of a [UNC] Board of Governors meeting where they were going to fake-discuss this bill. We had written a statement with a couple of workers who had become really involved. Everybody had the same statement, and we had students and workers and community members planted inside the room. Everybody would stand up and start reading the statement aloud and disrupt the meeting until security came and took you out. Then the next person would pick up where the last person left off. We had people on deck waiting outside so that when those people got removed, they would take their seats and be ready to pick it back up. I remember that I was trying really hard to keep myself busy outside because I didn't want it to be my turn to have to go in there and be the one speaking. I remember talking to the folks who did end up doing that and telling them that I was so impressed by how brave they had been, because I was terrified and decided to stay outside and coordinate the in and out of everybody. I'm just one of those kids that really liked getting As and being loved by the teachers and every person of authority. So it's really terrifying to me to disappoint people who I think are in positions of authority. Upsetting the president of the UNC system and the board of governors was not something that I wanted to do.

We got a meeting with [UNC system president] Tom Ross. He hosted a public forum and he claimed that it was all his idea. The truth is that he hadn't responded to a single email of ours until we disrupted the meeting. I realized that, without even really getting formal training, we ran a by-the-books campaign: We started with a petition. We asked for a meeting. They weren't responding to our emails. We emailed every single member of the board of governors multiple times, got no responses. We held actions in front of [the main administration] South Building and the Campus Y and invited faculty members to talk about the history, and we escalated. We delivered petitions to Tom Ross's house and were just ignored every step of the way. When we got shut out of [an earlier] meeting, they essentially gave us the reason to do what we did. And that was when they reacted.

My roommate first year and second year called herself a feminist from day one. We weren't allowed to say the word *bitch* in our room. You'd get kicked out of our room by Elizabeth if you said it. She convinced me then to live in a women's living-learning community at UNC, and that group was filled with a lot of self-identified feminists. They were the first people that exposed me to that. Before that I was always like, "I'm a woman. I can do anything I want." I just didn't see how my gender was relevant to my life and to my existence and to my experiences. So it had been on my to-do list, take a women's studies class, and I decided to go for it.

I remember thinking it was really weird to be in a class [Women in the Public Sphere, at Duke] with all women. That had never happened before. I can't remember a particular thing that triggered it, but it gave me gender as a way to analyze and see the world. I think it happened gradually. I was completely enamored with the stories of the women activists that we read about. I was in the middle of this campaign mostly working with housekeepers, women of color, and I was drawing all kinds of connections, especially once we started to read about labor.

One column [about Ai-jen Poo, founder and director of the National Domestic Workers Alliance] in *Time* magazine just completely blew my mind. I had been working with UNC housekeepers. They're women; they're cleaning after people. It's what women do. It's what my mom did in our house. It's what my dad never valued. Everything kind of just came together. So I sent Ai-jen this groveling email: "I have the money. Just let me come hang out with you for a summer." I ended up interning with the Domestic Workers Alliance in Oakland.

I remember pretty clearly the day that we came to class—we had finished the first phase of the class where we read all of the history stuff—and you came in and said, "What did these women do and use to achieve what they wanted?" I remember we filled the entire whiteboard with all of these strategies. They used humor, or they picketed, or they used their "maternal immunity" to demand welfare reform. So we filled up that whole board. I was furiously taking notes. I was like, "This is perfect. This is amazing." I was getting really excited. We were supposed to look at this "toolbox" of our foremothers, essentially, and decide what we were going to do for our project. We spent this whole class talking about how it's so obvious that we still have such a long way to go to achieve gender equality but we couldn't talk about these things [on campus]; we weren't finding space to have those kinds of conversations that would, in theory, turn the tide. We had talked about running a PR campaign for the Women's Center, and then you pushed us a little bit and asked us, "Why the Women's Center? Is the problem that people don't like the Women's Center, or is there something else?" And that's how we came up with [the idea that] the problem is that people have this horrible idea about what a feminist is.

I remember that when we started going down the path of this poster campaign, I was kind of a little bit upset about it because I was thinking, "I've lived on Duke's campus. I've spent a lot of time there, and poster campaigns at Duke are a dime a dozen." There are so many of them. They're all beautiful and colorful and really amazing, but I had seen so many of them and I didn't think that it was going to make a difference. This is all with the background that I'm in the middle of running this direct action campaign, right? I was like, "All right, fine. I'll do this poster campaign. It'll be fine, I can help with pictures, I can do stuff." And I don't think I was really sold on the idea when we started to do it. It wasn't until I got out there and started taking pictures—we just had some really amazing conversations with people when they came to take their pictures.

We wanted to get men and women of different races who were College Republicans and College Democrats, who were dancers and athletes and science majors and just people who ran in really different social circles. That was part of our goal; we were trying to be really intentional about that, with the intent of saying, "You can't put feminists and feminism in a box."

We had different teams; we had people on fundraising, on photography and design. We had people on outreach, who were getting folks to actually sign up for time slots. We had a group that was writing the op-ed that eventually got published in the [Duke] *Chronicle* the day that we put up the posters on campus. So all of these teams were doing their work simultaneously, and we started to take these pictures. We set up stations on different parts of campus, and I would go over to Duke and spend the afternoon, and people would just come. Sometimes random people would just be like, "What are you doing?" I would tell them and they'd be like, "Oh, I'll do it." I think we ended up with sixty pictures, maybe more. What was really amazing about it and made them really meaningful was that I was there when people sat down to think about what they wanted to write down.

We spent a lot of time putting them together on Photoshop and got them printed in the middle of the night the night before. They got plastered all over campus at the crack of dawn the morning that the *Chronicle* op-ed was going to be run. I wasn't living at Duke so I wasn't a part of putting up the posters, which I was really sad about because I had this vision of this feminist army just falling all over Duke. I wanted to be a part of the feminist army.

It was funny because we had spent so much time photographing other people, we didn't think to take a picture of ourselves, of doing our own "I need feminism because" sign. So [classmate Ashley Tsai] decided to take a picture [of herself] in her dorm. She posted it on the [campaign's] Facebook wall, and pictures then just flooded in. That first night, the pictures were just flooding in and our Facebook wall was being overtaken with both really positive things of people who were inspired and amazed by how great it was but also people saying horrible things. The posters on Duke's campus, some of them had been defaced, and Post-its that said "Make me a sandwich" had gone up. We decided to put pictures [of those] up on the Facebook page to show how bad the negative reaction was. I had this huge paper due the day that happened, and I was in the basement of my boyfriend's dorm hitting refresh, like, every second. I cried because I was so panicked. I was like, "Something bad is going to happen, one of these nutcases is going to hurt somebody."

It was really tough because our class was once a week, so all of this happened, we put up the posters at the beginning of the week, and we didn't see each other until a week later. We started to get our act together and have people monitoring the Facebook page as much as possible. We had two-hour shifts, and we even had shifts in the middle of the night. I remember when we actually walked into class, Kate [Gadsden] was on her computer as we were starting to talk about everything that was happening and what we were going to do, and a picture of somebody's penis popped up on the Facebook page and she said, "Oh, boy." And she hit delete and she told us what had just happened while we were sitting in class talking about all the trolls. It was really weird, just really scary. I wasn't excited at that point. I was just really scared.

We wanted to have dialogue. I was really concerned with this idea of democracy. We wanted people to not be afraid to bring out the little things they think about women and everything and to be OK saying that, so then somebody could refute it. Because if you're afraid to say it out of quote-unquote political correctness, then nobody's ever going to challenge you on it or to say something to you that might get you to change your mind. But then there were some really obvious cases where this is not productive dialogue. Saying "Go make me a sandwich" is not that kind of dialogue. So the whole process of coming up with a comment policy was really important because it helped us think about that.

I just had to understand what was the role of Who Needs Feminism and other campaigns like it and this bigger sphere of [online] feminist activism that in isolation probably doesn't mean a whole lot, but the reality is that our campaign didn't exist in a vacuum. It existed in a time that was really kind of politically important for women in the United States. There were so many other things happening around it; there were other people, other organizations, and other campaigns that were doing the direct action, that were doing the policy advocacy. Who Needs Feminism, in my head, is supposed to be a gateway, the kind of entry point that is then supposed to expose you and send you to all of these different organizations that are experts at doing that work. The thing that I heard from other people—and I believe made it successful—is that it felt like it was run by a bunch of college kids. It wasn't super glitzy or feel corporate or polished. It just was a social media campaign that was run by a bunch of college kids and started on a college campus and got really big, and I think that was exciting to a lot of people. I think the story of how it happened really captured people's imagination and made them think, "Wow, I can make a difference," as cheesy as that sounds.

What was really amazing is that then people naturally weren't just thinking, "I'm just going to run a Who Needs Feminism campaign on my campus." People were then thinking about "What am I going to do with it?" Doing something like what we did at Duke was a way to start a conversation on your campus about other issues. To learn about what other people care about so that you know about what issues you need to be focusing on, which issues are important to people, and then figuring out what to do about it. It was pretty amazing. Lots of students, really young students, middle schoolers, high schoolers, college students at community colleges and at Yale. Everything in between, and Oxford, just everywhere. There were students in Kazakhstan that did a campaign.

I helped some folks, walked them through the whole "people are being really mean" thing, this horrible backlash that happened. You can't do this alone. You need to do it with people that you trust and are going to support you, because it's not easy. Having people around you say these things that are horrible about you as a person and about all these things that you care so deeply about—that to me was the most important part of this whole thing. [It's] the reason that I, a year and a half, two years, out—I do my best to keep up with the inbox because I have this fear that I'm going to get an email from somebody in rural Kentucky who's trying to run a campaign by herself and doesn't know what to do with the backlash. That's the main thing for me, because it just wasn't so much about keeping the campaign and the brand alive. It's that people are doing this and they're living it and it's really scary, and I know how scary it is.

Ho Nguyen

PROGRAM OFFICER, PFUND FOUNDATION,
MINNESOTA, MINNESOTA

I very much knew in my core that I couldn't talk about myself as
being this gendered woman without talking about my experience as a kid of
refugees and a person of color and a first-gen[eration college student].

I met Ho Nguyen at the sunny, modern offices of the PFund Foundation in Min-neapolis. PFund serves as a "regional LGBTQIA grassroots community founda-tion," and Nguyen described herself as a "gay for pay." Sitting in a conference room on hard plastic chairs, neither of us knew that Nguyen would be laid off the very next day due to budget cuts. Later that summer she landed a position working on statewide policy at the Minnesota Coalition for Battered Women as its housing and economic justice program manager, a position that drew on her experience in the field of housing earlier in her career.

Nguyen's parents arrived in the United States in the 1980s as refugees after the Vietnam War. Of her four siblings, Nguyen was the only one born in the United States; the others were born in refugee camps. Her father was disabled by a wartime back injury and could not work. She grew up in Section 8 housing in Minneapolis, moving with her parents and three siblings from one "black and brown" neighborhood to another. Nguyen described herself as a "care-free" and "happy-go-lucky" child, whose father cared for the children while her mother worked hard to provide for them. Eventually their frugality allowed them to buy a house in a middle-class neighborhood. Nguyen's parents took education seriously and encouraged her to aim for college. But by the time she was a teenager, although she got good grades, she was disengaged and unhappy in school.

Nguyen's interview is a good example of how young activists both draw on and push forward the frameworks of their elders. She remembers how her in-troduction to second-wave feminists like Judy Chicago and Betty Friedan "blew [her] mind," but she also felt frustrated by what she saw as the limitations of much feminist work. She struggled to convey to older activists in the reproduc-tive rights movement that she valued their work but also wanted to broaden the movement to encompass a reproductive justice lens. She reflects on the roles of philanthropy and social media in community formation.

I was sort of that kid in high school that didn't really connect with any-body. I had a really hard time making friends, had a really hard time blending, I think. I never really hung out with any cliques. You know, high school is pretty cliquey. I just remember hanging out with a mix-ture between the theater kids, the potheads, and the goth kids. It was sort of like this hodgepodge crew. I think I was pretty unhappy and disengaged. My junior year of high school, I was talking to another classmate, and she was telling me about this thing called PSEO, which is Postsecondary Enrollment Options, and what that means is high school students can apply to take col-lege courses and you get college credit, and that was just like, "Oh my God, I need to do that. I need to get out of here."

I remember going to my high school guidance counselor and asking him about this, and the first thing he said was he thought I was being really "ambitious." He's like, "Do you think this is too ambitious that you're doing this?" I think maybe the teachers and counselors didn't really have a good cultural lens, not really understanding my experience and who I was and never connecting with me.

Anyhow, regardless of what the counselor said, I was like, "Well, I'm ap-plying anyway." So my senior year I took courses at Minneapolis Community and Technical College, and for the first time in my life, at that moment, I re-member just feeling like, "OK, this makes so much sense"—it was amazing. I took a bunch of women's studies courses. I took sociology courses. I took earth science courses. That was the first time in my life where I connected to something else. I connected to the students in my classes. I connected with the professors. Nobody knew I was in high school. I didn't tell anybody that I was in high school, because I was still buying my own books and had my own car at that time. I was seventeen or eighteen.

I remember taking a course and reading about this artist named Judy Chicago, and it just blew my mind. It was so radical. Then, in another course, they're talking about *The Feminine Mystique* and it was incredible, and in the sociology classes I took, I just felt on cloud nine. I loved it. I absolutely just loved it because, I think for the first time in my life, I had language. I had language to describe feelings, feelings of loneliness, feelings of notic-ing, feelings of sort of something greater, something greater is happening in the world than just me. I remember in high school I just knew that there were bad things happening in the world and there were injustices, and I just couldn't name them. I could see them and I could feel them, but I just had no words or language.

I ended up going to Hamline University. I actually wanted to go out of state, but my parents claimed that they would be pretty devastated and I felt really bad. My parents still dealt with a lot of language barriers and I just couldn't leave. Anyway, so I ended up going to Hamline, which I still think to this day was probably one of my best decisions.

That was one of the first places I ever really felt at home in my own body. There was a lot of support for students of color and especially for first-year students of color. That came out of our Multicultural Office, and the framing in which they welcomed first-year students was the first thing that made sense to me. I've never heard anybody else talk with this narrative of being a first-generation kid of refugees. That was the first time in my life in which I had heard that, and I was like, "Wow, that experience absolutely reflects me." There's a space in which they completely nourish that, and they can really sort of help you flourish and really help you figure out who you are. I think that, to me, was one of the first times I sort of stopped, like, hating myself.

I was probably a pretty stereotypical eighteen-year-old college student who just learned about activism the first time and I was like, "Oh, I'm going to save the world." Just learning about the political history of, What does it mean to be a person of color? What does it mean to be queer? What does it mean to be a woman? What does male privilege look like? What does white privilege look like? What does capitalism . . . ? I was inculcated with all that and really feeling like, "Oh my God, this is what's happening. Yes, this is what's happening and here are the words to describe what's happening."

My coming-out journey felt so much more complicated than my coming out as a person of color and political, you know. I actually had a girlfriend at fourteen, and I remember actually the first moment for me wondering was twelve. I was in sixth grade and I remember having a crush on my female teacher named Jamie, and I just remember being like, "Oh, man, Jamie is just so beautiful," and all the other girls were wooing over Kurt, who was the handsome male teacher. I had zero interest. But these were things which I kept, like, kind of tucking away, tucking away, tucking away. I kind of had this one foot in and out. I think it was until my midtwenties where I was just like, "OK, just be honest with yourself, Ho." At that point, I was just like, "OK, I am queer."

For me, queer is also political, it's not necessarily just a sexual orientation. I suppose sexual orientation—the closest thing would be, like, a lesbian, and I don't necessarily identify with that term, but it's more true than not. I started reading a lot of Audre Lorde, who very much identified as a black lesbian, a woman-loving woman, and I think there definitely is power in that, and I think there is definitely something really radical about that.

For me, I also really think about [the fact that] there are people who I have dated and fallen in love with that don't necessarily identify as female—you know, they've either identified as gender nonconforming or genderqueer—and still loving that person. Well, if I say I'm a lesbian, then what does that say about this person I love? So for me, *queer* always sort of felt more radical in the sense that it's more encompassing and it's wider, and it also sort of talks about how I see myself politically too.

Feminism for me, up to a certain point, felt very second wave, and it felt very white and very middle-class and very exclusive, and so during that time [in college], I was really dabbling in trying to figure out what does feminism mean to me, really trying to define that and think about that. I think it was either bell hooks or Audre Lorde that coined the term *womanism*, and that resonated more with me.[6] Now I think about it, and I think what was missing for me now that I can name it—then I couldn't—was that feminism in college lacked a certain amount of intersectional work, and I couldn't connect with it. Because for me, I very much knew in my core that I couldn't talk about myself as being this gendered woman without talking about my experience as a kid of refugees and a person of color and a first-gen[eration college student]. I couldn't talk about any of my experiences without talking about all of my experiences, and feminism in college, or that brand of feminism, didn't bode well with me.

In my senior year, I was working, I think, three jobs, and at some point my best friend at the time emailed me [and] this email probably changed my life. She emailed me, "There's this job posting you should check out. It definitely sounds like it's right up your alley," and it was a job to be a desk person at the shelter. I applied for it and I got it.

It was a transitional family shelter and people stayed there for about a month, and it was all families with, I think, boys under thirteen. So I worked there and I worked at another day shelter later. I worked at both simultaneously and that sort of launched me into the next six years of working in housing and homelessness and doing tenants' rights and crisis housing and mental health crisis housing and all that. I was pretty lucky that before I graduated that May of 2008, I had landed a full-time job at a mental health center being their housing specialist. Here I am, twenty-two, you know, just fresh out of college, and somebody's like, "Help mentally ill homeless people find housing," and I was like, "OK." I was up for the challenge and it was exhilarating. It was probably the most exhilarating, I think, four, five, years of my life, and I loved it. I loved it quite a bit, and it was during that time that I also started noticing that social services and direct service in itself was really problematic. I remember having this moment with myself and some of my friends. I said, "We just spend so much time case managing and putting out fires all day long. Do any of us actually think about why the fires are starting?" I also was pretty close to getting my master's in social work. Everybody else around me that was working at this organization—their next track was you get your master's in social work, and then you get your licensure, and then you become a social worker for the rest of your life. I was like, "Yeah, that's exactly who I'm going to be," and my dad was super excited about that. He said, "Yes, that's a great job for a girl," and I was just like, "Well, that's kind of weird, Dad," but, you know, my dad's old-school, so he still has some of his patriarchal stuff.

I remember having that feeling again that I had in high school where there was something missing I couldn't name. I think in college I learned language around identity and politics and stuff, but then it was during this time where I really started hearing people talk about systemic oppression and systemic racism, and I was just like, "I need to find out more."

I remember sitting on Facebook one day and somebody had posted something about Lobby Day from NARAL Pro-Choice Minnesota, and I thought, "I want to understand what that is." I did a ton of research on them and was like, "Oh my God, who is this organization and how do I get involved?" They ended up having a fellowship. It was through this Choice Leadership Institute, and I think that opened a door to me being able to do this work.

Choice is really about bodily autonomy, right? But if you don't have a house, you can't make this choice. If you don't have a job, you can't make this choice, right? If you are burdened by systemic racism and economic burden, you're not able to fully self-actualize. That's when I started getting into really heavy reproductive justice work.

I ended up doing that in conjunction with my master's thesis. We had to look at a real-life policy, and I ended up doing mine on something that our super conservative governor had passed years ago called the Positive Alternatives to Abortion. Essentially it was giving money to CPCs, which are crisis pregnancy centers.[7] I had to be neutral, just looking at the history of it, the implementation of it, how people apply, where the money goes, all that stuff. Two-point-something million dollars goes to CPCs and nobody really monitors anybody. I stayed connected with choice work and ended up getting a full-time job at a partner organization called Pro-Choice Resources doing their grassroots advocacy stuff there, working around abortion policy in Minnesota, working around grassroots stuff, building a base, educating people on reproductive justice, helping people make the connections, the intersectional connections, of the importance of thinking about reproductive health and rights as also a matter of socioeconomics and a matter of race and a matter of gender and not just this siloed issue of abortion or not.

Our base was predominantly middle-aged white women, and they were just like, "Who the hell are you?" We did extensive training and it was hard. It was a really hard conversation to have with people, to really say that the different waves of feminism were all incredibly imperative, that all that was important, and that broadening our lens and broadening the way in which we talk about this work doesn't necessarily—we're not trying to steamroll anybody's work. So really working through that reassurance to say, "No, that organizing that you all did back in, like, the 60s, that was important. That is important work, and now let's think about the work that we do broader. Let's think about the women that have not been a part of the work. Like, historically women of color had not been a part of mainstream feminist movements. Low-income women haven't been a part of mainstream feminist movements. LGBTQ people have not been a part of mainstream feminist movements." So, it was just about how do we make our movement smarter, stronger, and more efficient and more effective? But, yeah, it still took people a long time to get there and it was—it was hard. It was probably the toughest two years of my life, doing that work.

I remember learning about the third wave in one of my feminist study classes and thinking that third wave was sort of more open, more broad. Somebody said that we're entering another wave of feminism and I'm just like, "What is that—the fourth wave?" That's still something I struggle with. I mean, I still call myself a feminist, right, like I absolutely have no shame in that word. I also just want people to really parse it out, to really think about what that means. What does your feminism mean, and what is mainstream feminism lacking? I don't think that it's a dirty word, and I also don't necessarily feel comfortable with running around saying I'm a womanist. There's a part of me that feels like that's kind of co-opting. That framework came out of black women, and unless I understand a lot more, that's just not something I'm comfortable with. So, but yeah, I mean, I still definitely claim myself to be a feminist.

PFund is an LGBTQ foundation. It's a community foundation. At this point in my life, I was really interested in economic stability. I think two years of doing hard-core policy lobbying, then having a grant—my job pretty much almost taken away. I was just like, "This is a problem with nonprofits; it's not sustainable." You're in the groove, you're doing great work, and then the money is gone. The same thing when the Ford Foundation pulled their money from reproductive health and rights. That was millions of dollars for the entire national movement. I was just like, "What is happening?" Then I was curious. I wanted to understand what philanthropy is, and so when this position opened—"OK, I'll make the jump. I'm going to see what's on the other side," you know.

It is interesting. People do not think about philanthropy like I do. I walked into it really thinking about it as economic redistribution and sort of moving money around, and that is not how the field thinks of itself. I think philanthropy really sees themselves as the maverick of all the different fields to help communities propel themselves forward. I still don't know if I see it that way.

When I started, my counterpart and I, we were given the opportunity to revamp the [grant-making] program, and we were able to create the program that we thought was the most equitable in terms of the application, in terms of the questionnaire, in terms of money, in terms of accessing us as program officers, the foundation, all that stuff. So we were able to knock down a bunch of barriers. But what we're doing is not what is necessarily considered philanthropic best practices, because philanthropy has a set way in which they do it. You have an application. The applicant comes in. They have to give you a budget. They have to give you outcomes. They have to give you benchmarks. They have to do x, y, and z because trustees and the founders want to know where their money is going and what the impact is. We think about it differently—not that we don't care, but for me the impact is "You're an organization that has their own funding. We gave you funding. What you do with it, you're doing your work, and so we don't necessarily need all that." So when we are playing with other partners, it gets complicated because we try to push them and they're just like, "Whoa, whoa, whoa. You're so radical; why would you do that?" Then for us, it's "You're this big behemoth of an organization that's moving at this glacial speed and your community is suffering."

I think the movement, whatever that is, has become increasingly fragmented. We talk a lot about a feminist movement. We talk a lot about an LGBTQ movement. We talk a lot about Asian American movements, and if you really dig into it, none of those are quite real in the sense [that], I think, people in each of those categories are mobilizing hard-core separately. Especially, like, in Minnesota, it's quite decentralized, so we don't have any, I think, aside from the Women's Consortium, which is still pretty siloed— they're not necessarily working with a lot of racial equity or economic justice organizations.

I think within the feminist movement, within the social justice movement, whatever movements, it's fragmented, it's siloed. People always think that somebody is always going to quickly jump on another person for a wrong tweet, a wrong term, a wrong word, a wrong statement, a wrong sentence. It's come to the point where people are filtering themselves so much because people are worried somebody's just going to jump down their throat. We're just not as generous with each other to sort of let people fall and fail as much as we did at one point.

I think we are all becoming increasingly disconnected with each other. The way people think about community is so different. At some point, community meant coming together, literally coming together with your fellow humans. Now you can build community virtually, and I think because you can build community virtually, there is a certain disconnect when it comes to critique, criticism. I think it's a little more desensitized because you can post something and call somebody really mean names and then walk away, versus if you're in a community and you're fighting with somebody that you had to look in the eye, I think that feels different. That definitely looks different.

We are doing a better job than five years ago in talking about the intersections of a person's identity and how that affects their world view. I think that's still something that people have to work on.

Park Cannon

PROGRAM COORDINATOR, FEMINIST WOMEN'S
HEALTH CENTER, ATLANTA, GEORGIA

I hope that abortion access is considered vital to the feminist movement's future.

I first met Park Cannon when she was a student at the University of North Carolina at Chapel Hill and was editing the campus feminist journal, *Siren*. She had also participated in the Who Needs Feminism campaign at UNC. Cannon was clearly a leader on campus, and I remember being impressed by her energy and maturity (as well as her signature eyeglasses). At the time of this interview with graduate student Rachel Gelfand, Cannon was the coordinator for the Black Women's Wellness program and a health advocate at the Feminist Women's Health Center in Atlanta, Georgia. Cannon had been born in Albany, Georgia, and then moved to New York City as a young girl. She later moved back south to "reground" herself. In 2016, less than a year after this interview, Cannon was elected to the Georgia state legislature, as one of three openly LBGTQ+ representatives and, at twenty-four, the youngest.

The interview was conducted at her partner's dining room table. A passionate advocate for reproductive justice, Cannon expresses her gratitude for the commitment to women's dignity and value at the Feminist Women's Health Center and for the recent passage of the Marriage Equality Act. Her interview helps us think about the importance of place in people's lives, the impact of 9/11 on young activists, the significance of reproductive issues and justice, and the experiences and perspectives of queer black women in the feminist movement.

After living in Albany, Georgia, going to school there, definitely experiencing a good amount of racist stuff, we moved to New York, to Brooklyn. So that's where I grew up mostly. I spent about ten years living in Brooklyn. That was totally different. I was living with all these urban kids who were just mixes of Puerto Rican and black or Italian and Greek and helped me better understand that people are made up of so many different types, and it's not just white or black. So that was really nice.

We lived with my maternal grandparents in Brooklyn. They would take me to school every day. My grandfather was a taxicab driver who liked to gamble. My grandmother loved to go to church and cook. They were very in-fluential in my childhood. I was growing up hetero, a black, hetero, church-going, extracurricular-having girl. I was pretty happy. I was blissfully happy. I had no clue of anything that was going on in the world. I was not a child that was raised politically aware. I was made to believe that being black was fine and that no one had a problem with it, only people in the south, and we were in the north, so we didn't have to worry about it. I was rudely awak-ened because we moved to New York *right* before 9/11 happened, so when that took place, ideas of ethnicity and social class and being a citizen or not became really apparent to me because I saw all of that collide in violence, and it was a very confusing time. I think that's when I woke up, actually, now that I think about it. I started to realize that if people don't get their way or they feel like they're not listened to, they're going to stand up and do some-thing about it. I needed to reground myself, so I came back to the south. I am a southern gal. I was born here. I was taken elsewhere to learn about myself, but I think I needed to return to feel who I really am.

The concreteness of feminism came into my life in college [at the Uni-versity of North Carolina Chapel Hill]. I started taking women's and gender studies classes. I had this professor, Karen Booth, who has this purple hair, and she was just so honest and real and helped me see that the stuff that I was experiencing was worth studying. It was not to be discarded. And so that was really exciting and appealing to me. But I think that feminism has always been trickling in, in all the little ways that I interact with people. Like, I always knew that the way that men catcall women is ridiculous. So it's always been there, but it, feminism, became major to me in college, and I don't ever want to live without it.

UNC had Students United for Reproductive Justice, a student undergrad-uate organization. I just showed up at some meetings and went to a con-ference and started talking a lot more, getting on social media. My Twitter was big. I had a blog at that point, too, where I started to talk more about the importance of women having choice and women being able to access abortion and how 80 percent of the counties in North Carolina have these fake clinics, these crisis pregnancy centers, and like no percentage have abortion clinics. That was my main thing.

[After graduation, Cannon moved to Atlanta, where she got a job at the Feminist Women's Health Center.] My weekdays consist of working in our advocacy and empowerment network. That's our downstairs area, where we have a variety of different staff members work on policy or political en-gagement activities. For example, I work for the Black Women's Wellness program, creating a program where women who receive abortion services or need health insurance or just want to talk about sexual health can come and say, "Listen, I'm having these problems. I really need someone to talk to. I need a community." We set them up with five or six other women, have them come together, talk about it; now they have a network.

The weekends, I'm up in the clinic, and that's in the same building, just on a different floor. That's where we provide our gynecological care services. Our main one on weekends is abortion. We do up to 23.6 weeks, and that means we take the women through all the stages. They come in our door pregnant; they leave not pregnant. So whatever that takes. If that means that they need to speak with a health educator and talk through their decision and work with their family to have them understand why they're making this decision, we help them do that. If they have a fetal anomaly so the fetus is not viable or will not live outside of the womb, we help them find a way to cope with that and undergo surgery to not to have to deal with that anymore. Also if women are coming to us because they've been raped, [we're] helping them feel like they have a place that is safe to access these services where their perpetrator won't come and find them or know what they did or ask any questions. Yeah, it's just like a safe haven.

It's really cool. I love working there. We are such a close-knit family that when someone leaves to go back to school or for a new job, it's really sad because we experience so much together that we can't really explain to other people. We hold people's lives and make sure that they're breathing and they're happy and not crying, realizing that this is their choice. They don't have to be stigmatized about it. If this is something they need or want to do, we can do it safely.

Our doctors are awesome. They're Emory [University] doctors. They really care about women's lives and are willing to do whatever it means at the state capitol to make sure that women can access abortion, which I think is really important for the actual medical professionals to be advocates for this service, because sometimes, actually more so than not, the medical professionals just have to do what they do, walk out the door, and pretend like it never happened because they don't want to be scrutinized or impose danger on their families, which I understand. But for the future of abortion access, it's so critical right now. We're forty years away from it being legal. It's been that way since the 70s, but states are just moving back and back and back and making sure that women are denied access.

The south is already like a world of its own. I'm black. I live in the south. I'm passionate about black people thriving. Atlanta is generally thought of as this place where it's the black mecca. It's all these black people, and they seem to be doing good. But it's also a place where white people really want to resist it. So they do small things. The most recent thing that has really bothered me took place in Conyers, which is about forty-five minutes from here. KKK members were putting flyers on people's driveways and cars, recruiting for more members. And it wasn't necessarily in neighborhoods that were black, but it was just like, "Yo, we need to up our people because these black people are coming out and talking about all the injustices." It made the news for a hot second but was not something that was deemed important by our governor or our mayor. So that's been really frustrating for me. I have marched a couple of times in the past three months for different causes that have to do with either black women being beaten or black men experiencing unnecessary violence or being killed. I took my mom with me recently and we marched. It was awesome. We wore all white. It's definitely at the forefront of my every day.

So, luckily, working at a place like Feminist [Women's Health Center], we're talking about those things. We're on them, and it's not like, "Everyone close your Facebook, don't check that until after work." It's like, "No, post something right now. Make sure you retweet this, sign this petition, and tell other people to." So it's actually been helpful for me working at this type of organization, because I don't have to hold on to it all day and then bring it home. But at the same time, it's really hard for our organization to stand up for so many things at once. Abortion access in the south is already such a taboo topic, to then also bring in police brutality is just too much, [to] also bring in economic access and the need for funding is extra. It's a lot of strains on top of our organization. But I'm committed to it.

Social media is important when we're trying to reach out to organizations. Building credibility, showing that we support these types of issues, telling people about things. I did come of age with a lot of social media outlets, and it's cool. I enjoy it. But I also have a deep hatred for everyone knowing everything about everyone at all times. I have a lot of social media pet peeves, like people who check in every single place they go. I'm like, "Now they know where you're at; they're coming for you, they're going to kill you. Now they know what you're thinking."

But social media is powerful, too, because it gets you across the world. I have been able to be a part of the Women of Color Sexual Health Network, which is women all over the United States who do any type of work like this. And it's really good to look up, and that'll give you a lot of people to talk with. So it's helped me see that people are experiencing the same types of bullshit in different places and how if we actually talk to each other, we might be able to do something about it; whereas if we just felt like we were isolated here, then we might not be able to make as much of a stink, because we can compare ourselves to other places. So I think that social media is powerful in positive ways too.

Social media is also a place of harassment for us. We have to be really careful about how we respond to trolls and how we are vigilant with who gets access to our files. Hackers are real; they try and do what they can to shut us down at all times. Being careful with our password chains, and if we log in to something, making sure we log out. Whereas in other places you just might not have to worry as much. Literally none of us are allowed to have our cell phones die; we always need to have our phone in case something happens, especially in the time where right now we're having a lot of extra scrutiny and protestors.

They know that we do abortions on Fridays and Saturdays, so those are the main days that they come out. But I think they're lame. I had a lot of protestors in New York when I lived there and saw them at the Planned Parenthoods there. They had really graphic signs and were screaming curse words and trying to not let you walk in physically, and here they're just like, "Oh, please, can we help you?" So I think they're pretty lame.

That was my claim to fame in Chapel Hill; I shut them down. I shut the Genocide Awareness Project down. I was like, "There's no way you will be on our campus." I literally counterprotested for two days straight because it was ridiculous. I was standing in front of them with a bullhorn and signs, throwing condoms at all the students. We created a little space with balloons and blankets and coloring books and finger paints and nail polish and yummy foods, so that if people were feeling triggered by seeing that, they could just go be isolated from it. Yeah, those people, the Genocide Awareness Project, are really relentless with their decision to display graphic stuff. I taught sex ed at that point to sixth graders, and they happened to come on a field trip to UNC's campus that day, so they saw the stuff, and it had an effect on them that was really negative, which further pissed me off and made me stay longer.

Feminist Women's Health Center provides comprehensive gynecological care to all who need it, without judgment. We support who I call my rainbow family. Whatever it is you feel in your body, we support it. We have a Trans Health Initiative that's run by this awesome guy who does a lot of workshops.

We have been, as an organization, really excited about this new federal ruling that people can marry whoever they want, and it's important for my relationship because we've experienced a lot of confusion and hatred from our families because they're very conservative. And so, kind of having this federal truth is exciting for us. Marriage equality federally is really exciting.

Like the day that it happened, we went to this burger spot, and I get there before [my partner] gets there. And I have my flowers and my cupcakes, rainbow cupcakes, of course. And then she shows up, and she has the same flowers from the same store—they were called, like, freedom flowers. And she had a balloon, that little balloon right there that says thank you. So then we were happy and we were eating burgers and drinking four-dollar margaritas, and someone walks up to us and they're like, "What are you celebrating?" And we were like, "Equality." And the whole restaurant just cheers. It's like, "Yeah, this is awesome. This is fun. This is really cool."

It's also helped my mom come around a lot. She had some elevated levels of homophobia, and now they are decreased. So it's had a lot of implications that will continue to evolve, I think, because people are just realizing like, "Oh, I can't be racist anymore. OK, I won't be racist. Oh, I can't be homophobic. I won't be homophobic." So I'm excited about it. And our organization is too.

Obama's two terms, for women, has meant that he put a really strong black woman, Michelle Obama, in the forefront of everyone. He put two black girls [his daughters] also as admirable role models, and that's huge. But at the same time, he's never once spoken about the importance of matriarchs or not beating on women or defending abortion access. He just doesn't. I kind of understand it. He really can't rock the boat right now. There's just been too much conservative whiteness for all these years that he feels like he can't do it. He just needs to slowly make these changes.

I'm fine with people deeming me as in the third wave. I was at some meeting recently at Spelman College with my colleague Kwajelyn [Jackson], and the students were leading the meeting. The icebreaker question was "Tell your name and what kind of feminist you are." So some people started off with "Hi, I'm Sarah. I think I'm just, like, a regular feminist." "Hi, I'm Susie. I think I'm a womanist." "I'm Athena. I'm really Chicana feminismo." Then I was like, "I'm just Park and I'm a feminist." Like, chill; we're all in this. It's good to identify with certain struggles, but then you get back to the oppression Olympics and that's annoying. Saying that white feminism really doesn't get to the root of intersectionality; no, it doesn't, but that doesn't mean that white feminists suck, or you're better, or that you're a womanist because you read Alice Walker's *In My Mother's Garden* or whatever.[8] I think it's evolving naturally, and we should just be happy that people are interested.

I hope that abortion access is considered vital to the feminist movement's future. I also hope that we have someone in office who says *feminism* out loud once a day on a microphone. I also hope that more men begin identifying as feminists and start realizing that it's not a term just for women. I also hope that feminism is nurturing and is kind. My brother even said to me when I told him I was taking a women's studies class, "Ah, you're going to be one of those mad angry feminists. I hate that." In some regards, I hear what he's saying. I think that we have a right to be angry, and I always defend myself as an angry black woman, but at the same time I want it to be gentle with its people. I want it to be kind to the people who subscribe to it. I want it to be fun. Like, let's go out drinking and dancing. Let's go out celebrating. Let's dress up nicely if we want to; let's not. Let's protest. Let's look beautiful. Let's look sad and angry. Yeah, I want feminism to be fun.

Andrea Pino

COFOUNDER, END RAPE ON CAMPUS,
WASHINGTON, D.C.

Senator [Kirsten] Gillibrand had this very nice receptionist named Bo,
and we said we'd like to meet with someone to talk about sexual assault.
Bo looked at us in a way like, "Girl, that's not how it works."

Andrea Pino and Annie Clark both attended the University of North Carolina at Chapel Hill, a prestigious public university with a beautiful campus of tree-lined quads and rhododendrons that burst into pink and white blooms in early spring. Both survivors of sexual assault, they became famous when they rocked the bucolic academic world with their complaint to the federal Department of Education, arguing that UNC was not complying with Title IX because no student could equally access education if she did not feel safe from sexual violence. They and other students on campuses around the country worked together to demonstrate how campus rapes should be seen not as isolated crime stories but as the result of a culture of violence and misogyny and to show that universities were not taking the issue seriously enough. They cofounded End Rape on Campus, a direct-service organization through which they support victims and help them learn how to become activists. Senator Kirsten Gillibrand declared that they had inspired her to take up the issue of campus sexual assault, and they helped her write a bill, which she introduced to Congress. Their work was highlighted in a dramatic documentary, *The Hunting Ground*, which was released at the 2015 Sundance Film Festival.

In December 2015, Pino and Clark were living in a cozy house in Washington, D.C. The front porch prominently displayed a UNC banner, and I met them and their friendly dog in their small living room that was dominated by a Christmas tree. They had been living and working intensely together for three years by that point and had recently moved to D.C. from the West Coast in order to be closer to the legal and political networks in which they were now moving.

Pino's story is full of conflict, pain, and exhaustion as well as growing confidence, guarded optimism, and a coming to terms with her role in the world. The granddaughter of Cuban immigrants, she grew up in a tough neighborhood in Little Havana, Miami. Her father started a business but lost it in the crash of 2008. Until she transferred to a charter high school, her academic ambition was frowned upon and discouraged by her peers and unsupported or simply not understood by the adults around her. Driven to succeed, she made her way to UNC—which she had fallen in love with on a campus visit—through her own hard work, supported by scholarships and money she had saved by doing graphic design, something she taught herself in eighth grade.

Despite being valedictorian in high school and always succeeding in her leadership activities, adjusting to UNC as a first-generation Latina student was hard for Pino. She had a difficult time finding resources or meeting peers who could help her adjust to college life. After a troubling experience where she was pressured into drinking and then left behind at a party, Pino became cautious of her peers. Her confidence plummeted even further, and she began to experience severe anxiety.

When she returned to school for her second year, though, Pino started getting involved in student government, joined a program called Women Engaged in Learning and Leadership, took a course on violence prevention, and got involved with Project Dinah, an activist group on campus focused on sexual violence.

None of that protected her from a sexual assault. But together with her decision to reach out to Annie Clark, an activist who had graduated the year before, her training helped her see her own experience in a much broader context and planted the seeds for her approach to making change.

My grandparents are from a small town in a port area of Cuba called Gibara. They came over fifty years ago seeking employment opportunities. My grandfather, for a living, he painted warships. He raised us to be Democrats, meaning he's always believed that the government should be there for the people. He always instilled in me the desire to be politically active and to call out things that seemed to be unequal and unjust. He's definitely where I got most of my political drive from. Since growing up, he used to tell me, "Nunca, nunca, nunca pares de luchar." You never, never, never give up. He said despite what you might have to deal with, always remember that you can do what you set your mind to do.

My schedule throughout most [of] high school was I would wake up at four in the morning; I would study for the SAT; I would do research on a [college]; I would brush up on my notes for my classes. I would go to school at six, start school at seven thirty, and be in school all the way up until three o'clock. At three o'clock, I would take a bus or walk to the local community college to make my dual enrollment class—that's how I made up for not having access to AP classes. My day did not end until seven o'clock. That's when I went home and did my homework. That's because, in a way, to be able to compete in the marathon that is college admissions when you are a person of color, you have to make up for the fact that you don't have shoes. That's how I felt for a very long time. It wasn't about keeping up with people; it was the fact that you don't have shoes throughout most of the race. It was a commitment. I graduated high school top of my class.

It was hard to adjust as a first-generation Latina student at UNC. I felt lost. You have some people who are willing to help you, but you're very much on your own. That's very much what life is like when you have to navigate college as a first-generation student and as a student of color. There's nobody helping you out. I went from a valedictorian to feeling like I had to survive in my classes. It was difficult to talk about. It was something that my parents noticed when I went home for Thanksgiving. I wasn't really bursting with happiness like they had left me in August.

[In fall semester of sophomore year] I had taken a violence prevention class, Women's Studies 298. I began caring about sexual assault and gender-based problems. I became a peer educator for a bystander intervention program. I thought I knew everything about sexual violence prevention, the causes and what it looks like. I was training people. I was an advisor and educator. I was training women and men about how to notice the signs, how to be safe, and how to get resources. I guess in many ways I felt that people like me couldn't get sexually assaulted. I had a scary incident my first year, and after that I didn't go out to parties. I didn't get wasted. I didn't do these things because I realized that I really wasn't into the idea of blacking out. One experience is enough for me.

I had a friend, and she invited me to a party. It was right around spring break. I went to this party with her. I ended up being sexually assaulted. It happened to me at a party in which I knew the hosts; I knew someone going in there. They were also student leaders. They were people who should have seen the signs, who should have known that this was going on. In many ways, I thought for a long time that I must have put myself in a certain place. I must have not seen the signs. I must have been vulnerable in some way. I must have invited it in some way even though I was wearing black jeans and boots. I was very much in winter gear. It was March, after all.

I didn't know what happened. I remember waking up [in my bed] that morning, the morning after, in a pool of blood. I grew up in Little Havana. There were a couple of people around me who were *santeros*.[9] My grandfather used to always joke [that] if there was ever a dead animal in front of your house, then it must mean somebody was after you. He said that the worst thing that could happen is if someone left a goat head dripping in blood. I thought, "I guess this is what one of the severed goat heads would look like."

I remember not being able to understand what had happened. Who was there that night? Why was I in so much pain? Why did I have bruising and this amount of blood? I did not stop bleeding for a few days.

I didn't report anybody. I didn't go through the adjudication process. I didn't go to the police. I didn't go to the hospital. I didn't do anything that a good victim is supposed to do. I felt very guilty. For a very long time I felt, "How could a person like me speak about this issue if I didn't do what I was supposed to do?"

Later I saw these silver boxes that are fixed to the wall in the entrance of the women's restroom in the student union. It had this little sticker that said, "If you've been sexually assaulted or if you're a victim of interpersonal violence, consider anonymously reporting." I thought, "Huh." I remember getting the paper and taking it into the handicapped restroom. I was sitting on the toilet, not even going to the bathroom, sitting on the toilet and looking at it and reading it. I remember pulling out a pen, and I started to cry and I filled it out. I remember looking at the boxes and not really knowing what counted as rape. What was assault? What did that mean?

I Googled. What is this box? Who created this? Why didn't I know about this before? I read the article that was interviewing a then senior named Annie Clark, who had created these boxes for students. I ended up emailing her and saying, "You don't know me, but we have a couple of common friends, and I wanted to talk to you about the boxes that you put in the union." She said the reason she did that was because she had a bad experience. She wanted to give a space to people that might not know their attacker and might not feel safe coming forward or might not know how to articulate their experience. She wanted to give those survivors the space to be able to come forward.

I was appointed to the Title IX coordinator search committee; it happened to be that the student body president had read that I was interested in women's issues. He said, "I'm going to appoint you to this committee. It's somewhat important but I don't know what it's about." I said, "Title IX, interesting." I thought, "What does sexual assault have to do with Title IX? I'm very confused." It was then that I stumbled upon the "Dear Colleague" letter which was released by the Department of Education in 2011.[10] It was pretty recent. It was in reading it that I learned that universities are responsible for adjudicating sexual assault. I thought, "Interesting. I've never heard of this."

It made me think a lot about, What were we doing? How did I not know about this? How did I not know that I had a right to report to the university, that I had a process independent of the police? Then I Skyped Annie.

I remember asking her, "Have you heard about Title IX and its connection to sexual assault? Did you know that UNC adjudicates sexual assault in the Honor Court?" She said, "Yes. I've been to some of the hearings." I said, "This is insane and it's illegal." She said, "Yes. I had friends who lived through the process and nobody was found responsible." I said, "I don't think anybody's been found responsible. Ever."

Annie was the first person I told my full story to. She's the person who said, "You were raped." That for me was a transformative point. In accepting it and talking about it for the first time, I could come to terms with what happened and be able to translate that into doing something about it. I realize that I was like the majority of survivors: the ones who never come forward; the ones who don't really know what to do; the ones who don't think their incident is terrible enough to come forward. I realized that I wasn't going to seek any justice for myself. What I could do was I could influence how students were educated about this in the future. I could do something directly by helping hire the administrator who would change this policy.

I began taking more political science classes and I enrolled in Feminist Political Theory. We were assigned most of Catharine MacKinnon's readings and her work. I read that she had written a legal brief arguing that sexual harassment was a violation of Title IX. I thought, "Interesting. Everything is coming full circle. My classwork is coming full circle. What I'm doing in this committee is coming full circle."

When I read MacKinnon's work and I learned about the case she wrote that brief for, *Alexander v. Yale*, I began to realize that the arguments the plaintiffs brought forth against Yale in 1979 were similar to the ones survivors at UNC were arguing. I met dozens of other survivors at UNC and had never heard of a single case in which an accused assailant had been found responsible, much less expelled. That was the final straw for me. Then I realized that we could no longer work within the system. That was a very difficult decision. I loved my school. Since I got to Carolina I've worn the school's seal around my neck; getting into Carolina is still one of the happiest moments of my life. It was something that I worked so hard for. Everything about the Carolina Way and about the institution's history is something that is so integral to my identity.[11] I realized if I loved my school, I had to fight to change it. I never wanted to shame UNC. I never wanted UNC to get in trouble. I simply wanted things to change. It was when I was told the policy was set in stone, that this is how it had been for decades and that nothing was going to change, I realized that something had to change.

[From MacKinnon] I learned that you don't have to have an attorney to use Title IX. The cool thing about filing a federal complaint is that you simply write your complaint directly to the Department of Education's Office for Civil Rights. That's it. It's essentially as close to filing a lawsuit as you can without passing the bar. You could be a twenty-year-old and take on a 200-year-old university without legal help. That's what we decided to do. We weren't going to wait until we found an attorney who would take our case pro bono. We didn't have the time for it.

Annie and I decided to look up as much as we could around the case law of Title IX that happened until then, about the cases of the Jane Does and John Does that were not being covered. We were able to put together this framework arguing that sexual assault was a violation of Title IX because no student can feel safe if they are afraid of the fear of sexual assault. That's not to say that we were pioneers; this had been argued before. What made us a little different was that we were among the first students who filed a complaint publicly, not anonymously, and without legal representation.

We wrote a letter to [the student newspaper] the *Daily Tar Heel* and said that I, Andrea Pino, and Annie Clark were going to file a federal complaint in January of 2013. Everyone laughed at us. I had meetings with a couple of the higher administrators. They were promising that they were going to take it seriously and they were going to change their policy. I said, "I'm not confident enough that you are going to change anything." We filed our complaint in January of 2013. We did so with a press release that said that UNC is one of many schools that are struggling with this. At the time, we did not know this was going to become the movement that it did.

It wasn't so long after that we began hearing from other survivors. It was repeated across dozens of campuses time and time again. We realized that this was going to be way bigger than we ever imagined. We started talking with these survivors, and they reached out to us through Twitter, through Facebook, through LinkedIn even, wanting to do what we did. We developed this model of being able to teach survivors how to file complaints.

This is one of the times when I began to read more refined research on media framing in particular. I had a theory that a movement would happen if we could frame sexual assault as being thematic, not episodic. To do that, you would have to create a climate in which survivors felt safe coming forward publicly, using their names instead of being Jane Does. We know the media aren't trained to connect a story thematically, because they don't cover crime as being thematic. What if we could force them to do so? With sexual assault, it's often seen as the one case of which a girl possibly put herself in a certain place that made it happen. Whereas if you were to see thematic coverage, the media would have a better grasp that women are targeted on campus. It's not that the girl put herself in a bad place; it's a bigger problem beyond that. It's a culture of harassment and a culture of violence that is happening on every college campus.

The way we were going to solve this is, if the media were not going to cover our stories collectively, then we were going to force them to do so. We started connecting survivors across the country. We all did a public press conference and filed together. That became really powerful to get the media to cover it that way.

In March of 2013, I heard from [reporter] Richard Pérez-Peña. He reached out to me and said, "I've been following your social media and there seems to be a movement that's building." His article, which at the time I did not realize was going to be as big as it was, became one of the first thematic news stories around campus sexual violence. It was on the front page of the *New York Times* website when I was in my Women's Studies 101 class that semester. I remember clutching at my chest and thinking, "Oh my God, I'm on the front page of the *New York Times*." It was a photo of me and Annie.

Since then, it's only gotten more and more and more coverage. It went from the *New York Times* to be covered by *Time*, to be covered by MSNBC, and to be covered by CNN. It's something that completely exploded after that. So did the calls from survivors who were trying to get ahold of us.

My residence hall had been broken into on Easter Sunday [2013]. I began feeling very unsafe at Carolina. They had spray-painted on my bulletin boards with phallic symbols; they left a knife behind; and there were fingerprints across the hall from me. I decided I was going to take some time off. I moved out to Oregon to work with Annie. It was then that Annie and I, together with Alexandra [Brodsky], a former Yale student that filed a Title IX complaint in 2011, and Dana [Bolger], an Amherst student activist, began talking about formalizing and creating somewhat of a network. Alexandra and Dana ended up formalizing an awareness campaign called Know Your IX. Annie and I went on to create an organization called End Rape on Campus [EROC]. They are two different organizations that we created around the same time. Know Your IX was focused on more of a campaign educational approach informing students of their rights. EROC is a direct-service organization. We support survivors in finding counsel, in finding mental health care, and predominantly supporting them in taking action. That's what most of our work comes from.

One of the things that is most frustrating to me now is that while there seems to be a lot of interest in this issue, there doesn't seem to be a pipeline for funding it. My income in 2013 was $4,000 for the entire year. That was when Kirby [Dick] and Amy [Ziering] reached out to us and said, "Would you like to move forward with the work on this documentary [*The Hunting Ground*]?" Of course, to a theorist like me who works on media framing, what an awesome opportunity to create a documentary. Talk about perfect thematic framing, creating a documentary that can be used as a tool to propel the idea of the thematic problem of campus sexual assault. Of course I said yes and packed my bags for Los Angeles.

The PTSD had completely taken over my life. It wasn't just my assault; it was more the vicarious trauma of listening to some of these survivors. I didn't have money for therapy. Later, that fall, I got really sick—it turns out it was a severe staph infection. I was given prednisone to help with the inflammation that it was causing; I ended up having medical poisoning because of it. I became severely suicidal for about twenty-four hours. I ended up being taken to the psychiatric ward. Even though I wasn't admitted, being in the hospital even for a short time, I realized that I had given up everything to [that] point. Because of all this work, I did not have a body that was working for me anymore. That moment in the psychiatric ward completely changed how I was an activist thereafter. I was working twenty-four hours a day, if not with the film, it was with survivors. I had given up everything: my education, my life, and my body. It was some of the hardest times of my life.

These are things you don't really see in *The Hunting Ground*. What you don't really see in all the coverage about me is that I gave up everything to become an activist and to dedicate my life to this issue. The one thing that I gave up that really haunts me is that I gave up my education. When I returned to Carolina in January of 2014, I was told I wasn't going to graduate because I did not have the needed courses that I thought I had. It was three intro-level classes; it wasn't even a whole semester's worth. It was three classes that I had forgotten to take but I couldn't take when I was gone.

At the same time, when I was taking my finals, Annie and I decided to go to D.C. because we had a meeting with the White House. We decided to walk to the Capitol and then walk to the Russell Building. We stumbled onto Senator [Kirsten] Gillibrand's office. Senator Gillibrand had this very nice receptionist named Bo, and we said we'd like to meet with someone to talk about sexual assault. Bo looked at us in a way like, "Girl, that's not how it works." [*Laughter.*]

Then out came Brooke Jamison, who is the legislative director, and Alyson Kelly, the legislative aide at the time. They're looking at us like, "You're clearly in college. You're clearly a student. So what are you two talking about?" We told them how we were two activists, how I had given up everything to work on this issue and my life had really changed. Our schools weren't paying attention. You could tell they were [like], "Oh my God." We talked for forty-five minutes. We were in the middle of the hallway in the Russell Building surrounded by marble columns.

A few days later, Senator Kirsten Gillibrand gave a public speech and said, "I'm taking on campus sexual assault." She said, "These two young women came into my office a few days ago and they told me what was going on. I'm taking on this issue." Since then, we worked with her on writing a bill that she introduced to Congress. I often say that the year of my senior finals, I was in Washington talking to a senator and talking to the White House.

I didn't officially graduate, but I walked so that my family could be there. After the 2014 commencement, Annie and I took the car and we drove across the country and visited survivors. We went to seventeen different states and went to all these incredible natural landmarks. In a sense it was this cool cross-country college road trip. It was the first time that I began realizing that what we were doing was remarkable and it was successful. Although nobody saw it that way at first. Nobody saw that what we did would be anything but two women complaining about their sad experiences. It was seen as something that was just for attention. It wasn't seen as something that was radical. It was something about Kirsten Gillibrand and other activists— the Jaclyn Friedmans, the Emily Mays, the people we've met throughout our work—and kind of being in the same circles, we realized that we were activists, that we were part of this movement, that we were part of history. I think often about that Women's Studies 101 class and the fact that I was in that class when we were on the front page of the *New York Times*. A few months later, students who were taking that class messaged me and said, "I saw you during my lecture today, you're in the PowerPoint slide. We're learning about you. You're part of the curriculum."

This has happened so fast. I will be twenty-four in a few weeks, and this all started when I was twenty. It hasn't been that long since my assault. My life has completely changed. I never thought I'd be meeting all these incredible activists, speaking in the Senate, going to the White House on a regular basis, living in D.C., and running a nonprofit before I turn twenty-five without a college degree. One thing I thought that would happen: I would definitely have a BA. I have everything else. It's been hard. It's been hard to come to terms with the fact that my family isn't sure how to feel about what I am doing. My *abuelos* don't know I was sexually assaulted. I think, in many ways, I can't really articulate what happened to me in Spanish even though I'm fluent. There are certain things I don't have the words for to describe what happened. There's something about your mother tongue that makes things more real, that makes things more vivid. I feel like if I say that it happened in Spanish, I have to bleed all over again, in a way. Maybe, because they don't know what happened, they don't see all this as success? I don't blame them. They worked so hard for me to get my degree, and I don't have it.[12]

People have heard my story; they've seen the film. They've read what I've written. They've told me that "it's because of reading your story that I came forward." I often think about politics this way. It doesn't mean that I have to work with people individually to empower people. For me, it's balancing these options and thinking, "How much of a normal life will I have?" At the rate that I'm going, I'm never going to have a normal life, which is totally fine.

Rye Young

EXECUTIVE DIRECTOR, THIRD WAVE FUND,
BROOKLYN, NEW YORK

I'm interested in having a different conversation about how [cisgender
and transgender activists] work together, how our issues connect, how they're the
same thing often, and really be explicit about misogyny at the end of the day.

Rye Young grew up the child of Republican parents in Scarsdale, New York, and never felt like he fit in. I met Young in his shared Brooklyn apartment, where we talked more about his thoughts on the role of philanthropy in supporting activism than we did about his decision to transition to the man he is today. But his trans experience shapes his approach to and understanding of feminism and his ideas about how the movement needs to evolve.

Young is the executive director of the Third Wave Fund, the new iteration of an organization that dates back to the Third Wave Direct Action Corporation founded by Rebecca Walker in the 1990s, which then for many years operated as the Third Wave Foundation. The Third Wave Foundation raised money and gave money away in support of youth-led activism around issues of gender justice. Just before the economic crash of 2008, the foundation had its own office and a significant staff and had received two $1 million gifts, their first ever. But the effects of the recession were significant and led the group to restructure. When I interviewed Young, he was the only staff member for the Third Wave Fund, now operating as a fiscally sponsored fund at another organization. Like Ho Nguyen, Young explains how philanthropy both shapes and responds to the changing dynamics of movement activism.

I grew up in Scarsdale until I was seventeen, and oh my God, I don't know what I can say about Scarsdale that hasn't already been said. Scarsdale's kind of a joke of a place that's incredibly rich, incredibly college focused, a very homogenous environment in terms of race and class. There weren't even private schools in Scarsdale because the public school was so good. People would sacrifice a lot to send their kids to Scarsdale High School.

To me, it was socially disturbing and I hated it. I was very much a fringe-y kid. I was probably a different kind of kid since forever. I was the kid in middle school with blue hair and drumsticks in my tube socks. Always ran with a pretty queer or punk or goth crowd.

For a while, I was kind of Republican in my stance on things, not in a fully formed way, but my parents were Republican voting and their libertarianism sort of sunk into my brain. It was really the Iraq War that I think tipped the scales for me and made me see the light.

What happened was that I went to an alternative school. We were encouraged to do a senior project and mine was about "Can outside governments create democracy for another country?" I was just exploring that as a question, because to me that was a big question, but it was the whole premise of the Iraq War. I did a study on the history of attempts to bring democracy to other places. I did a lot of research and basically found that it never works. It literally never works, and I had this epiphany. That was when I just realized, "Whoa, our government doesn't live by any code or moral compass that I thought it did." I had a real breakup with the government.

I remember [9/11] was one of the first major international political things that put me at odds with my parents. I was out at some kind of alternative school bonding trip. We were out in the woods somewhere outside New York, or upstate New York, and we were told that we were going to leave early and go back home because the Twin Towers had been hit, and first of all, I was like, "Why are we going toward the city if there's a terrorist apocalypse happening?" I didn't know what was going on. Maybe I was sixteen. But a lot of people had parents who worked there and were really terrified, and I think that people just wanted to go home.

I remember thinking immediately about that the people doing this, what are the chances that they're all crazy evil people? I'm remembering thinking early on, "I think our job is to understand the forces that led to this and not respond out of anger. If sometimes resistance is OK, could this be one of those times?" I remember saying it out loud and people being like, "What the hell? What are you even talking about?" But I still feel that way.

I went to Bard [College]. I just was excited to be in a place where the norm is to be a little bit different and having a critical mindset is sort of normal. That felt exciting to me. At that point, I was pretty leftward leaning, not to the extent where I am now, but I was getting there. I studied Arabic language, culture, and literature. It was connected to 9/11 for sure, to the Iraq War more specifically, and to this kind of feeling I had that we're so arrogant in the way that we talk about cultures we know nothing about. I think I just wanted to learn as much as I could about why things are the way they are.

I've never taken a gender studies course in my whole life, which is funny because I feel so tapped into that right now. I never did LGBT work on campus. I always found it to be so apolitical and sort of removed from critical inquiry. It was often about throwing parties and distributing condoms.

I don't know if I identified as queer or genderqueer or dyke or something—it was waves of all of those things at different times. I wasn't trans identified in college, but I was definitely visibly queer and hung out with a queer crowd. And so, often the students would be like, "Why aren't you in the LGBT group?" And I was like, "Why aren't you in solidarity with any of the activism on campus?" It seemed like a social space, you know? I wanted a political space.

I never got the sense when I was at Bard that feminism was alive and happening and was a thing. I knew it to be an affiliation or a way I was being impacted and growing through, and thinking about my own body and my own life and sex was very affected by feminism. I probably identified as a feminist in a way, but it didn't seem to me to be a movement that was present or active.

Then I went straight to Third Wave as an intern right after Bard. I had never heard of it; I didn't know what it was. I just saw it [on Idealist.org] and was at the end of my rope. I had applied to a million things. Had no applicable skills for most things that I wanted. I wanted a job in the nonprofit field. I didn't want to do work internationally. When I found Third Wave's work, it just appealed to me as a way to continue doing racial justice work within a gender-focused space, and that was more appealing than anything I could have imagined for myself. I found Third Wave and started as an abortion fund intern.

It was really trial by fire. I got there. The intern that had been running the fund was there for the first five minutes I was there, and she was like, "Here's a notebook where you write things down. People are going to call you starting now, so answer the phone and give money away for abortions, and then call the clinic and tell them how much money you're giving. Tell Tara and she'll write a check." Day one, and I'm giving away money.

There were definitely really hard moments, because people would be telling you their lives, their life situations. And some of it was really hard. There was not a lot of time to feel, because it was so busy and it was a moving train. People would call constantly. There were way more people that needed funding than we could ever possibly fund, and so I felt like I had way too much power. It felt overwhelming to make decisions like that that affected people's lives so severely. But it also felt really rewarding to be able to say to someone that the $3,000 procedure that you need covered, we're going to pay for half of it and the clinic will discount the rest.

When I was coming up in the organization, there wasn't a ton of funding going to trans work. I think in part because it was so focused on reproductive justice, and there weren't a lot of trans groups really situating themselves as repro justice organizations. I was in culinary school in between being an intern and being hired as a part-time program associate. I went to school and then I took on a line-cooking job at the same time that I was working at Third Wave. I worked seven days a week for eight months, built up enough money to get top surgery, went and got the surgery done, and I think it was sometime around then that I was offered a full-time position. Then I was able to quit my line-cooking job and do Third Wave full-time as program assistant. Then I got a promotion to program associate. And then in 2010, there was a major round of layoffs, and in that round of layoffs my direct supervisor, who was the program director, was laid off due to budget cuts. That's when I became the program officer.

We announced [recently] that we're becoming the Third Wave Fund. We're pausing all programmatic activities and redeveloping our donor base. In addition to that, we set up at a fiscal sponsor institution, so we're now Third Wave Fund housed at Proteus Fund. We don't have an office; I have Skype meetings with interns and fellows. It's very, kind of, flexible and different. The grant-making programs are new and launching right now as we speak.

We're setting up two movement-building funds. We're not trying to create subissue categories or put work into boxes, because it just doesn't work. It really doesn't. That's the beauty of our grantees, is that they're multiple things. I think that's always been the beauty of third-wave feminism, is that it's not one thing; it's a multi-issue agenda. It's a multicultural agenda and intergenerational agenda.

The Mobilize Power Fund is a direct action rapid-response fund for urgent community-organizing needs. It's very flexible and open to non-501(c)(3)s, individuals, collectives, and pretty much any way that the work might pop off. It's really geared to be flexible, such that if all abortion clinics in Mississippi are going to close, we could fund direct action around that. If a trans woman of color is murdered on the street and there's a need to urgently respond, we would fund that. If black girls are organizing around state violence and the murder of black people in America, we're funding that. So I think it's putting our intersectional priorities into practice in a way that's responding to urgent needs. It kind of reminds me of the abortion hotline. It's like, OK, this isn't necessarily that long-term work, but this is where it's needed right now and we're going to be there for that.

We just created a new process that's really meant to be something that, if you're in a crisis, if you're a young person, if you're not versed in philanthropy, you have multiple ways that you can apply for funding. The proposal itself, it can be two paragraphs, it can be a list of bullet points. It can be a half-hour interview with us on the phone. It could be a selfie video that you and your members, whoever's applying, can respond to the questions in a video.

One of the things that we've done recently with this rapid-response fund, Mobilize Power Fund, is have crowdfunding platforms to support moving bigger grants to the field. We'll put up a grant, but we'll ask people to crowdfund to match that grant. So the idea is, if the work around Black Lives Matter [and] #SayHerName campaigns are taking off on the internet, there's a whirlwind of interest in that work and inspiration that is coming out of that organizing, but the organizers of the campaign are doing the work, they're not necessarily fundraising. Part of what we're trying to contribute with the rapid-response fund is to take some of that momentum and drive it into donor activism. Having this engaged, online network of people whose interests are evolving around specific real-time campaigns versus gender justice philanthropy and theory—this is something happening now; we're talking about it right now.

We want to plug into that whirlwind and sort of add a donor activist dimension to it and make sure people know that their five-dollar gift plus a retweet is going to have an effect of strengthening organizing through grassroots philanthropy. We've developed a network of communications social media leaders who are committing to playing an active role in the campaigns that we roll out. So we identified people who are sort of the most tapped into the things we do—people who favorite our things or retweet our things the most or share our posts on Facebook—and we've made direct interactions with them and have said, "You're awesome. People care what you have to say; we care what you have to say. Can we work out an arrangement where we can send you updates on our campaign work with specific asks around communications pushes and sample tweets and different ways you can support this growing movement?"

That's been really effective and so far almost everyone has agreed to do that, and so as we launch this new fund, we have this ready and willing group of people who are going to help our campaigns take off and hopefully go viral if that's possible. Integrating a somewhat sophisticated and pre-planned online approach to tying grassroots philanthropy to urgent campaign work and political activism is strong fuel.

I think our nonprofit field mimics our economy. A vast majority of them have no budget, are staffless, are essentially cash-poor institutions that have no resources, truly, but they're community efforts. The vast majority of grassroots groups are that: they're informal, maybe a part-time staff member, maybe not. That kind of thing. And then there's this precarious middle class that's evermore precarious. And I think we don't have a solution for that. It speaks to the real lack of commitment to building long-term social justice infrastructure in this country. That's the big question for us, is how to support groups that can really last and withstand a big funder leaving, which most of them can't. So a lot of groups that we find to be beloved organizations, grounded so deeply in our values and our vision, most of them close; if not while they're a grantee of ours, soon thereafter. It's often after a big jolt in funding that a group will close their doors. I think we are interested in convening conversations around that to think about what our responsibility is for groups that might have between a $200,000 and a $600,000 budget but they feel terrified like they always might close. Or if they rub a funder the wrong way, then they're gone, or if they have a leadership transition and people don't like that leader, then everything they worked for would go away. That's where a lot of groups find themselves. And they're considered successful! If that's our measurement of success in terms of the nonprofit model that we support, how do we create something different or fund differently to not create that constant crisis mode? I think it's a profound question and a challenge to some bigger foundations to change and to really fund long-term and to stop their self-serving rebranding that brings groups on and kicks them off. You know, it's a cycle of boom and bust.

I do think it's important that gender be explicitly talked about because it's so easily wiped off the map of funding priorities to organizations that might think about economics but they're not thinking about gender or vice versa. I think a lot of what we focus on is naming a gender justice frame. What does that look like? Third-wave feminism is not what we lead with, in part because it's not an effective way to lead any conversation to give a history lesson or talk about the genesis of ideas and movements. It's to say, "What is the agenda now? What do people care about?" In many ways, we're naming a feminist agenda, and that's politically important work but we don't talk about it like that. There's so much that we're trying to avoid. Some of the only ways to talk about feminist work is to have an inner battle about feminism in the media, and it's so sad to me because the media's interest in feminism is to look at it as a point of conflict and always being in a battle with itself and to make the movement seem funny and sort of sad.

I would challenge some of the current rhetoric makers and narrative makers to say, "How much are we playing into that? And why aren't we trying to build solidarity across issues of structural oppression? And why are we still having conversations with ourselves about feminism in an exclusive kind of way?"

That's one of the things I talk about as being a trans person running this foundation: I'm not interested in having a debate about trans inclusion in feminism. I'm interested in having a different conversation about how we work together, how our issues connect, how they're the same thing often, and really be explicit about misogyny at the end of the day. I think that somehow that gets lost in a lot of "Are trans women actually women? Can trans people be feminists? Can they be in this space or that space?" The reality of misogyny is absent from most of that conversation, and we try to bring it back and keep that at the heart of what we do. For us, it's more important than the label *third-wave feminist*. But I did keep the name in part because I think that legacy is important. I think we're really standing on those shoulders of people who invented intersectional ways of doing work. I think feminists of color invented intersectionality, and I think it's important as it goes off into the world that the legacy really stays there. I wanted to keep the name and the name recognition but rebrand it and brush the dust off and say, "This is relevant now." [To] point people to specific action that's happening, that young people are leading, and to say, "This is Third Wave in action right now. It looks like Black Lives Matter. It looks like Free CeCe McDonald."[13] That's what we hope to do now.

Alice Wilder

MEMBER, SPARK MOVEMENT, CHAPEL HILL, NORTH CAROLINA

*Harry Potter is the foundation for most of who I am as a person. A sense
of justice, to me, was imparted by those books: how you treat people who are
looked at as inferior to you says a lot about who you are; and what it
means to be kind; and when it's OK to break rules.*

Alice Wilder had just finished her sophomore year of high school when the final
Harry Potter movie hit the theaters. For Wilder, the Potter book series and the
communities that formed around it—both in person and online—were central
to her life, and the film's release felt like the end of an era. Depressed about that
and a recent breakup, she spent the summer of 2011 watching the television
series *Parks and Recreation*. Inspired by what she saw as a woman-friendly show
that took female friendships seriously, she started reading online and finding
feminism through the internet and an online publication called *Rookie*. *Rookie*
tweeted that applications were being accepted for SPARK, a "girl-fueled, intergenerational activist organization working online to ignite an anti-racist gender
justice movement" founded and run by Dana Edell (whose story appears in part
II of this book.) Wilder applied, seeing in it a way to combine her love of popular
culture with her budding feminism.

When I interviewed Wilder, she had just finished her sophomore year of
college and had participated in many key SPARK campaigns. In college she was
the editor of a campus-based feminist magazine and had been active in a variety of progressive causes. Feeling some burnout already, and wary of working for
advocacy organizations and nonprofits that she felt sometimes took advantage
of people's passion, she was starting to think about how she would integrate
her continuing enthusiasm for girls' activism with her own needs as an adult
who wanted to be able to "eat and go see a doctor."

Until I was three, we lived in Baton Rouge. That's where my parents met and got married. Then my dad got a job at the University of Rochester in upstate New York, and so we moved there.
I lived there for ten years, and then when I was fourteen—I was
going from middle school into high school, about to start ninth grade—we
moved to Charlotte, North Carolina.

I think the first year of high school I was floundering a lot, because it was like I had been taken away from my entire life, basically, that I had always known. It was a big transition to move to the south after having grown up in the north. It was a huge culture shock for me, but I think overall I liked high school. I went to a small arts magnet school, and so it was more intimate. I had friends, and I really liked a lot of my teachers.

I had [been] and continue to be a very deep and devoted Harry Potter fan. I mean, Harry Potter is the foundation for most of who I am as a person. A sense of justice, to me, was imparted by those books: how you treat people who are looked at as inferior to you says a lot about who you are; and what it means to be kind; and when it's OK to break rules. I really liked the idea that you could be like Hermione, who really likes school and likes to follow the rules, for the most part, which was who I was as a kid—I was very much a rule follower—but also there are times when you can kind of throw that out the window and be like, "Following those rules that this person sets out is not right, and so I should be breaking these rules."

I was rereading the books every time I got the chance, and when the last movie came out, in that moment I knew that it was a new period of my life, because this was this huge part of growing up for me. I had a lot of friends that I had made on the internet about Harry Potter and from Harry Potter conventions, and it was just this really solid part of my life. After that, it didn't end, but that chapter was definitely closed. I sort of was just like, "Well, what do I do now in terms of media consumption?" I started watching a lot of *Parks and Rec* and reading books by John Green and doing sort of the typical internet girl route to feminism. The internet kind of leads you quickly from one source of interest to another, and then you kind of go down that road, and so that's how I got to that internet location where suddenly I was reading posts about bell hooks and intersectionality and the wage gap.

My parents are liberal people. The Iraq War and surveillance and wire-tapping and stuff like that was something that we talked about in our home, about who was George Bush, and let's watch *The Daily Show* when you're eight years old. So I mean, obviously there's some feminism to that, but I think my parents didn't guide me to those sources. It was pretty self-directed.

For me, that first thing was just watching *Parks and Rec*. I think the thing that hooked me into it initially was that friendships on the show between women were not competitive or toxic, which was not something you see very often, especially when you're that age. It was really cool to see the characters of Leslie and Ann, who just straight-up love each other. Not in a corny way. It was also really funny and sincere and authentic. It was a funny show that I could watch without feeling like all the jokes were sexist or racist; that's always a plus as well.

I probably applied for [the SPARK team] late at night when I should have been asleep. I remember being very nervous. I had seen what they had done to petition *Seventeen* magazine to include more diversity in terms of race and body type and ability and then to also pledge to no longer Photoshop their images for girls.

At that point I had sort of identified within myself dual passions for media and feminism, and that is what SPARK is. I felt this divide between "OK, I really love this book series, and I really love TV. I think TV is great, and music, and all these things, but I'm feeling this disconnect between that and what I know of feminism." This seemed like a good way to sort of bring those two things together. And [to have] a nice, larger community, because I had friends in high school who were interested in feminism by that point, but they didn't want to talk about it all the time. So it was nice to know that I could possibly have this online community of girls who would want to talk about it all the time and also adult mentors as well.

Pretty soon after I joined, we got a message in our private Facebook group: "No one can say anything, but we know that *Seventeen* is going to publish this Body Peace Treaty, and who's ready to talk to the press? Who needs to rehearse?" It was very undercover: "We're talking to the *New York Times* in two days." Suddenly, I get to know these secrets, and that's so fun. I love secrets.

[As SPARK members] we would write posts. Basically, we would pitch to Melissa [Campbell] an idea that we had, and then she would tell us 99 percent of the time to go for it, and then I would just write it on a Google doc and share it with her, and then we'd kind of go through and make edits. This would be whenever I had free time at school or after or before homework. I was like, "Oh, I get to actually write and get feedback from someone who's a really good editor," which was something that I really enjoyed a lot.

[In 2013, YingYing Shang] and I were talking about how it would be kind of fun for the month of April to give evidence of how hard it really is to actually abide by the instructions that these magazines set out to just live by. And then we talked about it with Dana on a conference call, and she was so excited about it. So we made a plan. We basically just flipped a coin for who was going to get *Seventeen* and who was going to get *Teen Vogue*.

For each week of the month, we had a different theme. There was a beauty week, there was a fitness week, there was a lifestyle week—so basically just different sections of the magazine—and then we would basically live according to that for the week and then write about it on the blog. This was a Tumblr account that we both had access to, and it ended up getting over 1,000 followers or maybe more. By today's standards, it wasn't that popular, but back then it felt like a pretty huge deal.

I remember being hungry. I remember being really hungry during the health and fitness week. The whole notion behind the fitness activities they had in that magazine is that there's never a time where you shouldn't be working out. So they had "sneaky workouts to do in class." While you're in your math class, you should also be gripping the table in such a way that you're flexing your biceps. I knew I was doing it for the challenge, but it was also crazy to be sitting in class and just thinking, "OK, what are the exercises they were telling me to do, and how can I do them in class?" It also looks ridiculous when you do it in real life.

I think my favorite action that I actually got to be a part of was a reaction to the Steubenville case in Steubenville, Ohio. I think I was seventeen when this happened, and this was pretty soon after the first time someone who I was close to had disclosed being sexually assaulted. This was when sexual assault came onto the scene for me, in addition to the idea of just sexism in the media and body image. Not that that other stuff isn't serious, but it was also this feeling of "Oh, we're being killed and attacked and we don't have a lot of time. This is not something that you can just sort of wait around on because this is happening every day." So hearing about that case of the young girl, who was my age, who found out about her sexual assault because it was Instagrammed—we had a group Facebook chat about it, basically just to process it, because all of us were around that age and everyone was just kind of stunned. "We're all so angry and we feel powerless, and what is going on here?"

From that grew the Educate Coaches campaign. We petitioned—and this is not our most glamorous action, but it's one of the ones I'm the most proud of—the group that certifies high school coaches. We petitioned them to make sexual assault prevention training, or just sexual assault awareness training, a part of the certification process for their coaches. I don't think they actually made it mandatory, but by the end of the campaign—and this is a campaign that I worked on a lot and did a lot of things for—they ended up putting some of our workshops and some of our resources on their site that is visited and downloaded by millions of high school coaches. So that to me felt like, "OK, well, this awful thing happened, and we were all really mad about it, but look what we did."

When you've been doing something since you were fourteen, at a certain point it's easy to get burned out. First year and sophomore year [of college], the nature of what I was doing changed from activism that felt really fun and exciting to activism that felt just like wading into more trauma, especially the sexual assault aspect. It felt like "Oh my God, this is all just so painful and also so real." There was a point in my first year—because I had trained with the Orange County Rape Crisis Center, once people know that about you, they disclose to you a lot, which is something that I understand is a sign that people trust you and that they feel like they can come to you with things like that, which is something that I value, and that means a lot to me. But at the same time, it can definitely be pretty exhausting when you're just going about your day and then someone comes up to you and just sort of tells you that they've been raped. It's just like, "Whoa. This just completely shifted; now I'm in this crisis mode and working out all this stuff." I'm the coeditor of the feminist magazine on campus and I'm working on that, but it's not my main thing that I do in my life, mostly just because I have a part-time job.

I'm a pretty staunch defender of quote-unquote millennials because I think that we're very politically engaged, and maybe this is just the people I tend to be around, but I think for a lot of us there's a lot of cynicism about politics, especially because we all grew up in the Bush era. I mean, I haven't really decided how I feel long-term about Barack Obama yet, but I think there's definitely been a certain level of disappointment from a lot of people of, like, "Well, why is Obama still sanctioning these drone strikes in the Middle East that are killing lots of innocent civilians?" At least, that's what I've seen, a lot of cynicism around that. People are hyped about Bernie Sanders, which is, I don't know. I don't know if I would even define our political engagement by presidential politics, necessarily. I think at least my activist generation is much more actively engaged in politics around race and class and gender—and gender not just as women but as gender identity and fluidity and queerness. I've seen a lot of activism that's much more based from younger and younger kids. There was a girl who I mentored during our mentoring program in high school, and we're still Facebook friends, and she'll post about mental health stuff and about Black Lives Matter and about respecting genderqueer people, and that's really dope to see that the internet has given younger and younger kids access to learning and identifying privilege and oppression in their lives and taking action about it. That's something that just makes me feel very excited.

A lot of my friends in Rochester were employed by Xerox and Kodak, and those groups started to fold and lay off tons of people after the [2008] crash. There were all these news stories about young people and unemployment. It changed my perception of possible career paths. Especially now that a lot of my friends have graduated college and are underemployed or unemployed, my thought right now is just "Well, how can I put myself in the very best position by the time I've graduated, where I can have skills that are marketable and enough of a cushion that I feel like I can pay my rent?" And activist work just is not really going to be able to provide that for me. It doesn't mean it's not going to be a part of my life, but it's not going to be the main thing because, you know, I want to be able to go to the doctor and eat food.

I don't think there's anyone in the world that's braver or more powerful than teenage girls. When people ask me what I want to do, I'm just like, "Whatever teen girls need me to do. Whatever is most helpful to them is what I'll do." I think that when it's done right—and I think that SPARK did it right—when girl activist groups focus on girls and trust girls as leaders who know what they need the most, then they'll be successful. Where I personally don't find it fulfilling is groups where they have adults sitting you down and saying, "So you are thirteen, we'll teach you how to do these things, and we'll give you a task, and here's our plan for you." SPARK was much more like, "Hey, what are you all mad about right now? And how can we work together to work on that? How can we help give you the resources that you need and the skills that you want to learn?" I think as long as girls are in the driver's seat and have adults who are willing to support them and an amount of funding where they can hopefully make a stipend or some sort of thing off of their work, I mean, I just think teen girls are the best, and it's going to be fine.

CONCLUSION

An important part of oral history practice involves sharing completed interviews with our interviewees so they can check transcripts for accuracy and participate in interpretive reflection. As my interviewees looked back at the interviews we had undertaken a couple years earlier, some told me that even such a recent moment seems like long ago; that their thinking had changed due to their own experiences and the ways that the social, cultural, and political winds have shifted since then. But they agree that the stories presented here capture how they saw the world at that time. We share the belief that it is important not only to document what they thought then but also to grapple with how that helps us see what has changed. When I set out to do these interviews I hoped to capture a sense of "feminism today." But writing a book that tries to address "the current day" is complicated because time doesn't stay still. Even since I started this project, there have been significant changes in how we think about the state of the contemporary women's movement.

I started grappling in earnest with questions about "feminism today" in 2012. Part of what motivated my students to start the Who Needs Feminism campaign was their frustration with the then-popular notion that it was supposedly a "postfeminist" world, where young women had all the equality they needed and feminist anger and activism were outdated and silly. That trope made it even more difficult to confront a campus culture that included an egregious frequency of rape and sexual assault and instances of "everyday sexism."[1] Meanwhile, they were watching the "war on women" unfold on the national scene; that was the year when, in the run-up to the presidential election, Republican state legislatures unleashed a rash of anti-abortion bills, Missouri representative Todd Akin made his famous remark about "legitimate rape" not causing pregnancy, and right-wing radio host Rush Limbaugh vilified activist Sandra Fluke on air, calling her a "whore" for arguing that insurance should cover birth control. The outrageousness of Akin and Limbaugh touched a nerve among many women, including my students.[2]

The degree to which our project went viral that spring surprised all of us, but looking back, it now appears clear that we were tapping into a new level of feminist energy and action that was just being unleashed. In January 2012, the Komen foundation for breast cancer research and advocacy announced it was cutting funds to Planned Parenthood and then suffered the wrath of women from around the country who took to social media to excoriate it. The foundation was forced to change positions, but even before it did, Planned Parenthood received $3 million in donations. Together with Joan Walsh, journalist Rebecca Traister noted in *Salon* at the time that "for the first time in what feels like forever, passion and fury were being loudly, proudly given in a full-throated voice, on behalf of women—women as moral actors; women as citizens with rights, health, bodies, freedoms; women as people with families and economic concerns." They called it a "watershed moment in the contemporary conversation about reproductive rights."[3] *Ms.* magazine reported that the number of women calling themselves feminists increased from 50 percent in 2006 to 68 percent in 2012.[4] Suddenly a rash of female celebrities were debating the word, and the media endlessly covered which ones declared themselves feminists. Feminism, as a concept and a word, was occurring in the mainstream with increased frequency.

Whether or not 2012 was the kind of turning point Traister and Walsh suggested it could be, major events in the next few years revealed a degree of "success" for feminist ideas and endeavors that were not at all a given before then. Some of the most stringent antiabortion laws were overturned in part due to the efforts of the three female Supreme Court justices. President Barack Obama published a piece in *Glamour* about why he identified as a feminist.[5] In 2016, the Democratic party chose Hillary Clinton as its presidential nominee, and the national convention highlighted her connection to suffragists of the past and suggested she would finally smash that "highest, hardest glass ceiling."[6] It seemed clear as I was finishing up my interviews that feminism was in a very different rhetorical and political place than it had been before 2012.

I finished my interviews three months before the 2016 presidential election. During our conversations, most of my interviewees assumed that Hillary Clinton would be the next president of the United States. But looking back at their interviews after the election, I saw that their narratives were full of anger and worry over the tenacity and force of antifeminist resistance, which many of them had experienced firsthand. They assumed that Clinton would win, but they were worried about what could happen if she did, because they knew that misogyny was still very much alive, and they had seen backlashes before. Although the outcome was different than they expected, the 2016 election confirmed their worst fears about the existence of a powerful opposition to women's increasing power—something many of them identified before it was recognized by the rest of the world.

The nation's seeming embrace of a virulent form of right-wing populism shook many feminists to their core after 2016. But there were soon signs that Donald Trump's election had provided them with a shared "enemy" that helped overcome some of the internal battles that had long divided movement activists. The Women's March on Washington, the day after Trump's inauguration, was by many accounts the largest single-day protest in American history—and it brought together the women who had long been active in feminist causes with those for whom it was a newfound passion.[7] Half a million people congregated on the National Mall in Washington, D.C., and an estimated 5 million others protested at sites around the world. Many wore knitted pink hats shaped with cat ears in a playful effort to powerfully remind people of Trump's taped comments about grabbing women "by the pussy." The policy platform released by the organizers embraced a wide range of issues including immigration reform, LGBTQ rights, workers' rights, environmental rights, and health care reform—a deeply intersectional approach to "women's issues" that drew on years of progress among groups learning to think about the breadth of the topic in new ways, as we saw in the interviews collected here.[8]

Many of my interviewees, for instance, reveal that the Black Lives Matter movement had a major impact on them. I believe much of the success of the Women's March can be attributed to the lessons Black Lives Matter activists taught other feminists about the relatedness of issues, coalition building, and strategy. The years from 2014 to 2016 were a stark time, especially for African Americans. During those two years, just a few of the high-profile cases in which police killed black boys and men included the deaths of Eric Garner in New York City; Michael Brown in Ferguson, Missouri; Tamir Rice in Cleveland, Ohio; Freddie Gray in Baltimore, Maryland; and Philando Castile in Falcon Heights, Minnesota. The #SayHerName campaign, launched by the African American Policy Forum, sought to draw attention to the many black women, including Sandra Bland, who had also been killed by police. Several of the women I interviewed, especially those who were black, described in these interviews a sense of being under siege and the emotional toll the violence was taking on them. Although I did not interview any of the three founders of Black Lives Matter (Alicia Garza, Patrisse Cullors, and Opal Tometi), the activists I talked to were deeply affected by the way those women had approached the social, political, and even moral crisis represented by ongoing cases of police shootings, and they welcomed and joined their efforts to publicize and decry those murders. While devastated by the violence, the activists I interviewed focused on the promise they saw in the Black Lives Matter movement and on their belief that it offered a powerful example of what a social movement can look like and accomplish. Many described their organizations grappling with the implications of police violence for their own feminist work and how to support, interact with, and form coalitions with Black Lives Matter activists. I believe the results of those new conversations and connections were central to the success of the Women's March on Washington and the political organizing that has unfolded since then.

Since the Women's March, thousands of grassroots groups of politically active women and men have sprung up to resist a range of policies including travel bans, efforts to repeal the Affordable Care Act, tax cuts for the wealthy, unlimited gun rights, attacks on reproductive rights, and more. While they have not always been able to stop or overturn the policies they reject, the level of engagement remains strong.

What will come of this? On the anniversary of the first Women's March, in January 2018, hundreds of thousands of women and men turned out again in cities around the country. Stories abound in the media of the newly energized women who are engaging in ways they had not before.[9] Women are running for political office in record-breaking numbers and have already garnered attention for a number of surprising wins. Although the Center for American Women and Politics cautions that the results of "the pink wave" may not be as transformative as some hope in terms of gender representation, women's new political engagement is undeniably substantial.[10]

We also saw a profound cultural shift in 2017—a nationwide reckoning with the issue of sexual assault and harassment in the workplace via the #MeToo movement. On 5 October 2017, the *New York Times* published an article documenting thirty years of sexual abuse and harassment by Harvey Weinstein, the immensely powerful Hollywood producer.[11] Weinstein's subsequent fall from grace quickly morphed into an international movement. On 15 October, actress Alyssa Milano tweeted, "If all the women and men who have been sexually harassed, assaulted or abused wrote 'me too' as a status, we might give people a sense of the magnitude of the problem. #metoo." Suddenly, Twitter, Facebook, and other social media were inundated with hundreds of thousands of aching memories poured out from women and some men all around the country. Reporters at newspapers and magazines received endless calls from women who wanted to share their stories, either on or off the record. As Rebecca Traister wrote in November 2017, "This is '70s-style, organic, mass, radical rage, exploding in unpredictable directions. It is loud, thanks to the human megaphone that is social media and the 'whisper networks' that are now less about speaking sotto voce than about frantically typed texts and all-caps group chats."[12] And most startlingly, other powerful men swiftly lost their jobs, or at least their reputations, in entertainment, publishing, newsrooms, and famous restaurant kitchens.[13] The media focused, un-surprisingly, on cases that centered around the most well-known perpe-trators and victims.

But in another example of new coalitions across race and class in femi-nist organizing, on 10 November 2017, the Alianza Nacional de Campesinas, a national organization of women farmworkers, published a public letter in support of the many famous women who had come forward with their stories of abuse. "Dear Sisters," they wrote:

> Even though we work in very different environments, we share a com-mon experience of being preyed upon by individuals who have the power to hire, fire, blacklist and otherwise threaten our economic, physical and emotional security. Like you, there are few positions available to us and reporting any kind of harm or injustice commit-ted against us doesn't seem like a viable option. Complaining about anything—even sexual harassment—seems unthinkable because too much is at risk, including the ability to feed our families and preserve our reputations.
>
> We understand the hurt, confusion, isolation and betrayal that you might feel. We also carry shame and fear resulting from this violence. It sits on our backs like oppressive weights. But, deep in our hearts we know that it is not our fault. The only people at fault are the individuals who choose to abuse their power to harass, threaten and harm us, like they have harmed you.
>
> In these moments of despair, and as you cope with scrutiny and criticism because you have bravely chosen to speak out against the harrowing acts that were committed against you, please know that you're not alone. We believe and stand with you.

Two months later, 300 women and men in the entertainment industry an-nounced a new organization, Time's Up Now. Directly responding to the letter from farm-working women, they wrote "Dear Sisters. . . . Now, unlike ever before, our access to the media and to important decision makers has the potential of leading to real accountability and consequences. We want all survivors of sexual harassment, everywhere, to be heard, to be believed, and to know that accountability is possible. . . . We particularly want to lift up the voices, power, and strength of women working in low-wage industries, where the lack of financial stability makes them vulnerable to high rates of gender-based violence and exploitation."[14]

As part of the new initiative, they announced the Time's Up Legal Defense Fund, which at the time of this writing has raised $21 million to support low-wage working women seeking legal actions due to harassment.

This narrative of rapidly changing events shows how difficult it is to capture a snapshot of something as vital, shifting, and evolving as the feminist movement. As I write this, eloquent young women from high schools across the country are helping lead a national youth movement for gun control.[15] By the time this book goes to press, new developments may very well change how we see even the recent past. The oral history interviews collected here allow us to look back on a particular moment in time and to reflect on how individual women's personal decisions and political actions intertwine with the contexts in which they happen—familial, social, political, and global. They show how individuals contribute to shaping the world around them. They also help us see in detail how a movement grows; it does not simply emerge out of whole cloth from a particular event but builds on the connections, successes, and challenges of those who were active before. None of my interviewees could have predicted the immensity of the Women's March or the swift power of the #MeToo campaign. But those phenomena and the results that are still unfolding were made possible because of the work that these activists have been doing for so long and the networks they created with others around the country and the world.

ACKNOWLEDGMENTS

Writing a book can feel solitary at times, but it never really is. This is perhaps especially true when writing a book based on oral histories: The voices of those you interviewed are always in your head—not to mention in your email inbox and sometimes on the phone. I am responsible for any mistakes in this book, but whatever wisdom shines through is the result of my conversations with the remarkable activists I interviewed who shared their lives so graciously with me. My deepest debt is to them, and I am eternally grateful for their generosity. I might not have interviewed those activists, though, if it weren't for the creative, energetic, whip-smart young women who founded the original Who Needs Feminism media campaign. I am especially indebted to Ivanna Gonzalez, Ashley Tsai, and Kate Gadsden, who continue to think creatively about the power of the project they started and who inspire me with their commitment to seeking justice in the world.

The Schlesinger Library Oral History Grant made it possible for me to undertake the first of my interviewing trips, and I am grateful not only for the financial support but for the early enthusiasm Susan Ware and the selection committee expressed for the project.

I could not have written this book without the unfailing support of my colleagues at the Southern Oral History Program, the Center for the Study of the American South, and the history department at the University of North Carolina at Chapel Hill. Della Pollock and Renée Alexander Craft encouraged and inspired me. Malinda Maynor Lowery's generosity as well as support from Fitz Brundage and others made it possible for me to carve out time for scholarship and writing and to share my work-in-progress at conferences. Jaycie Vos and Sara Wood dealt with my absences from the office for research trips and writing with grace and infallible competence; their skill and commitment to the craft of oral history kept me both grounded and on my toes. Bill Ferris, Ayse Erginer, Emily Wallace, Emma Calabrese, Pat Horn, Terri Lorant, and Barb Call cheered me on and gave sage advice. I am forever indebted to Jacquelyn Hall, Bob Korstad, and Beth Millwood for introducing me to the generous, creative, collaborative world of oral historians and for welcoming me in with open arms.

Working with students is one of the joys of my job at the Southern Oral History Program. Rachel Gelfand, who at the time was completing her PhD in American studies at UNC, undertook the Atlanta, Georgia, interviews for me. I am grateful for her thoroughness and thoughtfulness in the process. Carol Prince of UNC's history department helped keep me organized, and Isabell Moore, also of UNC's history department, came to my rescue near the end of the process with her sharp attention to detail. Over the years, many other wonderful graduate and undergraduate students have come through the Southern Oral History Program and have joined me in classes. Their energy, questions about method, ethics, and theory, and their eager engagement in conversations about the art of oral history and the history of women's activism have sustained me in more ways than they realize.

Librarians and transcribers are often invisible colleagues in the world of oral history, and I thoroughly appreciate their care and professionalism. I want to thank especially Laura Clark Brown, Jacqueline Dean, Bryan Giemza, and Maria Estorino of UNC's Wilson Library and the Southern Historical Collection. Laura M. Altizer, who has worked as a transcriber with the Southern Oral History Program for many years, and the good folks at the Audio Transcription Center in Massachusetts literally made this book possible.

I am so lucky to have partnered with excellent colleagues at the University of North Carolina Press. Mark Simpson-Vos has consistently given me generously of his time and expertise, and I am grateful for his support for my work and belief in the project. Lucas Church, Jessica Newman, Jay Mazzocchi, and Iza Wojciechowska all brought their keen eyes and professionalism to the task of shepherding this book into the world, as well as others at the Press whose work is even more behind the scenes. I am indebted to Kathy Nasstrom and Annie Valk for their thoughtful, thorough, and insightful comments on the manuscript and for their friendship as fellow oral historians. They helped make this a much stronger work than it would otherwise have been. Thank you also to Mike Taber for the index.

Friends and family around the country gave critical support. Some opened up their homes to me during my research trips. For the warm welcomes, comfortable beds, delicious food, and especially for the lively conversations, I thank Brian Horrigan and Amy Levine, Lisa Baker and Steven Gelman, and Ken and Karen Seidman and Ulrike Palmbach. Michele Berger and Lisa Levenstein offered useful feedback on early drafts; Felice Belman went above and beyond the call of duty by reading multiple drafts and providing expert editorial advice. Others kept me going by asking me how I was progressing, when the book would come out, what I was discovering—or by keeping quiet about it at the right times. Jill Lepore discussed the complexities of the current world over cups of tea and walks around the pond, and her unflagging encouragement meant the world. Lisa Nagel buoyed my spirits via cheerful texts. Lisa Terrizzi often texted when she saw something maddening in the newspaper— "Who needs feminism?!?!"—making me both laugh and roll up my sleeves.

Writing this book has mostly been a joy, but the joy was interrupted by profound sadness and loss. My brother-in-law, Dan Broun, was a central figure in my Chapel Hill life. Kvelling about each other's children, talking Tar Heel basketball, and expounding about politics with equal passion was at the core of our relationship. He and I had bonded especially over our giddiness about the upstart young candidate Barack Obama, even traveling together to South Carolina to help get out the vote for 2008. Dan's eighteen-month illness and death from leukemia in 2017 punched a hole in our family that can never be filled. I am terribly sad that I cannot share this book with him—I know he would have been absurdly proud.

Our family, though, is resilient and provides a context of love and support that allows me to thrive. Becky, Susannah, and Eli Broun honor Dan's memory by continuing to love and laugh even through tears. Jeanette Falk and Peter Filene have always supported me as a scholar as well as a daughter-in-law. Alice Levenson, Mark Tetreault, Ethan Seidman, Rachel Gunther, and Elias and Theo Seidman are my home base (a metaphor I hope especially Theo will like). In more ways than just the obvious one, I could not have written this book without my beloved parents. My dad, Irv Seidman, is an expert interviewer himself and a scholar of the craft, and I cherish comparing notes with him about the pleasures and challenges involved in talking to people. I'm lucky that my mom, Linda Seidman, passed down her love for the written word, and I treasure sharing our thoughts on reading and writing together. The two of them raised me in such a way that feminism was simply obvious, which I deeply appreciate. I wish my grandmother, Ruth Levenson, were here to read this book; I'm pretty sure she would have loved it.

It's not always easy to live with feminism. I am so grateful to have a husband and two amazing daughters who support and never trivialize the work I do but help keep me laughing and hopeful. Benjamin is my fellow traveler between past and present; Eliza and Hazel are excellent guides to the future. Without them, I would be lost. With all my love, this book is for them.

A NOTE ON METHOD

The practice of oral history is more art than science. As oral historians we can learn how to do background research, prepare good questions, and use a digital recorder, but truthfully the most important tools in our kit are curiosity about and respect for our interviewees and their stories. Deep, careful listening is key to both undertaking and interpreting interviews—we need to listen for what our narrators are saying and what they are leaving out; we must pay close attention to body language, long pauses, deflecting laughter, or phrases meant for public consumption more than for revelation of personal truths. I encourage readers who are interested in the practice of oral history and the power of spoken testimony to listen to these interviews in their entirety; no edited collection of transcripts can convey the complexity of the original voices.

When I walk into an interview situation, I cannot predict how it will go, because an interview is always cocreated in the moment with my interviewee. I know that I can never get the whole story, or every story, or the only story. But I hope to give my interviewees the time and space to tell the story that is important to them at that time and the one that will help me understand my research questions more deeply. I recognize that the interview is inescapably shaped by the racial, class, gender, and cultural dynamics between me (a white, Jewish academic, born in 1966, who is heterosexual, married, the mother of two daughters, and able-bodied) and my interviewees. We both bring assumptions and experiences to the encounter; I do not see this as a problem so much as a reality of which to be aware and to consider when analyzing the results.

In identifying whom to interview for this project, I used what social scientists call the "snowball method," in which I identified some narrators through research into feminist organizations and networks in the locations I had chosen and then asked them whom else I should interview. I also sought names from other scholars and members of various feminist communities. I sought out activists who work in a variety of contexts: media, politics, academia, grassroots organizations, labor, and girls' organizations. The narrators I showcase here represent variation across age, race, class, ethnicity, sexuality, sexual identity, and geography.[1]

I reached out to potential interviewees via email or telephone, explained the project to them, and answered as many of their questions as I could. If they agreed to an interview, we met at their home, or their office, or in one case at a local public library. We went over consent forms together, and I made sure that they understood that they did not have to answer any questions that made them uneasy and that they would be able to decide, after the interview, whether they were comfortable with me archiving it and using a selection from it in this book.

We undertook life history interviews, meaning that, rather than zeroing in on their current work as feminists, I began by asking them about their grandparents, their parents, and their lives growing up. As we discovered in the process of talking about it, the histories of their families and their early educations were often deeply entwined with their own feminist awakenings. Although there was no single pattern, knowing those deep roots was clearly essential to understanding these activists' individual paths.

I used an interview guide created for each interview, a set of pre-devised questions based on my background research on the person and shaped by the kinds of issues I am curious about. Each guide focused on that person's family background, youth, educational experiences, and their work and activism. But oral history interviews are not surveys and the guide is not a script; I follow the lead of the interviewees in how they want to tell their story. I do not always get to all my questions, and often the most important questions are ones that I may ask as a follow-up to something they said, not ones I had prepared in advance. The interviews lasted anywhere from ninety minutes to several hours. I recorded them digitally, on a Zoom H4n recorder, and then had them professionally transcribed. I shared the full transcripts with each of my interviewees, giving them a chance to correct any mistakes or places where they thought the transcriber misrepresented them. In rare cases interviewees requested that we excise things they regretted including and did not want made public.

For this book, I edited down the fifty-to-seventy-five-page transcripts into excerpts of approximately ten pages. I think of these as short stories crafted from the epics of people's lives. I wrote introductions to each interview that briefly describe the location of our interview and in some cases the details about our interaction that I believe help the reader understand the person, the context for our conversation, or the practice of oral history. Some of these are longer than others when I thought that background material I'd had to cut out of the excerpt would be important for readers' comprehension of the narrative. In other cases, the introductions are quite short, where the excerpt needed less context.

In the edited transcripts presented here, I have not rearranged any pieces of the narratives, except in a very few cases where moving a sentence or two would help the reader understand the story's logic. While I have remained true to each individual voice, I have edited out repetitious verbal tics, such as the overuse of *like* or *kind of*, that, while authentic speaking styles, tend to distract a reader. I sent each interviewee the excerpt to review before it was included in this book and asked for approval and feedback if he or she felt uncomfortable with any omissions I had made.

Most of the time they had very few requests; in a few cases, we worked together to reach consensus on how to present the material.

Readers who are interested in hearing the audio or reading the transcripts of the full interviews are able to access them through the Southern Oral History Program, where they are archived and made available to researchers around the world.[2]

INTERVIEW INFORMATION

To listen to the audio or read the full transcript for any of the interviews excerpted in this book, as well as a few that I did not include here, see the Southern Oral History Program Project R.47, "Speaking of Feminism: Voices from Today's Women's Movement in the United States," in the Southern Oral History Program Collection (#4007), Southern Historical Collection, Wilson Library, University of North Carolina at Chapel Hill. Interview numbers and the dates of each interview are provided below. Note that the Southern Oral History Program Collection contains many other interviews of women (and men) whose activism spans the twentieth and twenty-first centuries, and they are available online as well.

COMPLETE LIST OF INTERVIEWS

Noorjahan Akbar (R-0871), 15 December 2015

Soledad Antelada (R-0872), 10 August 2016

Elisa Camahort Page (R-0888), 18 August 2016

Park Cannon (R-0874), 23 July 2015

Soraya Chemaly (R-0875), 15 December 2015

Dana Edell (R-0876), 6 July 2015

Kate Farrar (R-0877), 15 December 2015

Ivanna Gonzalez (R-0878), 28 February 2014

Tara Hall (R-0879), 23 July 2015

Trisha Harms (R-0880), 21 April 2016

Kwajelyn Jackson (R-0881), 24 July 2015

Holly Kearl (R-0882), 16 December 2015

Emily May (R-0883), 7 July 2015

Kenya McKnight (R-0884), 21 April 2015

Samhita Mukhopadhyay (R-0885), 10 July 2015

Ho Nguyen (R-0886), 20 April 2016

Katie Orenstein (R-0887), 7 July 2015

Patina Park (R-0889), 22 April 2016

Erin Parrish (R-0890), 19 April 2016

Andrea Pino (R-0891), 16 December 2015

Joanne Smith (R-0892), 9 July 2015

Rebecca Traister (R-0893), 9 July 2015

Alice Wilder (R-0894), 6 November 2015

Kabo Yang (R-0895), 20 April 2016

Rye Young (R-0896), 6 July 2015

LIST OF INTERVIEWEES BY PLACE

Atlanta, Georgia

Park Cannon

Kwajelyn Jackson

Tara Hall

Bay Area, California

Soledad Antelada

Elisa Camahort Page

Durham, Raleigh, and Chapel Hill, North Carolina

Ivanna Gonzalez

Alice Wilder

New York, New York

Dana Edell

Emily May

Samhita Mukhopadhyay

Katie Orenstein

Joanne Smith

Rebecca Traister

Rye Young

Saint Paul–Minneapolis, Minnesota

Trisha Harms

Kenya McKnight

Ho Nguyen

Patina Park

Erin Parrish

Kabo Yang

Washington, D.C.

Noorjahan Akbar

Soraya Chemaly

Kate Farrar

Holly Kearl

Andrea Pino

NOTES

ABBREVIATION

SOHP

Southern Oral History Program Collection (#4007),
Southern Historical Collection, Wilson Library, University of North Carolina
at Chapel Hill

INTRODUCTION

1. For more on the Who Needs Feminism project, see Rachel F. Seidman, "Who Needs Feminism? Lessons from a Digital World," *Feminist Studies* 39, no. 2 (2013): 549–62; Who Needs Feminism Facebook page, accessed 20 November 2018, https://www.facebook.com/WhoNeedsFeminism; and Who Needs Feminism Tumblr page, accessed 20 November 2018, https://www.tumblr.com/search/whoneedsfeminism. See also Ivanna Gonzalez, interview by Rachel Seidman, SOHP (R-0878), 28 February 2014, excerpted in part III of this book.

2. Rachel F. Seidman, "After Todd Akin Comments: Why Women—and Men—Still Need Feminism," *Christian Science Monitor*, 23 August 2012, https://www.csmonitor.com/Commentary/Opinion/2012/0823/After-Todd-Akin-comments-Why-women-and-men-still-need-feminism.

3. For more on the practice of oral history and documenting social movements, see Paul Thompson, *The Voice of the Past: Oral History*, with Joanna Bornat, 4th ed. (New York: Oxford University Press, 2017); Robert Perks and Alistair Thomson, eds., *The Oral History Reader* (New York: Routledge, 2016); and Donald A. Ritchie, ed., *The Oxford Handbook of Oral History* (New York: Oxford University Press, 2012). For an excellent example of how oral history can reshape our understanding of the feminist movement, see Finn Enke, *Finding the Movement: Sexuality, Contested Space, and Feminist Activism* (Durham, N.C.: Duke University Press, 2007). See also "Suggested Further Reading" in this book.

4. Most of these interviews I did myself; the interviews in Atlanta were undertaken by a graduate research assistant, Rachel Gelfand, who was at the time a PhD student at the University of North Carolina at Chapel Hill in the Department of American Studies.

5. See, for example, Marisa Meltzer, "Who Is a Feminist Now?," *New York Times*, 21 May 2014.

6. See, for example, Faye Dudden, *Fighting Chance: The Struggle over Woman Suffrage and Black Suffrage in Reconstruction America* (New York: Oxford University Press, 2011); Eleanor Flexner and Ellen Fitzpatrick, *Century of Struggle: The Woman's Rights Movement in the United States* (Cambridge, Mass.: Belknap, 1996); Rosalyn Terborg-Penn, *African American Women in the Struggle for the Vote, 1850–1920* (Bloomington: Indiana University Press, 1998); and Judith Wellman, *The Road to Seneca Falls: Elizabeth Cady Stanton and the First Woman's Rights Convention* (Urbana: University of Illinois Press, 2004).

7. See Nina Rothchild and Bonnie Watkins, *In the Company of Women: Voices from the Women's Movement* (Saint Paul: Minnesota Historical Society Press, 1996), for interviews with women about their experiences in the women's movement of the 1960s and 1970s. See also Stephanie Gilmore, *Feminist Coalitions: Historical Perspectives on Second-Wave Feminism in the United States* (Urbana: University of Illinois Press, 2008); Benita Roth, *Separate Roads to Feminism: Black, Chicana, and White Feminist Movements in America's Second Wave* (Cambridge: Cambridge University Press, 2003); Stephanie Coontz, *A Strange Stirring: The Feminine Mystique and American Women at the Dawn of the 1960s* (New York: Basic Books, 2012); and Enke, *Finding the Movement.*

8. For more on the third wave, see Jennifer Baumgardner and Amy Richards, *Manifesta: Young Women, Feminism, and the Future* (New York: Farrar, Straus and Giroux, 2010); Stacy Gillis, Gillian Howie, and Rebecca Munford, eds., *Third Wave Feminism: A Critical Exploration* (New York: Palgrave Macmillan, 2007); Melody Berger, ed., *We Don't Need Another Wave: Dispatches from the Next Generation of Feminist* (Berkeley, Calif.: Seal, 2006); Rory Dicker and Alison Piepmeier, eds., *Catching a Wave: Reclaiming Feminism for the 21st Century* (Lebanon, N.H.: Northeastern University Press, 2003); and Barbara Findlen, ed., *Listen Up: Voices from the Next Feminist Generation,* 2nd ed. (Berkeley, Calif.: Seal, 2001). See also Nancy Hewitt, "Feminist Frequencies: Regenerating the Wave Metaphor," *Feminist Studies* 38, no. 3 (2012): 658–80.

9. Kimberle Crenshaw, "Demarginalizing the Intersection of Race and Sex: A Black Feminist Critique of Antidiscrimination Doctrine, Feminist Theory and Antiracist Politics," *University of Chicago Legal Forum*, 1989, 139–68.

10. Hewitt, "Feminist Frequencies," 669.

11. Soraya Chemaly, interview by Rachel Seidman, SOHP (R-0875), 15 December 2015.

12. For suggestions that there is a "fourth wave" of feminism, see Pythia Peay, "Feminism's Fourth Wave," *Utne Reader*, March/April 2005, 59–60; Ealasaid Munro, "Feminism: A Fourth Wave?," *Political Insight* 4, no. 2 (2013): 22–25; Kira Cochrane, *All the Rebel Women: The Rise of the Fourth Wave of Feminism* (London: Guardian Books, 2013); and Nicola Rivers, *Postfeminism(s) and the Arrival of the Fourth Wave* (New York: Palgrave Macmillan, 2017).

13. Elisa Camahort Page, interview by Rachel Seidman, SOHP (R-0888), 18 August 2016.

14. Rebecca Traister, interview by Rachel Seidman, SOHP (R-0893), 9 July 2015.

15. For more on "Twitter wars," see Michelle Goldberg, "Feminism's Toxic Twitter Wars," *Nation*, 29 January 2014, https://www.thenation.com/article/feminisms-toxic-twitter-wars.

16. Susan Faludi, *Backlash: The Undeclared War against American Women* (New York: Broadway Books, 2006).

17. See, for example, Dorothy Miller, "The 'Sandwich' Generation: Adult Children of the Aging," *Social Work* 26, no 5 (1981): 419–23; and Kim Parker and Eileen Patten, *The Sandwich Generation: Rising Financial Burdens for Middle-Aged Americans* (Washington, D.C.: Pew Research Center, 2013).

PART ONE. ACTIVISTS IN THEIR FORTIES

1. Rebecca Traister, interview by Rachel Seidman, SOHP (R-0893), 9 July 2015.

2. Katie Orenstein, interview by Rachel Seidman, SOHP (R-0887), 7 July 2015.

3. Tara Hall, interview by Rachel Gelfand, SOHP (R-0879), 23 July 2015.

4. Patina Park, interview by Rachel Seidman, SOHP (R-0889), 22 April 2016.

5. Thunderclap was a social media platform that allowed users to share a message with all their supporters at once, "flash mob–style."

6. Hall, interview.

7. CARE is an organization focused on women's empowerment, food security, education, and health in impoverished regions of the world.

8. Assata Shakur is a former member of the Black Panther Party and the Black Liberation Army. She was arrested for the murder of a police officer in the 1970s and, after escaping from prison, fled to Cuba, where she obtained political asylum. She remains on the FBI's most wanted list. See Assata Shakur, *Assata: An Autobiography* (London: Zed Books, 2016).

9. Acronym for historically black colleges and universities.

10. Bring Back Our Girls was a social media campaign to rescue more than 200 girls abducted by Boko Haram in Chibok, Borno State, Nigeria.

11. Rebecca Traister, *Good and Mad: The Revolutionary Power of Women's Anger* (New York: Simon and Schuster, 2018).

12. Traister is referring to the nationally televised Senate confirmation hearing for Supreme Court nominee Clarence Thomas, whom Hill accused of sexual harassment.

13. Susan Faludi, "Death of a Revolutionary," *New Yorker*, 15 April 2013, 52.

14. The board of Hewlett Packard ousted CEO Carly Fiorina, who had been the first woman to lead one of *Fortune* magazine's Top 20 companies, in the wake of the controversial merger with Compaq. See the Pui-Wing Tam, "H-P's Board Ousts

Fiorina as CEO," *Wall Street Journal*, 10 February 2005, https://www.wsj.com/articles/SB110795431536149934. See Kevin Drum, "Women's Opinions," *Washington Monthly*, 20 February 2005, https://washingtonmonthly.com/2005/02/20/womens-opinions/.

15. The Move to End Violence is one initiative of the NoVo Foundation, a private foundation that works to end violence against women and girls around the globe.

16. The Indian Child Welfare Act was enacted in 1978, after studies showed that large numbers of Native American children were being separated from their families and communities by state welfare and private adoption agencies, even when willing family members were available to take them in.

PART TWO. ACTIVISTS IN THEIR THIRTIES

1. Dana Edell, interview by Rachel Seidman, SOHP (R-0876), 6 July 2015.

2. The 1988 play by Wendy Wasserstein won the Pulitzer Prize for Drama and deals with feminism and women's changing roles during the 1960s and after.

3. See Carol Gilligan, *In a Different Voice: Psychological Theory and Women's Development* (Cambridge, Mass.: Harvard University Press, 1982). Gilligan's book argued that Lawrence Kohlberg's theories on moral development did not take gender differences into account. She argued that girls develop differently and laid out an ethic of care. Her work was highly influential and controversial.

4. *Report of the APA Task Force on the Sexualization of Girls* (Washington, D.C.: American Psychological Association, 2007), http://www.apa.org/pi/women/programs/girls/report-full.pdf.

5. Change.org is a website on which activists can launch petitions and reach wide audiences through social media.

6. The Houston Plan of Action, officially known as the National Plan of Action, was drawn up at the National Women's Conference in Houston, Texas, in 1977. The Beijing Platform for Action was created at the UN Fourth World Conference on Women in 1995. Both include advocacy and support for a wide range of issues. For the Minnesota Women's Consortium's own compilation of the two platforms, see "The Houston Plan of Action & Beijing Platform of 1995," Minnesota Women's Consortium, accessed 15 November 2018, http://www.mnwomen.org/wp-content/uploads/2012/11/Houston-Beijing-One-page.pdf.

7. The Women's Economic Security Act, signed by Governor Mark Dayton on Mother's Day 2014, strengthened workplace protections and flexibility for pregnant women and nursing mothers, expanded employment opportunities for women in high-wage, high-demand occupations, and sought to reduce the gender pay gap through increased enforcement of equal pay laws. See "Women's Economic Security Act FAQs," Minnesota Department of Labor and Industry, accessed 15 November 2018, https://www.dli.mn.gov/business/employment-practices/

womens-economic-security-act-faqs; and "Minnesota Session Laws – 2014, Regular Session; Chapter 239 – H.F.No. 2536," Office of the Revisor of Statutes, accessed 15 November 2018, https://www.revisor.mn.gov/laws/2014/0/Session+Law/Chapter/239.

8. In Hmong traditional spirituality, a shaman communicates with the Otherworld to understand why someone is sick, explains what he has learned to the patient and the patient's family, and then heals the patient.

9. See Brittany Lewis, "At the Margins of the American Political Imagination: Black Feminist Politics and the Racial Politics of the New Democrats," in *Race and Hegemonic Struggle in the United States: Pop Culture, Politics, and Protest*, ed. Mary Triece and Michael Lacy (Madison, N.J.: Fairleigh Dickinson University Press, 2014), 111–28.

10. In 2015 the Obama administration announced a $100 million, five-year funding initiative by Prosperity Together to improve economic prosperity for low-income women and an $18 million funding commitment by the Collaborative to Advance Equity through Research—an affiliation of American colleges, universities, research organizations, publishers, and public interest institutions to support existing and new research efforts about women and girls of color. See "Fact Sheet: Advancing Equity for Women and Girls of Color," Obama White House archives, 13 November 2015, https://obamawhitehouse.archives.gov/the-press-office/2015/11/13/fact-sheet-advancing-equity-women-and-girls-color.

11. Now called Family, Career and Community Leaders of America, the original Future Homemakers of America began in 1945 to unify the work of home economics clubs from white high schools across the country. The New Homemakers of America was a parallel organization of students from black schools. The two organizations merged in 1965. For more information, see Megan Elias, *Stir It Up: Home Economics in American Culture* (Philadelphia: University of Pennsylvania Press, 2008).

12. On 17 June 2015, Dylann Roof, a twenty-one-year-old white man who identified as a white supremacist, murdered nine African Americans during a prayer service at Emanuel African Methodist Episcopal Church in Charleston, South Carolina.

13. See Holly Kearl, *Stop Street Harassment: Making Public Places Safe and Welcoming for Women* (Santa Barbara, Calif.: Praeger, 2010). See also Holly Kearl, *50 Stories about Stopping Street Harassers* (self-published, 2013), CreateSpace; Holly Kearl, *Stop Global Street Harassment: Growing Activism Around the World* (Santa Barbara, Calif.: Praeger, 2015); and Stop Street Harassment, accessed July 10, 2018, http://www.stopstreetharassment.org.

14. See Anna Jane Grossman, "Catcalling: Creepy or a Compliment?," CNN, 14 May 2008, http://www.cnn.com/2008/LIVING/personal/05/14/lw.catcalls/index.html.

15. Kristin Mapel Bloomberg is a professor of women's studies and holds the Hamline University Endowed Chair in the Humanities. In addition to Harms, Mapel

Bloomberg also taught Erin Parrish. Ho Nguyen and Patina Park also attended Hamline University.

16. Senator Paul Wellstone represented Minnesota from 1991 to 2002, when he died at age fifty-eight in a plane crash. He was a member of the Democratic-Farmer-Labor Party and a leader of the progressive arm of the Democratic Party. See Paul Wellstone, *Conscience of a Liberal: Reclaiming the Compassionate Agenda* (Minneapolis: University of Minnesota Press, 2002).

17. Justice Scalia died in February 2016, just before a case was heard about whether nonunion public school teachers in California had to pay fees if they did not join the union. Because of Scalia's death, the justices were split 4–4 over whether or not to overturn a 1977 ruling known as *Abood v. Detroit Board of Education*. However, as Harms feared, a case in 2017, *Janus v. American Federation of State, County and Municipal Employees, Council 31, et al.*, 16–1466, undercut that victory once Justice Neil Gorsuch joined the court.

18. The American Legislative Exchange Council (ALEC) is a nonprofit made up of conservative policy experts and lawmakers who draft and share ideas for state-level legislation.

19. National Abortion Rights Action League, now known as NARAL Pro-Choice America.

20. Originally the British Universities North America Club, BUNAC is a youth travel organization.

21. Pete Seeger and his wife Toshi Seeger's sloop *Clearwater* was the centerpiece of their nonprofit organization Hudson River Sloop Clearwater, Inc., founded in the 1960s and dedicated to cleaning up the Hudson River and surrounding wetlands.

22. Freddie Gray and Eric Garner were both black men killed by police. Eric Garner died in July 2014 in New York City, after police officers put him in a headlock and he died from being choked. Freddie Carlos Gray Jr., twenty-five, of Baltimore died in April 2015 after being transported in a police van, where he suffered injuries to his spinal cord. Both men's deaths, along with many others', resulted in large-scale demonstrations.

23. The Hyde Amendment bars the use of federal funds to pay for abortion except to save the life of the woman or if the pregnancy arises from incest or rape.

PART THREE. ACTIVISTS IN THEIR TWENTIES

1. Ho Nguyen, interview by Rachel Seidman, SOHP (R-0886), 20 April 2016.

2. Alice Wilder, interview by Rachel Seidman, SOHP (R-0894), 6 November 2015.

3. Ivanna Gonzalez, interview by Rachel Seidman, SOHP (R-0878), 28 February 2014.

4. Since this interview, Free Women Writers became a registered 501(c)(3) with a team of volunteers in Afghanistan and the diaspora, and it reaches 70,000 people every week through its website and social media.

5. For more information on the Who Needs Feminism campaign, see Rachel F. Seidman, "Who Needs Feminism: Lessons from the Digital Age," *Feminist Studies* 39, no. 2 (2013): 549–62.

6. "*Womanism*" is a term coined by Alice Walker. See Alice Walker, *In Search of Our Mothers' Gardens* (New York: Harcourt, Brace, Jovanovich, 1983).

7. Crisis pregnancy centers are generally run by Christian anti-abortion organizations and have been criticized for deceptive advertising, suggesting that they provide abortion services when they do not and actively discouraging women from seeking them. For example, one study of crisis pregnancy centers in North Carolina found that 86 percent provided false or misleading information. See A. G. Bryant and E. E. Levi, "Abortion Misinformation from Crisis Pregnancy Centers in North Carolina," *Contraception* 86, no. 6 (2012): 752–56.

8. Walker, *In Search*.

9. Practitioners of Santeria, a Caribbean religion.

10. The Office for Civil Rights sent a "Dear Colleague" letter to colleges and universities asserting that sexual harassment and assault "interferes with students' right to receive an education free from discrimination." They reminded educators that Title IX prohibited discrimination on the basis of sex and that sexual harassment of students, including acts of sexual violence, is a form of sex discrimination prohibited by Title IX. https://www2.ed.gov/about/offices/list/ocr/letters/colleague-201104 .html, accessed 2/07/2019.

11. The Carolina Way is a phrase coined by famous former basketball coach Dean Smith to describe a way of playing basketball that emphasized sportsmanship and team togetherness. Over the years, it came to be associated by Carolina alumni with their school more broadly, and although interpreted differently by different people, it generally means doing things "right" with a focus on community and generosity.

12. Pino received her degree from UNC in 2017.

13. A movement to free CeCe McDonald, a trans woman who was attacked while walking with friends and was imprisoned for killing a man while fighting back. Trans actress and LGBTQ advocate Laverne Cox was the executive producer of a film about the movement called *Free CeCe*.

CONCLUSION

1. See Laura Bates, *Everyday Sexism: The Project That Inspired a Worldwide Movement* (New York: St. Martin's Griffin, 2016); and Everyday Sexism Project, accessed 7 March 2018, http://everydaysexism.com.

2. See Rachel F. Seidman, "After Todd Akin Comments: Why Women—and Men—Still Need Feminism," *Christian Science Monitor*, 23 August 2012, https://www.csmonitor.com/Commentary/Opinion/2012/0823/After-Todd-Akin-comments-Why-women-and-men-still-need-feminism.

3. Joan Walsh and Rebecca Traister, "Susan G. Komen's Priceless Gift: A Radical Decision Woke the Country Up to an Alarming Rightward Drift, and Gave New Life to Women's Health Advocacy," *Salon*, 4 February 2012, https://www.salon.com/2012/02/04/susan_g_komen%E2%80%99s_priceless_gift.

4. "The Feminist Factor: More Than Half of 2012 Women Identify Themselves as Feminists," *Ms.*, 18 March 2013, http://www.msmagazine.com/media-center/press/feminist-factor-in-2012.html.

5. Barack Obama, "*Glamour* Exclusive: President Barack Obama Says, 'This Is What a Feminist Looks Like,'" *Glamour*, 4 August 2016, https://www.glamour.com/story/glamour-exclusive-president-barack-obama-says-this-is-what-a-feminist-looks-like.

6. In her concession speech after her loss to Barack Obama in the Democratic primary for the 2008 presidential election, Clinton noted that she might not have cracked the "highest, hardest glass ceiling," but she and her supporters had put 18 million cracks in it. See Dana Millbank, "A Thank-You for 18 Million Cracks in the Glass Ceiling," *Washington Post*, 8 June 2008, http://www.washingtonpost.com/wp-dyn/content/article/2008/06/07/AR2008060701879.html.

7. See, for instance, Erica Chenoweth and Jeremy Pressman, "This Is What We Learned by Counting the Women's Marches," *Washington Post*, 7 February 2017, https://www.washingtonpost.com/news/monkey-cage/wp/2017/02/07/this-is-what-we-learned-by-counting-the-womens-marches/?utm_term=.c7ed3 3a3862c.

8. "Unity Principles," Women's March, accessed 7 March 2018, https://www.womensmarch.com/principles.

9. See, for example, Charlotte Alter, "'It's a Women's Wave Coming': The Women's March Is Turning into a True Political Force," *Time*, 21 January 2018, http://time.com/5111480/womens-march; Anna North, "How the Women's March Made Itself Indispensable: Over the Past Year, the March Has Become a Crucial Hub for Left-Wing Organizations, and a Potent Political Force for 2018," *Vox*, 19 January 2018, https://www.vox.com/identities/2018/1/19/16905884/2018-womens-march-anniversary; Erica Chenoweth and Jeremy Pressman, "The Women's March Could Change Politics Like the Tea Party Did: Donald Trump Came to Power on the Heels of a Rightwing Movement Rooted in the Tea Party Protests; The Women's March Could Pull Off a Similar Feat," *Guardian*, 31 January 2018, https://www.theguardian.com/commentisfree/2018/jan/31/womens-march-politics-tea-party; and Christina Cauterucci, "The Women's March Was Just the Beginning: All across the Country,

Activists Inspired to Fight Trump Are Building a New Kind of Feminist Movement," *Slate*, 17 January 2018, https://slate.com/news-and-politics/2018/01/the-womens-march-was-just-the-beginning.html.

10. Kelly Dittmar, "'Pink Wave': A Note of Caution," *Footnotes: A Blog of the Center for American Women and Politics*, 26 January 2018, http://cawp.rutgers.edu/footnotes/pink-wave-note-caution.

11. Jodi Kantor and Megan Twohey, "Harvey Weinstein Paid Off Sexual Harassment Accusers for Decades," *New York Times*, 5 October 2017, https://www.nytimes.com/2017/10/05/us/harvey-weinstein-harassment-allegations.html.

12. Rebecca Traister, "Your Reckoning. And Mine: As Stories about Abuse, Assault, and Complicity Come Flooding Out, How Do We Think about the Culprits in Our Lives? Including, Sometimes, Ourselves," *Cut*, 13 November 2017, https://www.thecut.com/2017/11/rebecca-traister-on-the-post-weinstein-reckoning.html.

13. Rebecca Traister, "Our National Narratives Are Still Being Shaped by Lecherous, Powerful Men," *Cut*, 30 October 2017, https://www.thecut.com/2017/10/halperin-wieseltier-weinstein-powerful-lecherous-men.html.

14. "Our Mission," Time's Up, accessed 7 March 2018, https://www.timesupnow.com/home#ourmission-anchor.

15. After a former student killed seventeen students and staff members at Marjory Stoneman Douglas High School in Florida on Valentine's Day 2018, students launched the Never Again movement, focused on gun control. See Charlotte Alter, "The School Shooting Generation Has Had Enough," *Time*, 22 March 2018, http://time.com/longform/never-again-movement; and Emily Witt, "How the Survivors of Parkland Began the Never Again Movement," *New Yorker*, 19 February 2018.

A NOTE ON METHOD

1. My choices were not the only ones possible, and other researchers I hope will fill in gaps that I have left. I interviewed one trans man, but no cis men; I encourage another researcher to interview male-identified feminists. I interviewed people mostly in urban settings where I could find significant numbers of feminist organizations and activists. While a few of my interviewees discuss rural women, that is not the focus here. However, for more interviews with rural women activists, see the Southern Oral History Program's project on the long women's movement in the American south, which includes many women who have been active since the 1970s and in some cases are still leaders in their communities.

2. The interviews with women in New York City, which were supported by the Radcliffe Oral History Grant, are also archived at the Schlesinger Library at Radcliffe, Harvard University.

SUGGESTED FURTHER READING

Oral history and women's history are rich, vibrant fields of scholarship with excellent articles and books being published all the time. The following short list is a sampling of works that provide more context and deeper examination of some of the themes and issues raised in this book. In the section on twenty-first-century feminism, I have also included some works from the popular press that have helped shape or reflect the conversation about feminism in today's world. This is by no means an exhaustive bibliography but a guide to further exploration.

ON ORAL HISTORY METHODOLOGY, THEORY, AND PRACTICE

Blee, Kathleen. "Evidence, Empathy, and Ethics: Lessons from Oral Histories of the Klan." In *The Oral History Reader*, 3rd ed., edited by Robert Perks and Alistair Thomson, 424–33. New York: Routledge, 2016.

Borland, Katharine. "'That's Not What I Said': Interpretive Conflict in Oral Narrative Research." In *The Oral History Reader*, 3rd ed., edited by Robert Perks and Alistair Thomson, 412–23. New York: Routledge, 2016.

Boyd, Nan Alamilla, and Horacio Ramírez, eds. *Bodies of Evidence: The Practice of Queer Oral History*. New York: Oxford University Press, 2012.

Gluck, Sherna Berger, and Daphne Patai, eds. *Women's Words: The Feminist Practice of Oral History*. New York: Routledge, 1991.

Iacovetta, Franca, Katrina Srigley, and Stacey Zembrzycki, eds. *Beyond Women's Words: Feminisms and the Practices of Oral History in the Twenty-First Century*. New York: Routledge, 2018.

Oral History Review. The premier journal for oral history research in the United States and an excellent resource for scholarship in the field.

Perks, Robert, and Alistair Thomson, eds. *The Oral History Reader*. 3rd ed. New York: Routledge, 2016.

Ritchie, Donald, ed. *The Oxford Handbook of Oral History*. New York: Oxford University Press, 2011.

Thompson, Paul. *The Voice of the Past: Oral History*. 3rd ed. New York: Oxford University Press, 2000.

Yow, Valerie. *Recording Oral History: A Guide for the Humanities and Social Sciences*. 3rd ed. Lanham, Md.: Rowman and Littlefield, 2015.

OVERVIEWS OF U.S. WOMEN'S HISTORY AND THE WOMEN'S MOVEMENT

Brown, Leslie, Jacqueline Castledine, Anne Valk, and Nancy A. Hewitt, eds. *U.S. Women's History: Untangling the Threads of Sisterhood*. New Brunswick, N.J.: Rutgers University Press, 2017.

Cott, Nancy F., ed. *No Small Courage: A History of Women in the United States*. New York: Oxford University Press, 2000.

Evans, Sara. *Born for Liberty: A History of Women in America*. New York: Free Press Paperbacks, 1997.

Freedman, Estelle. *No Turning Back: The History of Feminism and the Future of Women*. New York: Ballantine Books, 2002.

Guy-Sheftall, Beverly, ed. *Words of Fire: An Anthology of African-American Feminist Thought*. New York: New Press, 1995.

Hewitt, Nancy. *No Permanent Waves: Recasting Histories of U.S. Feminism*. New Brunswick, N.J.: Rutgers University Press, 2010.

Hewitt, Nancy, and Suzanne Lebsock. *Visible Women: New Essays on American Activism*. Urbana: University of Illinois Press, 1993.

Orleck, Annelise. *Rethinking American Women's Activism*. New York: Routledge, 2014.

Stansell, Christine. *The Feminist Promise: 1792 to the Present*. New York: Modern Library Paperbacks, 2011.

ON THE NINETEENTH- AND EARLY TWENTIETH-
CENTURY WOMEN'S MOVEMENT ("FIRST WAVE")

Cott, Nancy. *The Grounding of Modern Feminism*. New Haven, Conn.: Yale University Press, 1987.

Dubois, Ellen. *Feminism and Suffrage: The Emergence of an Independent Women's Movement in America, 1848–1869*. Ithaca, N.Y.: Cornell University Press, 1999.

Dudden, Faye. *Fighting Chance: The Struggle over Woman Suffrage and Black Suffrage in Reconstruction America*. New York: Oxford University Press, 2011.

Flexner, Eleanor, and Ellen Fitzpatrick. *Century of Struggle: The Woman's Rights Movement in the United States*. Cambridge, Mass.: Belknap, 1996.

Terborg-Penn, Rosalyn. *African American Women in the Struggle for the Vote, 1850–1920*. Bloomington: Indiana University Press, 1998.

Wellman, Judith. *The Road to Seneca Falls: Elizabeth Cady Stanton and the First Woman's Rights Convention*. Urbana: University of Illinois Press, 2004.

ON THE WOMEN'S MOVEMENT 1945-1980S ("SECOND WAVE")

Allured, Janet. *Remapping Second-Wave Feminism: The Long Women's Rights Movement in Louisiana, 1950–1997*. Athens: University of Georgia Press, 2016.

Cobble, Dorothy Sue. *The Other Women's Movement: Workplace Justice and Social Rights in Modern America.* Princeton, N.J.: Princeton University Press, 2004.

Cobble, Dorothy Sue, Linda Gordon, and Astrid Henry. *Feminism Unfinished: A Short, Surprising History of American Women's Movements.* New York: Liveright, 2015.

Coontz, Stephanie. *A Strange Stirring: The Feminine Mystique and American Women at the Dawn of the 1960s.* New York: Basic Books, 2012.

Enke, Finn. *Finding the Movement: Sexuality, Contested Space, and Feminist Activism.* Durham, N.C.: Duke University Press, 2007.

Faludi, Susan. *Backlash: The Undeclared War against American Women.* New York: Anchor Books, 1992.

Gilmore, Stephanie. *Feminist Coalitions: Historical Perspectives on Second-Wave Feminism in the United States.* Urbana: University of Illinois Press, 2008.

Levenstein, Lisa. *A Movement without Marches: African American Women and the Politics of Poverty in Postwar Philadelphia.* Chapel Hill: University of North Carolina Press, 2010.

Maclean, Nancy. *The American Women's Movement, 1945–2000: A Brief History with Documents.* Boston: Bedford/St. Martin's, 2009.

Roth, Benita. *Separate Roads to Feminism: Black, Chicana, and White Feminist Movements in America's Second Wave.* Cambridge: Cambridge University Press, 2003.

Rothchild, Nina, and Bonnie Watkins. *In the Company of Women: Voices from the Women's Movement.* Saint Paul: Minnesota Historical Society Press, 1996.

Swinth, Kirsten. *Feminism's Forgotten Fight: The Unfinished Struggle for Work and Family.* Cambridge, Mass.: Harvard University Press, 2018.

Valk, Anne M. *Radical Sisters: Second-Wave Feminism and Black Liberation in Washington, D.C.* Urbana: University of Illinois Press, 2008.

Wilkerson, Jessica. "'The Company Owns the Mine but They Don't Own Us': Feminist Critiques of Capitalism in the Coalfields of Kentucky in the 1970s." *Gender & History* 28, no. 1 (April 2016): 199–220.

ON FEMINISM OF THE 1980S AND 1990S ("THIRD WAVE")

Baumgardner, Jennifer, and Amy Richards. *Manifesta: Young Women, Feminism, and the Future.* New York: Farrar, Straus and Giroux, 2010.

Dicker, Rory, and Alison Piepmeier, eds. *Catching a Wave: Reclaiming Feminism for the 21st Century.* Lebanon, N.H.: Northeastern University Press, 2003.

Findlen, Barbara, ed. *Listen Up: Voices from the Next Feminist Generation.* 2nd ed. Berkeley, Calif.: Seal, 2001.

Gillis, Stacy, Gillian Howie, and Rebecca Munford, eds. *Third Wave Feminism: A Critical Exploration.* Basingstoke, UK: Palgrave Macmillan, 2007.

Henry, Astrid. *Not My Mother's Sister: Generational Conflict and Third-Wave Feminism.* Bloomington: Indiana University Press, 2007.

Lindsey, Treva. "Ula Y. Taylor's 'Making Waves: The Theory and Practice of Black Feminism.'" *Black Scholar* 44, no. 3 (2014): 48–51.

TWENTY-FIRST-CENTURY FEMINISM

Barker-Plummer, Bernadette, and David Barker-Plummer. "Twitter as a Feminist Resource: #YesAllWomen, Digital Platforms, and Discursive Social Change." In *Social Movements and Media*, edited by Jennifer Earl and Deana A. Rohlinger, 91–118. Studies in Media and Communications 14. Bingley, UK: Emerald Publishing Limited, 2017.

Berger, Melody, ed. *We Don't Need Another Wave: Dispatches from the Next Generation of Feminists.* Berkeley, Calif.: Seal, 2006.

Chozick, Amy. "Hillary Clinton Ignited a Feminist Movement. By Losing." *New York Times,* 13 January 2018. https://www.nytimes.com/2018/01/13/sunday-review/hillary-clinton-feminist-movement.html?action=click&contentCollection=Politics&module=RelatedCoverage&region=Marginalia&pgtype=article.

Crossley, Alison Dahl. "Facebook Feminism: Social Media, Blogs, and New Technologies of Contemporary U.S. Feminism." *Mobilization: An International Quarterly* 20, no. 2 (June 2015): 253–68.

———. *Finding Feminism: Millennial Activists and the Unfinished Gender Revolution.* New York: New York University Press, 2017.

Ebbert, Stephanie. "Kavanaugh's Victory Is a Disheartening Moment for Many Women." *Boston Globe,* 6 October 2018. http://libproxy.lib.unc.edu/login?url=https://search-proquest-com.libproxy.lib.unc.edu/docview/2116640524?accountid=14244

———. "A Year after the First Women's March, What's Changed?" *Boston Globe,* 20 January 2018. https://www.bostonglobe.com/metro/2018/01/20/year-after-women-march-what-changed/OZOYrsPHwMf9vveRr1oowL/story.html.

Keller, Jessalynn, Kaitlynn Mendes, and Jessica Ringrose. *Digital Feminist Activism: Women and Girls Fight Back against Rape Culture.* Oxford: Oxford University Press, 2019.

Martin, Courtney. "You Are the NOW of Now! The Future of (Online) Feminism." *Nation,* 2 November 2011.

Mendes, Kaitlynn. *Feminism in the News: Representations of the Women's Movement since the 1960s.* Basingstoke, UK: Palgrave Macmillan, 2011.

———, ed. *Gender and the Media.* Critical Concepts in Media and Cultural Studies. Abingdon, UK: Routledge, 2017.

———. *SlutWalk: Feminism, Activism, and Media*. Basingstoke, UK: Palgrave Macmillan, 2015.

Nazneen, Sohela, and Maheen Sultan. *Voicing Demands: Feminist Activism in Transitional Contexts*. London: Zed Books, 2014.

Silva, Kumarini, and Kaitlynn Mendes, eds. *Feminist Erasures: Challenging Backlash Culture*. Basingstoke, UK: Palgrave Macmillan, 2015.

Taft, Jessica. *Rebel Girls: Youth Activism and Social Change across the Americas*. New York: New York University Press, 2011.

Traister, Rebecca. "Fury Is a Political Weapon. And Women Need to Wield It." *New York Times*, 29 September 2018. https://www.nytimes.com/2018/09/29/opinion/sunday/fury-is-a-political-weapon-and-women-need-to-wield-it.html.

Valenti, Jessica. *Full Frontal Feminism: A Young Woman's Guide to Why Feminism Matters*. Berkeley, Calif.: Seal, 2007.

SELECTED RECENT BOOKS BY WRITERS
INTERVIEWED FOR THIS COLLECTION

Akbar, Noorjahan, Maryam Laly, and Free Women Writers. *You Are Not Alone*. Self-published, CreateSpace, 2017.

Chemaly, Soraya. *Rage Becomes Her: The Power of Women's Anger*. New York: Atria Books, 2018.

Kearl, Holly. *Stop Global Street Harassment: Growing Activism around the World*. Santa Barbara, Calif.: Praeger, 2015.

Mukhopadhyay, Samhita, and Kate Harding. *Nasty Women: Feminism, Resistance, and Revolution in Trump's America*. New York: Picador, 2017.

Traister, Rebecca. *Good and Mad: The Revolutionary Power of Women's Anger*. New York: Simon and Schuster, 2018.

INDEX

on Campus, 194, 200; Facebook campaign around, 16–18, 20; "legitimate," 1, 217; of Pino, 196–98, 201, 202–3. *See also* sexual assault and violence

rape crisis centers, 215

Reddit, 18–19

refugees, 24–25

Refugee Women's Network, 22, 24–29; microenterprise program of, 26, 27

religion, 84

reproductive justice, 155–56, 179, 183–84, 188

Republican Party, 86

Roiphe, Katie, 11, 48

Roof, Dylann, 43, 44–45, 237n12

Roots, 166

Ross, Tom, 174

Sacred Journey program, 67–68

Safe Harbor program, 68

Safety and Free Speech Coalition, 18

Said, Edward, 166

Salon, 46, 50–51, 149, 218

Sandberg, Sheryl, 16, 17

Sanders, Bernie, 215

San Francisco, Calif., 75–76, 119, 132, 134, 147

San Jose Mercury, 119

Santa Clara Community Action Program (SCCAP), 119

#SayHerName campaign, 208, 219

Say It How It Is, 77

Scalia, Antonin, 130, 238n17

second-wave feminism, 3–4, 91, 131, 182

Seeger, Pete, 147

Seneca Falls, 3

September 11th attacks, 49–50, 71–72, 76, 119, 139–40, 161, 188, 205

Seventeen, 80, 213

sexual assault and violence, 77–78, 117; as campus issue, 120, 201–2; media framing of, 199–200; Pino experience of, 196–98, 201, 202–3; SPARK activism around, 213–16; trauma from, 15, 20–21, 24, 25, 68, 102–3, 201. *See also* domestic violence; rape

sexual assault prevention, 81, 214

sexual harassment, 16, 77–78, 112, 123, 221; on campus, 198, 239n10; in journalism, 47, 49. *See also* street harassment

sexualization, 78

sexual orientation, 181–82

Shakur, Assata, 39, 235n8

Shang, YingYing, 213

SheKnows Media, 59

Siren, 187

Sisters Proud of Knowledge Evolving (SPOKE), 103

Slack, 81

Smith, Joanne, 38–45; background and youth of, 39–41; and black feminism, 12, 39, 42; and Girls for Gender Equity, 38, 41–42; and lesbianism, 40, 41; online threats received by, 44

smoking bans, 140–41

social justice activism, 72, 119, 154, 155–56, 171; and feminist movement, 129, 185–86; lack of funding for, 86; women's stake in, 129

social media: and activist campaigns, 78–79, 81, 87, 122, 150, 190–91, 199–200, 213, 214, 218; feminist disputes in, 5–7, 9, 53–54, 90, 150–51; harassment and threats in, 5, 15–16, 110, 176–77, 191; and Hmong, 96–97; and #MeToo movement, 220; and nonprofits, 86–87. *See also* Facebook; Twitter

CPSIA information can be obtained
at www.ICGtesting.com
Printed in the USA
LVHW091141101119
636876LV00010B/266/P